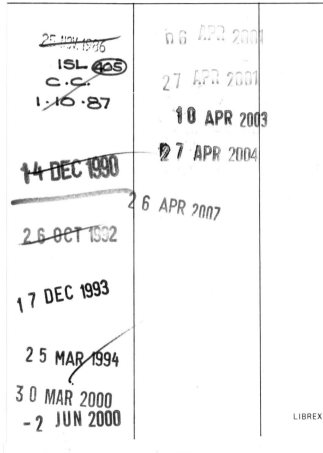

From Brown to Bunter

From Brown to Bunter

The Life and Death of the School Story

P. W. Musgrave

Routledge & Kegan Paul
London, Boston and Henley

First published in 1985
by Routledge & Kegan Paul plc
14 Leicester Square, London WC2H 7PH, England
9 Park Street, Boston, Mass. 02108, USA and
Broadway House, Newtown Road,
Henley on Thames, Oxon RG9 1EN, England

Set in Bembo, 10 on 12pt
by Columns of Reading
and printed in Great Britain
by St Edmundsbury Press Ltd.
Bury St Edmunds, Suffolk

© *P.W. Musgrave 1985*

Library of Congress Cataloging in Publication Data

Musgrave, P.W. (Peter William)

From Brown to Bunter.
Bibliography: p.
Includes index.
1. English fiction – History and criticism.
2. Education in literature.   3. Schools in literature.
4. Children's stories, English – History and criticism.
5. Boys – Books and reading.   6. Public schools, Endowed
(Great Britain) – History.   I. Title.
PR830.E38M87 1985   813'.009'355   85-1891

British Library CIP data also available

ISBN 0-7102-0529-5

Contents

v

Acknowledgments

My interest in school stories was not born in my youth despite a public school education. I realised that there was much scope for working in the field when writing *The Moral Curriculum* (1977) and whilst searching for evidence of the moral values taught in schools around the turn of the century. At the time I was working in Cambridge and much of the research for this book has been done there, using the collection of the University Library and as a guest of Corpus Christi College.

To both of these institutions I owe my thanks. I also want to thank:

The Publications Committee of Monash University for financial assistance towards publications.

Professor R.J.W. Selleck and Emeritus Professor W.F. Connell who made helpful comments at various times during the writing of the papers out of which this book was born.

The Lutterworth Press, Guildford, for permission to examine and to quote from the archives relating to the Religious Tract Society.

The Editors of the *Australian and New Zealand History of Education Society Journal*, *Children's Literature in Education* (copyright 1979, Agathon Press, Inc.), and the *Australian Journal of Education* for permission to quote in extenso in Chapter 6 from the papers listed in the Bibliography as P.W. Musgrave (1978, 1979 and 1981).

The Editor of *Melbourne Studies in Education, 1982* for permission to use the title of my paper published there as the title of this book.

Acknowledgments

Mrs C. Stuart, my secretary, for once again producing a typescript from my almost illegible manuscript.

Finally, one convention used throughout this book should be explained. Since most of the books and stories cited have been published in various forms I have, except where otherwise stated, referenced all such quotations to the chapter and where relevant, part of the book concerned.

1

The problem and the approach

No book . . . has any meaning on its own, in a vacuum.
D. Lodge (1981:3)

Introduction

This book is a case study of the life and death of one minor literary genre, the boys' school story. The genre was conceived around the middle of the last century and was almost dead before the Second World War. In this study an attempt will be made to discover the reasons why this literary form was born, flourished and had come near to death during that period; to describe the meaning of it for those alive then and, finally, to uncover its structure and the ways in which this was linked to the wider society.

Throughout history literature has had many forms and these have had changing popularity. In Greek times drama played a major part in society; for the cultivated Roman verse and oratory were given major prominence. For some centuries in the western world fiction has been growing in literary importance so that now one type of fiction, the novel, has come to be a predominant literary form and this is still true despite contemporary doubts about the health of this way of writing. Within this literary form there are a number of recognised choices of how works of fiction will be presented. There are, for example, romances, thrillers, and biographical novels. These genres have no necessary existence. They may die and new genres may be born. The Gothic novel of the Victorian time is now rarely read and never written, whilst science fiction is a major literary phenomenon. There is no study of the whole of the life-cycle of any literary genre, although Palmer (1978) has provided an excellent account of the birth and development of the thriller, a genre that is still thriving. Here the intention is to fill this gap by examining the whole biography of what will be claimed to be a minor genre, namely the boys' school story.

There has been some criticism of the concept of genre because it is said to imply an essentialist approach by assuming a number of inherent characteristics in the literary works grouped in any given example. Romance, for example is marked by 'the development of a love relationship, usually between a man and a woman' (Cawelti, 1976:41). In this study, however, genre is seen to be defined socially. A set of characteristics comes to be seen by readers, writers, by publishers and by all the others who comprise the literary world, for example, critics, to constitute a recognised type of literary work. At any time people expect to be able to read literary productions of certain types. Although these types come and go those that have relative permanence are here seen as genres. The position taken may be presented provocatively by saying that genres have temporary essence, and it is to a conclusion of this nature that we shall come at the end of the consideration of this genre.

In order to provide something of the flavour of the conclusion that can be reached by this approach, which is sociological rather than literary critical, part of Palmer's conclusion to his study of the thriller will be quoted:

> Structural analysis revealed a dominant procedure composed of a competitive hero and a pathological conspiracy; literary historical analysis specified a date for the emergence of the genre, the mid-nineteenth century, and a set of contributing components; social historical/sociological analysis has ascribed reasons for this date – the emergence of a specific class structure in a *laissez faire* economy and the adoption of a new perspective in criminality. (Palmer, 1978:202)

Almost all the thrillers produced within the set of expectations for that genre have been of low quality in the eyes of literary critics, though many have been 'best sellers'. The same is true of school boys' stories, although at least two are considered classics – Thomas Hughes's *Tom Brown's Schooldays* (1857) and Rudyard Kipling's *Stalky and Co.* (1899).

This predominant lack of what is usually seen as literary quality highlights the problem to be tackled here; why did a number of literary productions, not necessarily marked by perceived literary quality, come to be commercially successful, grouped together and seen as a genre and why did this genre flourish for about fifty years before gradually sinking, so that today it occupies a totally different position? Indeed, there is some interest in speculating whether, if the genre was not a fact of recent history, those boys' school stories that remain in circulation and any new school stories now written would be seen to form a group of works marked by common characteristics.

The production of genres

There is the danger in this approach either of treating any writer as completely determined by the social forces working upon him or of being accused of doing so. This is not in any way an inevitable implication of seeing genres as social productions. Writers take part in a complex set of relationships, more or less stable, but capable of change by any of the parties involved, all of whom have expectations for others and for themselves. This structure has been named 'the relations of expectations' (Sharrett, 1982:311). Even writers who are deemed to be very creative work within this framework. They have freedom over the content of what they write and they may even create new modes of expression or new ways of presenting their material, but, if they attempt to make a radical break away from current expectations, their writing will not be accepted or will only be accepted by a small minority – the position of, perhaps, Beckett today – or even may not be accepted till a much later date, as was the case of the novelist Jean Rhys, writing mainly before 1939, but accepted only in the 1950/60s – or even only accepted after the writer's death.

Because of the constraints of these relations of expections 'the writer always reveals or writes from a certain *position* . . . in relation to [the] ideological climate' (Macherey, 1978:195). He will, knowingly or not, represent part of an ideology and he will be read, consciously or not, through ideological spectacles. Individual creativity can only operate within such a setting. Macherey has summed up these constraints on the creativity of a writer: 'The way in which the conditions of its possibility *precede* the work (a fact which is so obvious, but which centuries of criticism have ignored) systematically consumes in advance any psychology of inspiration' (Macherey, 1978). Inglis puts the same point in a less abstract and academic way: 'Dickens was, of course, a genius; but he took his chances from Victorian society'

(Inglis, 1981:36). Furthermore, once a writer has written what he wishes, however much regard he pays to the expectations of others, as soon as his work is published it passes out of his control. His words will be read, worked on and made sense of by others in ways which he may not have intended. Out of this interaction of authors and readers the meaning of what is written emerges. The relations of expectations at any time put pressure upon the action of those involved in any literary network. Well-accepted forms, genres, emerge. These are coherent responses to contemporary social circumstances or to the circumstances of the recent past, since change is often slow to come. In this connection Sharrett has compared genres to organisations in that both 'are solutions to problems' (Sharrett, 1982:313). Because of this the intentions of any writer become critical. What set of circumstances has he in mind when he is writing? An answer to this question will help us to understand the contemporary significance of his work.

Analysis is complicated by the fact that in capitalist societies there stands between writer and reader the publisher whose continuing existence depends upon financial success. As might be expected writers have felt different degrees of independence of publishers. In a study of writers who were born or died between 1860 and 1910 Laurenson (1969) studied their biographies in the *Dictionary of National Biography*, and then characterised those in her sample as either 'institutionalised' or 'individualistic', though within each overall category various modes were possible. Thus, amongst institutionalised writers Trollope was strongly influenced by his market situation, Dickens wrote primarily for an audience, and Wells took a 'common sense approach', whilst among the individualistic Katherine Mansfield showed lack of concern for the market, Joyce was unconcerned with any popular audience and Henry James was very introspective in his work.

Without publication of some form, even though this be but a public reading, writers can not meet readers and no public creation of meaning is possible. Publishers, usually working for profit in capitalist societies, 'choose, manufacture and distribute' (Escarpit, 1970:400). The process of selection is important, because, whereas publishers have to survive and, therefore, to choose what they believe the market to want, they do from time to time also make judgments about what the public ought or ought not to have. Such judgments may relate to the presentation of innovatory work or be governed by their own moral values or their view of what the public's values should be. Sometimes they hope to produce a best seller to meet the wide and heterogeneous audience that makes up the market for popular work; sometimes they plan to sell to a more limited market, as would be the case with an academic work such as this book; and sometimes they aim to change the market either by presenting a new type of work which they hope will be acceptable in the future or by preventing work reaching the market that would strengthen the hold of presentations with which they do not agree. Publishers also clearly operate within and upon the relations of expectations.

In all societies, capitalist or otherwise, there are other middlemen who stand between author and reader and who operate within and upon the existing relations of expectations. Certainly since early in the last century the literary critic has played an important part as a mediator between the writer and his potential readers. The critic has used his own past experience to build up a critical apparatus with which he evaluates work coming forward and also from time to time he will revalue the work of times gone by. He makes judgments about the values that he sees to be represented in a work, on its craftsmanship and upon the apparent message contained in the work (Lang, 1958). The writings of such critics as Matthew Arnold in the last part of the nineteenth century and F.R. Leavis in the middle third of this century have been very influential upon their contemporaries, whether writers or readers, upon the development of young writers, and upon those studying to be teachers, who could have very wide influence upon future readers and writers. In specific fields, particular academic specialisms, critics have much power to make or mar the future of a book. This is more true when they are acting as publisher's readers, advising upon the acceptance or not of a manuscript submitted for publication. The writings of critics can, therefore, both control what is published and also shape the tastes of readers, thus limiting both what is read and how it is read.

Thus far the words writer, reader and book have been used carefully but without any detailed explication; the words author and text have not been used at all. All these words are crucial and their exact usage in this study must be clarified. A writer writes a book, a material object, that is words on a page, but he does not become an author until that material is worked on by a reader. Furthermore, as soon as the reader works on a book he begins to construct a text which may or may not match either what the author thinks that he presented or the text constructed by any other reader. Readers impose different meanings on books according to the varying social positions they occupy. A very clear case of this is the different view taken by a student of a novel studied for an examination and by someone reading the same book for pleasure. The two texts that are constructed in these cases might well have been written by two very different authors.

Reading a book, then, can be seen as a construction by readers from varying social positions of a text, presented by an author, whose original intention may or may not be sustained in the process. This approach to literature forces an analysis of why a particular interpretation is made at one historical moment. In Chaney's words the aim is to move 'beyond fiction as something meaningful through purporting to be pictorial representation, to *a group of narrative stories which are tellable*' and 'to concentrate upon the milieu in which that performance becomes conceivable' (1979:12-3). We must first ask the general question: what are the present relations of expectations? And then, following Chaney, within those expectations what stories can writers present that will be readable?

The relationships between author and readers are very complex, even before inserting any middlemen into the picture. Sharrett (1982:87-8) has shown how the word 'author' may be used in four senses: first, in an almost legal way to cover his contractual relationship with his publisher; next, as the one who writes the book; third, as the author of the text that he hopes will be constructed; and last, as the author of the text read by some reader. In a similar manner the word 'reader' may be seen to be used in three senses: first, as the one who constructs the text; next, the constructor of a text for himself; and last, the reader seen by the writer when writing the book. Oddly, perhaps, for an academic Sharrett omits one possibility, in a way the obverse of his first sense of 'author'. A reader, particularly a student, may occupy an almost contractual position in constructing a text, as when preparing for an examination.

As if this situation were not sufficiently complicated, the text that results from any particular reading must not be seen as necessarily final and unchangeable. Common experience should remind us that, after re-reading some book or passage, we often make some such remark as 'It seemed different the second time through'. Meaning changes through time – in the short term because we appreciate nuances not perceived in a first reading and in the longer term because we or later readers bring a different set of expectations to a second reading. *Tom Brown* read in 1857 resulted in one text; in 1910, after *Stalky and Co.* had been written and became public knowledge and after important political and economic changes, it was read in a totally different way; and today in a radically altered milieu the text is wholly different again.

Genres and change

The contemporary relations of expectations include within their structure those genres presently acceptable to authors, middlemen and readers – all know what a thriller is, though all may not hold the same view and such disagreement is one possible cause of change. There is some, but comparatively little room for manoeuvre within the present definition of any genre. Whatever changes will occur will be small and will not cause change to the groups involved in the particular genre concerned. Slow change may take place if all the acceptable minor changes occur at one end of the range of tolerance. This is what has happened over the last century in the case of the novel; there has rarely been a major change, but a whole series of minor changes, all acceptable within current expectations, has meant that Murdoch, Amis and Fowles have in some sense replaced Thackeray, Dickens and Trollope as contemporary literary exemplars. Styles used, material presented, and moral values upheld have all shifted totally over the period. But major and more sudden shifts have also occurred. For example, during the last part of the nineteenth century the influence of such French realist novelists as Zola affected writing throughout the western world. Quite major changes in content and manner were or became acceptable relatively quickly. The question to be answered really is: how much and what will the reading public tolerate? What are their bounds of tolerance?

This question can be considered using Williams's (1977) terms: the 'residual' and 'emergent'. The residual is that set of expectations formed in the past, but still active in the present; included here are the definitions of what various genres are. Inasmuch as those with political power succeed in preserving the residual hegemony exists and the place of any genre in ensuring hegemony merits attention, since those ruling a country may wish to support or eliminate a given genre because of their view about its political significance. This may particularly be the case where the genre under consideration is read by children, since political socialisation into the status quo is often seen as an important function of childhood. The resultant culture will not only be the dominant one, but will also influence the form of any counter-culture, in that the latter will be presented as an attack on the former.

By 'emergent' Williams refers to the creation of new relations of expectations which challenge the residual. The term tends to be used to cover two situations. First, there is the emergence of new ideas that are acceptable within the present set of expectations without any major change, the situation referred to above, when change occurs within the present range of tolerance. Second, there is the creation of really new ideas that require some shift in the relations of expectations. In this study emergent will only be used to cover this second meaning. Once such emergent ideas have been accepted they do, however, become part of the normally learnt expectations. In short, they become residual. Brecht's dramatic innovations, developed in the 1930s, imported to Britain in the 1950s, are now no longer emergent.

Such changes, rooted in literature, can, as was the intention with Brecht and as was perhaps the case, lead to questioning of the political status quo. 'Literature, to a greater or lesser degree, "rocks" the solidity of ideology, revealing the fault lines or fissures' (Bennett, 1979:126). This may be because of the invention of new forms or because a writer uses the old forms to mock at the status quo. Satire is, indeed, a very strong instrument for change, since revolutionary ideas can be presented in a form that has some chance of being acceptable. Yet new ideas and new forms have still to be accepted into the operative relations of expectations if change, whether hegemonic or anti-hegemonic in nature, is to result. What makes for this acceptability is little explored and in this case study attention must be given to what may be called prefigurative authors, those authors whose ideas or forms, though new in themselves, were yet not too far different from the residual that they had no chance of becoming emergent. A case will be made out here that such authors play a very real part in creating and standardising a genre.

8

Method

Genres come and go. In Elizabethan times drama took the form of verse plays. This has not been the case for more than two centuries, despite attempts by a number of writers, including Eliot and Fry, to revive this genre. The picaresque story, born in seventeenth-century Spain, has also disappeared, though elements of this genre appear in contemporary works. In the nineteenth-century narrative poems, for example, those by Wordsworth, Byron and Tennyson, were popular; today poems tend to be short, metaphoric and without any particular story. In other words, genres are born, live – well or with difficulty – and die. They have biographies.

In this study we shall examine the birth, life and death, that is, the biography of the boys' school story. The accepted version of the biography of this minor literary genre is that it was born, suddenly and apparently without parents, with the publication in 1857 of *Tom Brown's Schooldays* by Thomas Hughes, following which there was a flood of similar school stories. Ultimately, this popular view holds, these stories became much more easily available in such weekly magazines as the *Magnet* and the *Gem*. According to this version of the biography of the genre there is no end, although there is no doubt that school stories for boys are rarely published today, and that the *Magnet* and the *Gem* ceased publication by 1940 and no similar magazine has taken their place.

Briefly, then, the historical picture will be presented in some detail in five stages. First, the roots of *Tom Brown's Schooldays* will be sought in previous literature for adults and children; because there were a few stories about schools, written and widely read, for both adults and boys, before 1857. Next, both *Tom Brown* and Dean F.W. Farrar's *Eric*, published in 1858, will be analysed in some depth. The career of both authors, the events of publication, the nature of each book and their reception will be presented in detail. Third, the development of the boys' school story in the 1860s and 1870s, the period when the flood might be expected at least to begin, will be examined; this research appears to show that whatever flood occurred was in nature not quite as might be expected from an examination of *Tom Brown*. Fourth, we shall consider a writer seminal for the full development of the genre, Talbot Baines Reed, writer of a number of boys' school stories, one of which, *The Fifth Form at St Dominic's* (1881) became very famous, Finally, attention will be given to the period 1890 to

1940, during which the genre became both diversified, in that stories were written for adults as well as for adolescents, and in that some stories became critical rather than supportive of the schools as they were, and also standardised, in that stories were produced literally to a formula, so that the genre was emptied of moral meaning and became devoid of what was usually seen as literary merit.

The presentation of this material, both literary and social historical in nature, is essential as it forms the basis upon which any sociological analysis can be undertaken. The eventual sociological conclusions will relate to three sub-fields: the sociologies of literature, of culture and of education. But, in addition, the collection of historical evidence will in itself permit certain social historical conclusions to be drawn.

In the preceding paragraphs the course of the analysis has been outlined, but method has been ignored. Four main methodological points must be made. The first relates to the concept of genre. Clearly the prime need must be to establish that the genre, the boys' school story, did exist. The nineteenth century was par excellence the age of the novel. This period correlates with the end of the rise to unchallenged power of the bourgeoisie in Britain and, indeed, more than one analyst has attributed the development of the novel to the rise of the bourgeoisie (Watt, 1957). The characteristic novel of the time had a definite plot – often supported by several sub-plots, portrayed character in a concrete way, and was by and large optimistic in its tone of feeling. Certain material, for example, detailed accounts of sexual relationships, and certain modes of speech, for example, explicit use of swear words, were not acceptable to middlemen and to readers. In brief, there were very definite expectations of what a novel was. The preeminence of this literary form will be taken for granted. What has to be isolated is that set of additional characteristics which were seen at that time to constitute boys' school stories as a separate genre. We shall look for a structure, peculiar to these stories, of plot and of feeling that is found in most part in all the works seen at the time as examples of the genre.

Emphasis has been put, so far without comment, on the perception by contemporaries that a genre existed. This approach, phenomenological in essence, forces us to examine, as far as is possible at this historical distance, contemporary evidence of what people read, of who read any given book, of what was said and thought about these works, and of what the critics and other middlemen, including those *in loco parentis*, felt about them. In other words, we must try to see how readers at that time and since constructed these texts. Genres are socially constructed and socially sustained. In addition, further evidence relating to the development of the genre will be found in the uses to which the books were put and from within the books themselves.

A second methodological issue follows directly from the last point. For this and other reasons there is need for what academic literary critics often call a 'close reading' of a number of representative books from the genre. Only by such a course can the characteristics of the genre be isolated and, more especially, only in this way can we uncover 'the structure of feeling' that is, 'the characteristic elements of impulse, restraint, and tone' (Williams, 1977:132) presented by these writers. Macherey has drawn a distinction between two forms of critical reading. There is, on the one hand, 'la critique comme appreciation' through which writers like Leavis work the writing before them in order to discover the truth it holds. In this method the assumption is that there is an essential element in what is written that must be constituted to read the true text. There is, on the other hand, 'la critique comme savoir'. By this method the reader constitutes his own text which he then criticises, making very clear as he goes along what he is doing. In this way, just because he is not looking for some preconceived essence, the critic is more likely to uncover the taken-for-granted assumptions in the book before him. The second critical method demands that the book be seen in its social setting, that we know something of the author's career and background, and that something of the characteristics of the readership and of currently powerful middlemen be known. All these points will be borne in mind when 'closely reading' representative books from the genre.

This leads directly to the third methodological consideration. A number of exemplars of the genre must be chosen for analysis. Which shall they be? Clearly for historical reasons and because of its phenomenological standing *Tom Brown's Schooldays* (1857) must be the first choice, but, as already indicated, its close peer in time, *Eric* (1858) has also been selected, again in part also because of its great importance when published and in the years since, but also because analysis of boys' school stories written and published after 1857/8 and before the work in the 1880s of Talbot Baines Reed shows that some features found in *Eric*, but not present in

Tom Brown, played a predominant role, so that until the 1880s the genre almost seemed to have been sired by Dean Farrar, not by Thomas Hughes.

In view of the claim made earlier that Talbot Baines Reed firmed up the genre one of his books must be analysed in detail. The intention is to present a close reading of *The Fifth Form at St Dominic's*, but also, because of the importance attached to this writer, to refer in more limited detail to a number of his other school stories.

Finally, there is a plethora of material, written during the period of diversification from 1890 to 1940, amongst which to choose. Largely because there are limits to the length of a book of the genre within which this is written, but also because the necessary points can be made by a narrow choice, two books have been selected. The first is Kipling's *Stalky and Co.* (1899). This book is generally accepted as a classic; it was innovatory in technique and critical in tone, both of the public schools of the time and of boys' school stories in themselves. The second is Alec Waugh's *The Loom of Youth* (1917), the remarkable product of a seventeen-year-old, which caused a major literary and educational furore on its publication (Musgrave, 1979). This latter book is important in that it was severely critical of public schools and, though in passing, of school stories themselves; it was also written primarily for adults, a tendency which has been hypothesised above to have grown in importance in this period and which should, therefore, be exemplified in detail here.

The final methodological point concerns the historical and literary nature of the evidence used here. Selection of evidence is a tricky matter in sociological studies of a retrospective nature. There is always a temptation to choose data that will fit the case being made and to ignore or not seek contrary evidence. In this study this is doubly the case. First, it is so because of the historical nature of the method implied by the question asked; if one is to write a biography, historical material must be used. But, in addition, the sociology of literature has been plagued by various forms of 'correspondence theory'. Books are seen to reflect social values in what in logical terms is really little more than the qualitative equivalent of a statistical correlation. In Raymond Williams's words attention 'is directed towards instances of formal or structural homology between a social order, its ideology and its cultural forms' (Williams, 1977:106). Such work cites material chosen to illustrate the correspondence, forgetting any contrary examples.

Clearly one must always try to cover as much of the relevant literature as is possible. In addition, facile explanations of a homological nature may, at least in part, be avoided by keeping in mind throughout the analysis the fact that different social institutions have different saliency for different social processes at different periods of time. The middle class that arose in the early eighteenth century and has been seen as so crucial in the development of the novel was a different social class from that also named the middle class whose sons read *Tom Brown* and different again from that who with their sons read *Stalky and Co.* Conceptual tools like class or religion or the polity must be related to the social structure of the time not to some preconceived, constant and oversimplified view when using historical and literary material in sociological analysis.

Children's literature

Most of what has been said so far has assumed that anything that can be said about literature or about adult literature applies without any reservation to children's literature. Is this a wise assumption? First of all we must ask: what is children's literature? Even this question is difficult to answer, because if we say children's literature is what children read, we dodge the issue in that children do read much that is or was originally intended for adults. Examples are Bunyan's *Pilgrim's Progress* and Swift's *Gulliver's Travels*. Furthermore, some books are written for both audiences; John Buchan's novels fall into this category. Yet despite all this there are books that are clearly written for children. The great English classics in this genre include the books of Beatrice Potter, Kenneth Grahame's *The Wind in the Willows* and Rudyard Kipling's *Jungle Books*.

What differences are there between these books and those written specifically for adults? In asking this question we are turning attention from the relations of expectations in general to those particularly relating to children's literature. C.S. Lewis, who amongst his other work wrote a number of well-known children's books, said that he wrote for children

> because a children's story is the best art form for something
> you have to say; just as a composer might write a Dead
> March not because there was a public funeral in view but

13

because certain musical ideas that had occurred to him went
best into that form (C.S. Lewis, 1969:208)

Thus there seem to be no restrictions other than those con-
straining any writer whether for adults or for children on the
ideas and material that may be presented to children. In this
respect the same relations of expectations operate on all authors.
Whatever a child has experienced or can imagine may be
examined in the literature for him and this means that the gap
between adult and children's literature will lessen as he grows
older and even in pre-adolescence be quite small.

However, in the passage quoted above, C.S. Lewis does
acknowledge some difference in 'form'. Children's books that are
recognised as such seem to be characterised by a number of
conventions that differentiate them from adult books. In an
incisive passage Inglis (1981:101-2) names six. In books written
specially for them children are the protagonists, not so much so
that the readers may easily identify with the heroes, but so that
they may easily recognise them as people like themselves. There is
less concern with probability than in adult books in plot and in
circumstances; this convention enables the author to remove
parents and other awkward adults from the scene, but also allows
the employment of coincidence, hair-breadth escapes and even
those irrational devices so common in the stories for the very
young, fairies and ghosts, whose use probably exercise the
reader's imagination (Cook, 1969). Children's books are now, but
were not necessarily always, shorter than those for grown-ups,
partly to match their readers' stamina. But this characteristic also
in part depends upon another convention, namely that the
children's story is marked by 'its conscious limitation on formal
intricacy'. The syntax too is less difficult. Finally, Inglis notes the
'greater simplification (though not superficiality) of moral issues'.
McDowell (1973), whilst covering in one way or another all these
characteristics, adds three others. She believes that the tone of
most writing for children is optimistic, that the writing is
presented in an active, rather than a passive, way and, finally, that
there are a number of conventions relating to techniques or to the
forms of the narrative that are often found to play an important
role; these include time-travel, initiation into adulthood and the
rise and fall of fortune.

McDowell's inclusion of optimism as a leading characteristic of
writing for children raises an important point to which reference

will have to be made again in the concluding chapter. The general theoretical question may be asked whether expectations for a minor genre can become opposed in some respect to the major genre of which it is a part. In more specific terms can novels for children in some respect develop according to expectations that are different from the major genre, novels for adults? Thus, whereas in the nineteenth century adult novels were by and large optimistic in tone yet by the mid-twentieth century, and perhaps even since the 1914-1918 war, this was no longer the case, though children's stories, certainly until the birth of what may be called the American adolescent problem novel, have continued to be so. This lack of match between the relations of expectations of the major and minor genres must be considered as one possible reason when we come to account for the near-death of boys' school stories after about 1940.

These characteristics are, as noted, part of the relations of expectations which influence the writing, production, purchase and reading of children's and other books. They can and do change through time. Australian adolescent fiction, for instance, showed a marked change in the mid-1960s. There was a switch in what was written, published and read from chummy stories about bush holiday adventures to stories marked by a growing awareness of such social issues as conservation, mental and physical handicap and social disadvantage (Musgrave, 1982a). Publishing has become very dependent upon its market among the young. About one quarter of all books are now for the school-age audience, though many of these are textbooks. This dependence does, however, mean that the middlemen influencing expectations, whether in support or to change them, become crucial both for writers and publishers and for sociologists examining this part of the literary scene.

There are now literary critics who specialise in evaluating children's literature. The quality daily press in Britain and Australia carry regular features on children's books, often associated with the annual award of prizes for such works, prizes sometimes sponsored by the newspaper itself. The *Times Educational Supplement* and the general educational journals publish similar regular sections. Finally, specialist journals like *Children's Literature in Education* have been started to deal with this topic alone. In all these places 'specialists' work upon the current expectations of children's literature.

The question has to be asked who these critics hope to

influence. They naturally are aiming at very different targets. Those writing in daily papers may be read by parents or others who are near to the child and who may influence his reading by advice or by giving him books as presents. Others, however, stand *in loco parentis* and teachers are important here. Critics in specialist journals work on this set of expectations but so too do those who train teachers. All primary teachers teach their pupils to read and, hence, inculcate, consciously or otherwise, some literary standards. Any secondary teacher may comment on his pupils' English as our schools depend upon oral and written communication, but those teaching English are deeply involved in inculcating literary standards. Therefore, those in the colleges or universities where teachers are trained who are responsible for the methods used to teach English can have a crucial role in preserving or changing the relations of expectations covering children's literature.

There has been a growth recently in children's libraries, both in schools and as part of general libraries, so that the place of librarians in this process has to be considered. These professionals buy the stock of any library and advise on its usage. Their values, therefore, are important in influencing what books children may read. Furthermore, specialist children's librarians are now not uncommon, both in school and in other libraries. Thus, the training of these new specialists becomes a further point where the construction of the relations of expectations is influenced.

The place of the mass media is also important in several ways. Children's demands for certain types of books may be affected by the programmes seen or heard and this may extend to individual works. In this context there is some interest in noting that in recent years a number of the stories central to the argument of this book have been made into and shown as television serials. These include *Tom Brown's Schooldays*, Anstey's *Vice Versa*, and *Stalky and Co*. On the whole the didactic function of television for children has been realised now. But all literature can be didactic and children's literature is meant to be read at the period of maximum intended teaching when important structures of experiences are felt which it is hoped will order all future experience. What is seen on television is experienced very vividly. Those responsible for programming are seen here as another form of middleman and all the middlemen who operate in this field have an important cultural role which must be borne in mind when presenting and analysing the data in subsequent chapters.

Children's literature has been examined in the past for a number of purposes. Psychologists, often writing in the psycho-analytical tradition, have looked on it, for instance, as a source of violence (Wertham, 1954). Literary critics have evaluated specific books for children, as did Empson (1935) in a famous essay on *Alice*. More recently Quigley (1982) has examined in literary terms the merits of a number of the main school stories. Social historians have used children's books as primary sources, admittedly to be interpreted with great care. One of the consequent debates that is relevant here is that about how true a version of Rugby School in the 1830s/40s is depicted in *Tom Brown* (Scott, 1975). One of the best examples in this tradition is the work of Mack (1941) who in a classic study used school stories, those for boys and those for adults, as an indicator of the values held by members of society about the public schools in England between 1860 and 1940.

Sociologists have always been interested in values, however much they have argued about their place in social action or about how to measure them. Since children's literature is didactic it must by definition be a repository, in a literate society almost the quintessential source, of the values that parents and others hope to teach to the next generation. Therefore, one can express some surprise that this possible avenue for sociological analysis has been very largely ignored. One recent book (O'Dell, 1978) has examined the part played in the socialisation of Russian youth by the literature made available to them in school and elsewhere. O'Dell's pathbreaking work, however, suffers from some of the difficulties that also constrain this case study. Unlike in this work her focus was upon the effects of reading literature. But only in one case was she able to trace a clear effect of a book for children upon the way in which Soviet society operated. The Timurite movement was named after a hero in a book in which a group of children co-operated to help the war effort. The events described in the book were, almost immediately after its publication, imitated by groups throughout the USSR and since the war similar groups have continued to help those in hardship, especially war victims. O'Dell's difficulties were due to the fact that she had to work largely, though not entirely, from primary source material; she was totally unable to measure at first hand what the effects of reading any specific material were and she was able to interview very few of the middlemen whose position in the USSR is obviusly of much greater influence than their western

17

equivalents. Her restrictions were political and due to limited resources. Here similar problems exist because the case study is historical, so that access to the construction of the text of the books concerned in periods of more than a century past is very difficult.

Although the main aim is to learn something of the way in which genres develop, the evidence analysed, being didactic in nature, inevitably makes some conclusions possible about the values held during the period studied. We are, as it were, reading backwards from the books given to the young, from which they were meant to learn, to the values of those with some power over them. Rockwell (1974:23) has put the point aptly: 'The didactic function of the "literature of initial socialisation" is a key to the values of the society which produces it.' Particularly important is the nature of the hero or the heroes of these books, since they are the exemplars of the values being put forward for imitation. Relevant at this point is a finding of O'Dell's; in some children's writing in the USSR there are no heroes and this matches the national ideology. However, in non-socialist societies heroes are not merely permitted, but encouraged. One specific type of hero has been well represented in children's and other fiction, especially in the latter half of the nineteenth century. This is 'the boy who made good'. Harrison (1957) has called this genre 'success literature'. Books written in this genre, and school stories will be seen to have some of their characteristics, press very strongly a set of values seen as worthwhile at that time and in that society.

Children's literature, therefore, has some differences from, but many similarities with writing for adults. The expectations are that it will be somewhat simpler, but much of the material will be much the same as that produced for adults, hence the fact that much literature is read by both adults and children. However, there is a tendency for more overt didacticism and this is important for this study both in itself and because additional middlemen, each possibly having different sets of values, are available to work upon the relations of expectations for children's literature.

Conclusion

Although much of the evidence deployed here can be used directly to draw conclusions about, for example, the structure of values in late nineteenth- and early twentieth-century Britain or about the operation of the British educational system – and, inded, such substantive findings will be noted in the concluding chapter – yet the main questions asked will concern the biography of one minor literary genre, the boys' school story. In passing, the point might be made that comparison is possible with girls' school stories, a genre that was born and died slightly later than its male equivalent (Cadogan and Craig, 1976). This may be true, but would demand a case study about twice the size of this, a project hardly feasible for one worker, whose knowledge and interests are in slightly other areas than are needed for such a study. Girls' stories and girls' interest in boys' stories will, however, receive mention at several points throughout this book.

The way in which material is presented here will be governed by the choice of the concept of the relations of expectations as the main tool of analysis. At each stage of the argument authors, middlemen and readers and their changing expectations will be considered as far as the available evidence allows. In each case the basis for their actions must lie outside books themselves. Social pressures govern the ways in which writers become authors and readers construct texts out of the books that are presented or suggested to them by various middlemen. In a free society there is little or no co-ordination of what O'Dell in her study of the USSR called 'the agents of character education' (O'Dell, 1978:20), but middlemen in democracies are none the less very important agents in this respect, and nowhere is this more the case than when considering didactic literature such as much of that for children.

The relations of expectations is a very complex and constantly changing structure, hard to pin down except by taking snapshots of it at regular intervals in time. Here this will be done by focusing upon major representatives of the minor genre under consideration. Readers, in particular, constitute a many-faceted aggregate. Traditionally, and probably rightly in a capitalist society, major attention has been given to their social class, but readership of any one book overlaps classes; one result of this may well be that readers from different social classes construct rather different texts – even, for example, in the same classroom – of any one book. However, here all social institutions must be taken into account. In addition to social class, the demographic, economic, political, religious, educational and military frameworks of British society during the period must be considered in the development of any explanation of changes in the genre.

The relations of expectations are sustained by routine writing, but are altered by the successful publication of innovatory works. The exceptional author, amongst whom Thomas Hughes in this context must be numbered, are crucial in the development of any genre, major or minor. Sociologists must by the nature of their mode of thought have difficulty with individuals. Here exceptional writers are seen as those who slot into some space available to them in the structure of the culture, but by their occupation and development of this space they change the relations of expectations that ruled beforehand. Lucien Goldmann has written of these writers: 'the work [of such authors] constitutes a collective achievement which will afterwards reveal to the group what it was moving towards without knowing it, in its ideas, its feelings and its behaviour' (Goldmann, 1973:115). These prefigurative writers can be seen as the causes or the mediators of forces that are responsible for many of the major changes in the relations of expectations of a genre, but not of all changes, as will be seen when we come to analyse why this minor genre died in or around the 1930s.

2

Precursors of *Tom Brown* and *Eric*

In this chapter a brief account will first be given of children's literature in the early nineteenth century with the aim of showing both the tradition within which writers were working at the time and the minor part played then by school stories. There were, however, some mentions of schools in novels for adults and it must be remembered that by the 1850s the novel was entering what many would see as its great age. This situation was a manifestation of the ruling *relations of expectations* which were supported by the contemporary *social structure*, each of which will be considered in the second half of this chapter.

Children's literature

Nursery classics

Three books, written around 1800, have been described by Avery as 'the foundation stones of the nursery library of the next hundred years' (1965:13). There were Thomas Day's *Sandford and Merton*, Mrs Trimmer's *Fabulous Histories* and Mrs Barbauld's *Evenings at Home*. Each was republished many times in the next hundred years, an indication in itself of their continuing popularity, at least with adults, as reading material for the young.

Thomas Day published *Sandford and Merton* in three parts (1783, 1786 and 1788). His intention was to present the philosophy of Rousseau's *Emile* to English children, perhaps particularly to boys. He believed that there were not suitable reading books for young children at the time, and he wrote a series of little stories, some of which were based on classical myths, for example, 'Leonidas, King of Sparta' and 'Androcles and the Lion'; others were tales with a moral, for example, 'The good natured little boy' and 'The ill-natured boy'; some of the remaining narratives contained accounts of natural phenomena. These were linked by the presence throughout of three characters: Harry Sandford, the honest and bluff son of a farmer; Tommy Merton, the snobbish and somewhat effete son of a rich landlord; and Mr Barlow, their master. The tone is priggish to a late twentieth-century reader, but two considerations must be borne in mind: the book was avowedly didactic and the age was one when children had to be good, not mischievous, so that to contemporary readers these stories probably seemed interesting and acceptable material.

Mrs Trimmer's *Fabulous Histories* was published first in 1788 with the subtitle 'Designed for the Instruction of Children Respecting their Treatment of Animals' and was dedicated to HRH Princess Sophia, one of George III's daughters. It consisted of twenty-six brief chapters and the first edition contained 215 pages, much shorter than *Sandford and Merton*. The Introduction described the book as 'a series of FABLES, intended to carry out moral instruction applicable to children'. The 'story' is about Harriet and Frederick aged eleven and six years old respectively, children of Mr and Mrs Benson, and a pair of robins who have four young, called Robin, Dicky, Flapfy and Peckfy. Mrs Trimmer was opposed to fantasy so that her material is very down-to-earth, but the Christian and moral flavour of the didacticism can be judged by quoting her concluding sentences:

> Happy would it be for the animal creation, if every human being, like good Mrs Benson, consulted the welfare of inferior creatures, and neither spoiled them by indulgence, nor injured them by tyranny! Happy would mankind be, if every one, like her, acted in conformity to the will of their Maker by cultivating in their own minds, and those of their children, the *divine principle* of UNIVERSAL BENEVOLENCE.

Evenings at Home or The Juvenile Budget Opened, subtitled 'consisting of A Variety of Miscellaneous Pieces for the Instruction and Amusement of Young Persons' was written by Mrs Barbauld and Dr Aiken and published between 1792 and 1796. It contained a series of pieces, varying in length from one to ten pages, with such titles as 'Dialogue on How Things be Learned',

'Wines and Spirits', and 'The Boy without a Genius'. It was a mixture, rather like *Sandford and Merton*, of facts, stories and moral and religious teaching.

Two other books must be added to this list of early nineteenth-century nursery classics. Maria Edgeworth's *The Parents' Assistant* or *Stories for Children*, the first edition of which was published in 1796, and which was reissued as late as 1897 with an introduction by Anne Thackeray Ritchie, the novelist's daughter. This book consisted of a series of stories that followed the method used by Mrs Barbauld in that there was no connection between the individual items. Mrs Edgeworth, interested as she was in educational theory, did, however, set out to make her material not merely didactic, but also entertaining so that her readers would both learn more easily and be amused, though like Mrs Trimmer she distrusted the effects of 'pamper[ing] the taste early with mere books of entertainment'. In the stories she also set out to present a very rational approach to life and to moral situations. Two stories were about schools and to them we must return later.

The other book which must be mentioned is Mrs Sherwood's *History of the Fairchild Family*, published in 1818 and still in print early in this century. This is the story of Henry, Lucy and Emily Fairchild. They do many naughty things and are always punished. Moral lessons follow one another in a terrible and inevitable succession. This type of book, much more so than the others referred to, remind us that one other important source of reading material for children, particularly for girls, was such tracts as were published by the Religious Tract Society, an organisation that will be found to play a crucial part in the development of the boys' school story. By the middle of the century a number of mainly women's magazines were specially published for 'Sunday reading', a contemporary genre, and these included sections for children. Between 1848 and 1852 eight cheap religious papers were started (Dalziel, 1957: 65-6). The Religious Tract Society founded *Leisure Hour* in 1852 and *Sunday at Home* in 1854, both popular in late-Victorian Britain; the latter was aimed particularly at teenagers, especially non-church goers (Bratton, 1981: 44-5). The tone of this writing for young people was more earnest and unrelievedly moral even than the five books outlined above.

Adventure stories

By about 1840 some commentators had noted that the type of

book of which *Sandford and Merton* was still the outstanding example no longer met the needs of young readers, but that nothing had yet taken its place. Thomas Arnold, headmaster of Rugby, just before his death in 1842, had written, 'Childishness in boys, even of good abilities, seems to be a growing fault, and I do not know to what to ascribe it, except to the greater number of exciting books of amusement like *Pickwick* or *Nickleby*'.

There were a few writers trying to fill this need by producing books less overtly didactic in style and containing more appropriate material for young readers. Catherine Sinclair in 1839 wrote *Holiday House; a Book for the Young* in which she told of the adventures of Laura, Harry, Frank and Graham, their father, Sir Edward and their governess Mrs Crabtree. Their mother was dead, a characteristic very common in Victorian children's literature. In the introduction she displayed what were then revolutionary sentiments:

> In these pages the author has endeavoured to paint that species of noisy, frolicsome, mischievous children, now almost extinct, wishing to preserve a set of fabulous remembrances of days long past, when young people were like wild horses on the prairies, rather than like well-broken hacks on the road; and when amidst many faults and eccentricities, there was still some individuality of character and feeling allowed to remain.

Yet she still was writing somewhere within the expectations of the age since she was 'conscious of a deep responsibility, for it is at this early age that the seed can but be born which shall bear fruit into eternal life.'

But by the 1830/40s there was one major addition to the types of books available for older children, particularly for boys. There was a start to the writing and publishing of what became a long line of adventure stories. *Robinson Crusoe* (1719) provided a model, of which even Rousseau had approved. In passing we should note that Defoe originally wrote the book not for children, but for adults. One late twentieth-century way of reading *Robinson Crusoe* finds in it many characteristics of personality seen to be immoral and inappropriate for young people to learn today. Yet in the 1830s *Crusoe* was not read in this way. Rather, Defoe's tale of a hero overcoming many trials in strange surroundings was seen to allow the presentation of morality and information in a manner more attractive to contemporary youngsters than was possible in traditional children's books. The first well-known nineteenth-century adventure story for boys was Captain Marryat's *Mr Midshipman Easy* (1838). In 1829 Marryat retired after twenty-four years at sea in the Royal Navy. He was an unusual naval officer in that he had been elected Fellow of the Royal Society in recognition of the work he had done in signalling. He decided to write in his retirement and, though initially aiming at an adult audience, his work, marked by simple narration, fascinating detail about strange places and nautical matter, and by implicit rather than explicit moralising, was almost at once taken over by boys.

Marryat's example was soon followed by a number of writers who from the start aimed at the adolescent boy. Two will be considered here: W.H.G. Kingston and R.M. Ballantyne. Kingston (1814-80) wrote two school stories that will be considered in Chapter 4, but was a prolific writer of adventure stories for boys. In 1851 he wrote *Peter the Whaler*, an adventure tale very much in the Marryat tradition. Of the many stories he wrote over the next two decades this was the most famous and successful, being republished many times. R.M. Ballantyne is better remembered today, particularly for *Coral Island*, which first appeared in 1857, the year in which *Tom Brown* was published. He had already written *The Young Fur Trader* (1856), *Ungava* (1857) and was to publish *Martin Rattler* (1858), all books still readily found in libraries. *Coral Island* tells the story of three boys, Ralph, Jack and Peterkin, castaways on an island, who survive because of their initiative and memory of useful early reading. Much exotic and scientific material is presented and in the main the moralising is implicit in the story, though some overt Christian lessons are included, so that sentences such as 'when a man has done all he *can* do, he ought to leave the rest to God' (XIII) are included from time to time.

One other adventure story must be mentioned, Charles Kingsley's *Westward Ho!* (1855). He dedicated *Westward Ho!* without their knowledge to Sir James Brooke, first white rajah of Sarawak, and Bishop Selwyn, known for his pioneer work in New Zealand, as an expression of his admiration for 'that type of English virtue, at once manly and godly, practical and enthusiastic, prudent and self-sacrificing which . . . they have exhibited'. Kingsley had a very definite purpose in mind in writing this tale about Amyas Leigh, a Devon lad, who went to sea in Elizabethan times to fight the Spaniards. He, a Church of England curate, was concerned at both the apparently rising strength of Roman Catholicism in Britain at the time and the current poor showing of our forces in the Crimea. He therefore wrote this swashbuckling tale of English armed success over the Infidel which ironically was soon taken over as a boys' adventure story (Martin, 1959). Kingsley portrayed Amyas as physically strong, brave, straightforward, slow to speak, patriotic and Protestant. This view of a young hero was almost anti-intellectual and put far more stress on the physical than previous authors who were read by boys had done. In this respect Kingsley was an important innovator, though this tendency could already be found in the tales of Marryat and Kingston.

The corollary to these changes in writing for boys can be found in the books, very popular with adolescent girls, of C.M. Yonge. Charlotte Yonge wrote two very widely read works in the 1850s: *The Heir of Redclyffe* (1853) and *The Daisy Chain* (1856). These are realistic and eventful tales of family life as lived by contemporary English gentry. The moralising is somewhat more obvious than in Marryat or Ballantyne, but nevertheless is not frequent or laboured. Charlotte Yonge intended to appeal to middle-class girls as did the male writers to middle-class boys. These writers of both sexes succeeded in their intention of providing more entertainment in their books and in doing so helped to shift the expectations of children's literature away from the sole aim of improvement towards the twin aims of improvement and amusement.

School stories

In Maria Edgeworth's *Parents' Assistant* (1796) two of the stories were, as noted above, about schools. One 'Eton Montem' was in dramatic form, was marked by some inaccuracies, and its two heroes were intended to be examples of two types believed to be common at Eton, the first an extreme snob and the second an honest independent. The other story, 'The Barring Out', some fifty pages in length, is probably the first recognisable English school story and tells of a revolt of boys against masters. In the 1865 edition there is a footnote that 'the custom of "BARRING OUT" was very general (especially in the northern parts of England) during the seventeenth and eighteenth centuries.' Dr Johnson, it was said, connected Addison with one such successful occurrence, referring to the custom as 'a disorderly privilege, which in his time, prevailed in the principal seminaries of education'. In Maria Edgeworth's story a new boy, Archer, aged sixteen or seventeen, arrives from a public school at Dr Middleton's very happy small private school. Archer challenges the authority of De Grey, the senior boy, and as a result two 'parties' are formed. Dr Middleton for good reasons that he is unprepared to divulge closes the boys' theatre. Archer with a dozen or so boys 'bars out' the staff from the school room. De Grey is sent in to reason with Archer's party who soon end their sit-in. Dr Middleton gives them light punishments except for one boy, Fisher, who is expelled because he lied about 2s 6d of theatre funds entrusted to him, but spent on food for the siege. Quite clearly Maria Edgeworth hoped to persuade her readers that authority must be obeyed at school as well as at home. In her preface she claimed that she wanted to point to 'the errors to which a high spirit and the love of party are apt to lead'. Furthermore, she showed herself conscious of the way in which her tale might be read if she did not write with care, since she hoped to avoid 'the common fault of making the most mischievous character the most *active* and the most ingenious'. Perhaps over-optimistically she added, '*Unsuccessful* cunning will not be admired, and cannot induce imitation.'

In 1841 Harriet Martineau, a prolific writer in many, but mainly social fields, wrote *The Crofton Boys*, a full-length story for young adolescent boys. This book had enough appeal to be republished as late as 1895. In it she told of how Hugh Proctor, the eight-year-old son of the owner of a chemist's shop in the Strand is sent to Mr Tooke's Crofton School, some thirty miles outside London and near to his uncle's mill. He is the youngest boy in the school and Mr Tooke accepted him because he was so keen to come and because his brother, Phillip, was already there. On arrival Hugh is bullied a little, but refuses to tell anyone about this and is settling down well when in a snowball fight he is pushed from a wall by Mr Tooke's son, a fact which Hugh never reveals, and suffers a very serious injury when a coping stone crushes his foot. Ultimately, 'the surgeon took off his foot. As he sat in a chair, and his uncle stood behind him and held his hand and pressed his head against him' (VIII). The matter-of-fact courage demanded by early nineteenth-century medicine is here put in a nutshell. After convalescing he returns to school believing that his ambition of sailing round the world as a soldier or a sailor is now thwarted, but the father of a friend, Holt, promises him a

27

place in commerce in India. So the story ends with Hugh working hard at Crofton to gain entry to 'the India college'.

Many of the characteristics to be found in later school stories are to be seen in *The Crofton Boys*. References to Christianity and especially to prayer, particularly in public by the bedside: Mrs Proctor says to Hugh, 'My comfort is, my dear, that you know where to go for strength when your heart fails you' (III). After he loses his foot Hugh realises that many of the pleasures of the body will not be his as an adult, but 'this is nothing to the pleasure there is in exercising one's soul in bearing pain – in finding one's heart glow with the hope that one is pleasing God' (VIII). Character development is a constant focus. Manly independence is encouraged by the ways the boys treat each other. As Dan Firth, an older boy tells Hugh, when teaching him to climb trees, 'Yes, little boys are looked upon as girls in a school till they show that they are little men' (V). But they must be strong, silent men where emotions are concerned. On another occasion Firth tells Hugh, 'You will find in every school in England that it is not the way of boys to talk about feelings – about anybody's feelings. That is the reason why they do not mention their sisters or their mothers' (VII). Nor do they commit what came to be the major schoolboy sin, that is, to 'sneak'. 'A very slight hiss was heard from every form near, as he came down the room. "O Holt! you have been telling tales!" cried Hugh' (VI). School work, however, is not to be made much of; Firth tells Hugh, 'you will lose ground if you boast about your lessons out of school' (VII). These examples make clear the tone and the substance of the moral teaching that were to be a central feature of boys' school stories when they became more common.

Adult novels

Despite the growth in novel writing and novel reading in the early Victorian era no school story for adults had yet been written. Disraeli used about an eighth of his *Coningsby* (1844) to describe Eton. It was there that Coningsby as a teenager saved the life of Millbank who was to be so central a figure in his later life. Disraeli also included a very laudatory description of the festivities at Montem. Thackeray in *Pendennis* (1850) in passing refers uncritically to Charterhouse, his own old school. One novel by the minor novelist, Albert Smith, entitled *The Fortunes of the*

Scattergood Family (1831), the sixth edition of which appeared in 1887, was in its early chapters extremely critical of Merchant Taylor's School. Bullying (X), poor food – 'a very remarkable infusion, humanly called tea' (X), poor teaching, and caning – 'the constant strokes of the canes, which echoed in the vast room, sharp and distinct as the crack of a rifle, resembled the irregular firing of a body of soldiers' (XIV), are all described in a way perhaps more prefigurative of the *Gem* and the *Magnet* than of *Tom Brown*. Perhaps not surprisingly the suffering Scattergood boy ran away.

This unusually vicious attack on a public school more resembles Dickens's better-known account in *Nicholas Nickleby*

The Internal Economy of Dotheboys Hall

(1839) of Dotheboy's Hall, an exemplar of the infamous schools about which in his Preface to the First Cheap Edition (1848) Dickens wrote 'There are very few now'. In passing one may note that when the news that their master, Squeers, was a criminal reached Dotheboys Hall, the boys immediately rebelled (LXIV). In *Hard Times* (1854) Dickens attacked not the physical conditions or the cruelty in private schools of poor quality, but the crushing of imagination and individuality by the subordination of the pupils to a pedagogic system exemplified in Mr Creakle's school and based on the same principles as the burgeoning factories of the times. Even Dickens could find some good schools and Dr Strong's school in *David Copperfield* (1850) was excellent. Probably Dickens's long-term effect was rather on the contemporary idea of the child than of the school. He challenged the romantic image of Blake and Wordsworth by his realism, but the danger was that sentimentality too often could take over (Coveney, 1967). Even though the death of a child was a fairly common experience for most families then, Dickens's famous descriptions of, for example, the deaths of Paul Dombey or little Nell were marked by a sentimental streak, very different from that found in George Eliot's account of the drowning of Maggie Tulliver. But Dickens's voice was a powerful one.

Charlotte Brontë is better known for her writing about governesses, but she too described schools *en passant*: her own school, Lowood Hall, and a village elementary school in *Jane Eyre* (1847) and a girls' school in Brussels in *Villette* (1853). Her focus was on the development of the character of her heroines and she was little concerned in schools as such. The relationships involved in the position of a governess were a more important focus for her since these could be used to show the forces at work upon individuals and the restrictions imposed by middle-class society upon most women.

In 1850 a minor, but by no means unknown novelist, Frank Smedley, wrote a long novel, entitled *Frank Fairleigh or Scenes from the Life of a Private Pupil*, which tells of the adventures of the half dozen or so pupils of Dr Mildman, a country clergyman, who took private pupils, aged from about fourteen to eighteen. Frank says,

My ideas of a private tutor, derived chiefly from 'Sandford and Merton' and 'Evenings at Home', were rather wide of the mark, leading me to expect that Dr Mildman would impart instruction to us during long rambles over green fields, and in the form of moral allegories to which we should listen with respectful attention and affectionate esteem. (I)

In fact, the pupils had great freedom and learnt academically by traditional teaching methods from their tutor and much socially from each other. This book was considered still to have enough appeal to be reprinted in 1897.

One other adult novel must be mentioned, since it was about Rugby School and was published in 1857, the year in which *Tom Brown* first appeared. George Lawrence, the author of *Guy Livingstone*, was the son of a clergyman who had married a wife related to half the peerage. Lawrence was a contemporary of Thomas Hughes at Rugby (Ellis, 1931: 197-8). In his novel, later translated into French, the early chapters tell of Guy's time at Rugby. The tone, very different from that of *Tom Brown*, can be judged from one passage, supposedly based on a true incident in which he himself was involved when at Rugby. Guy flirts at dinner with the young wife of Tait, Arnold's successor, and carries off as a gage a flower she had worn at dinner. This novel was very popular at the time, but it, and this is true of all those mentioned here, was not by any stretch of the imagination a school novel.

The relations of expectations

Writers

The novelists who were considered great at the time and whom we still see as great used their own personal experience as a source from which to quarry material for their works. Those that had been to public schools wrote about them, on the whole uncritically, and in doing so they were not usually trying to make points about schools, because their work was more often individual in its focus. Dickens was the great exception in that he was deeply concerned about childhood, for Dickens was dedicated, as a result of his own experiences as a child, to preserve innocence against evil and saw clearly that in early Victorian England social institutions, including schools, were often not organised to achieve this aim. His influence was wide and did affect the view held of the child which in its turn changed expectations of the way in which authors might write about children.

However, the main body of those writing for children were lesser figures and largely were women, the majority of whom had been governesses. Mrs Barbauld and Mrs Trimmer, like Charlotte Brontë, had been governesses, and had, therefore, some experience of young persons, especially girls. Charlotte Yonge is important here for a number of reasons. Her career was long, lasting until 1900. She both wrote for adolescent girls and about children's literature, and was well known at the time for both these activities. She had firm views about the contents, moral and otherwise, of children's literature. In her novels she always portrays as the heroine a girl of good breeding, a member of an old county family, who is serious, intellectual and dedicated to good works under the inspiration of Christianity. Charlotte Yonge saw the family as the centre of affection and also as the object of obedience, particularly by girls to their father. This set of expectations was present in her work and was influential before Hughes wrote *Tom Brown*.

Charlotte Yonge, for whom writing was not a part-time occupation and who could be called a professional writer, and those like her had to assume a middle-class readership. Except for some religious tracts and some stories in religious magazines this was the case for literature for both girls and boys. Kingston may be taken as an example of a professional writer for boys. Born in 1814 he spent his childhood in Oporto. From 1824 to 1833 he was in England for his education after which he went back to Portugal to work in the family business. He returned to England and in the 1840s became interested in emigration. During this period he began to write boys' adventure stories. He travelled in the USA and Canada in 1853 and in 1856 was influential in the founding of the Mission to Seamen, becoming honorary secretary of the committee (Kingsford, 1947). During his useful, busy, adventurous and Christian life he wrote more than one hundred books for boys, the vast majority of which can be called adventure stories, exciting, but emphasising overtly the approved moral qualities of initiative and endurance and covertly a broadly Protestant view of Christianity. These books were popular at the time and, though now not seen as of equal quality, they were in the tradition of Marryat and Ballantyne.

Middlemen

In the autobiographies and letters of most Victorian novelists there are many stories of publishers – of difficulties and also of kindnesses. But, whatever the topic, throughout can be seen the power of publishers in selecting what will be published and in influencing very often the style in which it will be presented to the public. From contemporary sources Webb (1958: 206) has calculated that 'roughly 45,000 books [were] published in England between 1816 and 1851' and of these 'well over 10,000 were religious works, far outdistancing the next largest category – history and geography – with 4,900'. Fiction was third with 3,500 titles. At that time very many books, especially fiction, carried at the end a catalogue of other titles published by the same firm. By the 1840/50s these catalogues had become finely differentiated lists of books of different types at differing prices for each market that the publisher hoped to tap. In 1846 the hundredth volume of Bentley's Standard Novel Series was published at 6*s*. In the same year Simons and McIntyre of Belfast brought out their Parlour Novelists, fourteen volumes at 2*s* or 2*s*6*d*. In 1849 Routledge introduced their Railway Library; this was the year that W.H. Smith launched their first railway bookstall. The phrase 'railway literature' was born (Dalziel, 1957: 79-80).

In 1851 in a leader 'The Literature of the Rail' *The Times* attacked some of these books as being in bad taste. The concern was more over cheap periodicals than cheap books, because the former were felt to be more easily accessible to the lower classes. The argument of the leader writer represents a classic illustration of the ideological position of the ruling class of the time. To read certain works was recreation for the upper and middle classes, but to read the same book put a member of the working class in danger of corruption and so must be controlled.

There were at the time no public libraries, but there were circulating libraries, run for profit by businessmen and many sales of books, especially novels, were to circulating libraries. As early as 1824 a Scot, James Nisbet, founded in London a 'Select Theological Circulating Library'. His catalogue for 1832 included a list of tracts, carefully selected novels, books for young children and 'more than a hundred titles which represent the growing area of fiction for older children and young persons'. There were a few school stories, adventures set in exotic places, historical tales, especially stories of Judaism and early Christianity (Bratton,

1981: 57-9). In 1840 Mudie's famous circulating library was founded and we know that the influence on publishers of this library was immense (Grist, 1970). Mudie's would buy hundreds of copies of a successful writer, so that publishers felt that to publish what was unacceptable to such a client was likely to be an uneconomic proposition. Novels were usually published in three volumes at half a guinea a volume. They were, therefore, lengthy and beyond the pocket of all but the wealthy.

This was also the great age of the quality periodical – *Fraser's Magazine*, the *Quarterly Review*, and the *Edinburgh Review* are three amongst many. They carried influential book reviews, to some of which reference will be made in later chapters. Quite often the reviewers were clergymen and they were obviously very influential in controlling the contents of the periodicals published by such bodies as the Religious Tract Society. One such magazine was the *British Mother's Magazine*, published between 1851 and 1855. It carried frequent articles on light reading and in its pages is demonstrated the very stringent views of many early mid-Victorians on novels. Fiction for children should on the whole be avoided, because 'it wasted time, unfitted the reader for better literature, and imparted false ideas of life, stimulating without feeding the mind and the imagination, and blunting the sensibilities to real horrors because they are less extravagant than fictitious ones' (Dalziel, 1957: 53). Novels by the eighteenth-century founders of the British tradition, for example, Richardson or Smollet, were seen as immoral in the extreme.

Care had, therefore, to be exercised over what children read. The age was a didactic one and there was no difficulty for all middlemen – publishers, critics, those running circulating libraries and parents – to insist on didactic material, in both fiction and non-fiction, for the young. Indeed, Thackeray spoke of the 'young girl standard', saying that writers must 'suppose the ladies and children always present' (Ray, 1945: 161). All these middlemen had an interest, often financial, in preserving this climate of moral didacticism, based in Christianity. No attempt was permitted or encouraged, except in the case of boys' adventure stories, to create a special form of writing for children other than literature similar to *Sandford and Merton* or *The Parents' Assistant*, and even adventure stories were in spirit, and often openly, didactic. And this was so despite the fact that some, Thomas Arnold for example, had noted that this type of literature did not match the felt reality of childhood at any class level.

Readers

Novelists like Charlotte Yonge succeeded in large part because they had a clear view of their readership. They saw it as middle-class and when writing for children aimed at the child in the Christian and respectable family. Writers at the time did not try to write for the huge anonymous market addressed by those writing best sellers today. The material that was aimed at working-class homes was simpler in style, shorter in length, melodramatic and even more moralistic in tone than that for middle-class readers. Neither group was likely to benefit from reading the other's literature. Many cheap magazines, such as the *Penny Magazine*, catered for the cottage market, though the level of literacy amongst the working class at the time was not high, probably around 50 per cent, and furthermore hours of work were so long that literate workers often had little leisure or energy available for reading.

There was, therefore, around 1850 a mutually related network of expectations ruling in literary circles and amongst readers or their surrogates which supported a specific type of writing for children. This was characterised by an almost missionary-like zeal to teach a set of moral standards that seems to us today to be narrow and puritanical in the extreme. Writing to meet what we would see as the real needs of childhood was rare. The next stage in the argument is to try to discover the roots of these relations of expectations in the contemporary social structure.

Social structural supports

Those who held these relations of expectations did so within a changing social structure. What must now be traced briefly is the nature of and changes in the parts of the social structure salient for expectations as they then related to children's books. Four social institutions will be considered. First, no sociological analysis of Victorian Britain, Marxist or not, can fail to take account of the rapidly changing capitalist economy. Next, already in this chapter enough has been said to show that religion was a central social institution at the time. Third, similarly the family has also been seen to be important. Last, both the didacticism of contemporary children's literature and the focus of this study on *school* stories demands consideration of education outside the family.

The economy

The economic legacies for Britain of the Napoleonic wars were of many kinds. Manufacturing industry might have grown greatly, but only at the cost of social and fiscal dislocation. The latter could be overcome, it was believed, by a return in 1819 to the gold standard, but the former could not so easily be cured. Nor did those affected allow their rulers to forget their troubles and throughout the years from 1815 until 1848 there was a series of riots of varying degrees of seriousness and of disorders over social and economic conditions. Yet despite Cobbett's thundering, the clamour over Catholic emancipation and parliamentary reform, and the long drawn-out Chartist troubles the standard of life of the working man was slowly rising.

This was seen, certainly by the wealthy, to be due to the benign workings of the *laissez-faire* system which under the circumstances of the times did bring benefits. Implicit in the better conditions of the working class were profits for the industrialist and for those in commerce. The early Victorian years were marked by the rise of an increasingly wealthy middle class. In addition, there was a growing professional and commercial section of the middle class. This built on the by then traditionally strong position of London as a commercial capital and serviced both the new industrial trade and the old agricultural wealth of Britain. The development had begun of that long finely graduated system of social positions, closely associated with Victorian England, that stretched from the working class through the skilled craftsman to the aristocratic landowner with his seat in the Lords. The *laissez-faire* economy encouraged aspiration to upward social mobility. The system of status encouraged claims for the status conventionally associated with higher positions. Many successful businessmen claimed the position of gentlemen, if not for themselves, at least for their sons or their sons-in-law. One crucial step in achieving this claim was to ensure that their children were properly, that is conventionally educated, and in the case of English, though not yet Scottish, boys this meant attending a public school.

The *laissez-faire* system in its pure form implied that the central government withdrew from any attempt to steer the economy. No revenue, except to fund the armed forces and such minimal bureaucratic functions as the Foreign Office, was needed, so that taxes, which anyway distorted free trade, were almost unnecessary. When the disorder of the Chartist era ended those in power felt secure enough to extend the freedom already given to trade to the flow of information. A number of excise duties on the free flow of information were, therefore, abolished in the 1850s; these included that on advertising (1853) and the stamp duty on newspapers (1855). In 1861 the excise duty on paper was abolished. These remissions encouraged the publication of books and papers; for example, the *Daily Telegraph* was started in 1855.

The books and other goods produced by capitalist Britain found a market throughout the world, but particularly within the second Empire, another economic legacy of the Napoleonic Wars. Furthermore, the running and defence of these widespread possessions created a new and, as the Empire was developed, a growing demand for dependable soldiers, professionals, and bureaucrats, both in government and commerce, who under the social circumstances of the times must be supplied from Britain. In addition, the defence of this Empire, so much a part of the British economy, and of its lines of communication could and did lead the Mother Country into European and other international wars. The Crimean War (1854–6) to which reference has been made in connection with Kingsley's *Westward Ho!* is a case in point.

Religion

Kingsley's book also had religious aims and could at the time very easily be read in this way as religion was an abiding interest of the Victorian middle and upper classes, though perhaps of less crucial importance to the latter than the former. Except for a very few Roman Catholics the ruling class were and had been Anglicans for centuries, whereas a high proportion of the rising middle class were Protestant nonconformists. In 1828 the repeal of the Test and of the Corporation Acts, which prohibited dissenters from holding national or municipal offices, and the emancipation of Catholics, apparently political acts, all had immense implications for religious institutions. The period from 1830 to 1860 was marked by much religious ferment and a number of new positions were taken which were very influential at the time.

Two basic positions emerged in the 1830s in the Church of England, though a third evolved in the 1850s. The first was that of the Evangelicals and was largely under the influence of former members of the Clapham Sect who had been and still were deeply involved in the problem of slavery, especially in the Empire. Thus, Wilberforce and Hannah More, who had herself written many tracts for cottage children, were important in this group. They tried to recapture and build on the emotional intensity of Christian belief in the early part of the century. They claimed a literal interpretation of the Bible and stressed the need for purity of conduct as a sign of commitment to God. They believed strongly in the existence of an after-life in which Heaven or Hell formed rewards for earthly life. Those supporting the second position were usually known as Tractarians because of their connection with the Oxford Movement whose members had produced a controversial, but influential series of *Tracts for the Times*, beginning in 1833. These Anglicans were also sometimes loosely called High Churchmen because of their tendency towards the Roman, rather than the Nonconformist, position in doctrine and liturgical practice. They emphasised salvation by the grace of sacraments administered by clergy ordained by bishops and saw the Church of England as part of the ancient Catholic church. They were, therefore, much concerned with those ceremonies and beliefs that had been rejected at the Reformation.

Two events increased the distrust felt between supporters of these positions. The first was what has been called the Papal Aggression of 1850. The Pope declared his intention of establishing regional dioceses in Britain. There were, in fact, some doubts about whether this action was legally permissible at the time, but certainly it brought out all the latent anti-Catholicism of many and this was used by the Evangelicals, both amongst the Anglican and the Nonconformist communities, to stir up feeling against the Roman Catholics. This unpopularity rubbed off on the Tractarians. In 1851 a second event occurred which increased interest in religion. As part of the decanal census a count was made on 'Census Sunday', 30 March, of how many persons attended a place of worship. This count showed that 'not less than 47 per cent, but certainly not more than 54 per cent of the population of England and Wales of ten years of age and over went to church' (Best, 1971: 177). This finding led the churches to a belief that they must set about 'rechristianising' the population, especially, though not only, the working class.

The third group mentioned earlier becomes important at this point. This group was known as the Christian Socialists and is important not only because of its place in English social and religious history, but also because both Charles Kingsley and

Thomas Hughes were prominent members of it. The key figure for Christian Socialism was F.D. Maurice. From 1840 to 1853 Maurice, a clergyman, was Professor of English Literature and History at King's College, London, founded by the Church of England as a college of London University. In 1853, because of the radical nature of the theological doctrines that he had recently published, he was dismissed by the council of the college. When at Oxford, to which he went after taking his degree at Cambridge, Maurice had been much influenced by Coleridge's *On the Constitution of Church and State* (1830). In this work Coleridge assumed that a social ethic was implicit in Christianity. Maurice and the other influential Christian Socialists developed this belief. They tried to create a third position between that of the High and the Low Churches and, hence, were sometimes referred to as Broad Churchmen. In opposition to the Evangelicals who emphasised the future state of grace of the individual almost to the exclusion of any interest in contemporary social abuses, and in opposition to the Tractarians who appeared so absorbed in the details of their Patristic inheritance that they overlooked the contemporary sufferings of their fellow men, the Christian Socialists focused on the application of broad Christian principles to the lives of human beings today. They were particularly interested in the problems of the new industrial classes and of the rural workers who were suffering from the dislocations both to the hand textile industry because of the growth of British manufacturing industry and to agriculture due to the increasing competition from cheap food crops grown overseas.

Regardless of any internal argument about theological positions the Church of England was still very much the established church in England and Wales. This can be seen very clearly in its reaction to the great events of the period. 'National Days of Fasting and Humiliation' were proclaimed in 1853 on a bad outbreak of cholera, in 1854 on the outbreak of the Crimean War and in 1857 because of the Indian Mutiny. The Church still legitimately claimed to act on behalf of the conscience of the nation.

Writers worked within a field in which these strongly-held positions were constantly being presented at all levels of sophistication to the reading public. Dickens with great skill managed to present 'a good religious note without committing himself beyond the common stock of Christian phrases' (House, 1942: 110). This was the position which most acknowledged great novelists managed to take up and, indeed, their success could in part be attributed to their striding along a knife edge of religious susceptibilities without giving offence to the various positions on either side. Some writers, however, either were not so successful or wrote to press their position. Charles Kingsley, an avowed Christian Socialist, was one of the latter. Many lesser writers also fell into this category, particularly those who wrote for the various religious bodies that published tracts or periodicals. Yet the body that became the most prolific publisher of these works, particularly for children, the Religious Tract Society, took a stance somewhere between the Broad and Evangelical position without affecting Evangelicals or High Churchmen by affirming the more socialist beliefs of some of Maurice's followers. Their fiction could, therefore, be realistic in focusing on social, rather than individual situations, but didactic in a general Christian way without an excessive concentration upon points of religious doctrine.

The family

The family, and its foundation in marriage, no doubt had immense economic and social implications particularly connected with the ownership and transmission through time of property, but for the middle-class and for the 'respectable' working-class Victorians these were almost sacrosanct institutions, seen as religious, and hence Christian, in their roots. Whatever the truth of the evidence about the double standard of Victorian family life (Marcus, 1966), the external impression of the earnest and morally upright family had to be preserved and many novels portrayed struggles to hide black sheep from the gaze of the world.

This moral ambition was allied to the ambition for status referred to earlier, but the circumstances of mid-nineteenth-century life had begun to make more difficult the establishment and preservation of the type of family home considered proper for the middle class. Banks (1954) has shown by a study of Trollope's novels and of such guides to domestic economy as the various editions of *Mrs Beeton* that there was considerable concern in the mid-nineteenth century about the rising costs of establishing and maintaining a home. The wages of servants, the costs of keeping up a carriage, the prices of food and the increasing cost of schooling, now more necessary if a son was to succeed in professional or commercial life, all gave cause for concern. Indeed Banks, and his position has been generally accepted, gives this concern as the major cause of the start of the fall in the birth rate of the middle class from about the 1870s.

It was through the family, especially in the early years of childhood, that the religious and moral values of the time were transmitted. There was a firmly held set of views concerning the position of men and of women in the family and in life in general. The family was seen as the social agency which taught and supported these moral views of the sex roles. Furthermore, society was strongly hierarchical and the family was also the place where that obedience to authority so basic to the social fabric as a whole could be taught and preserved. The Victorian family was, therefore, a social and educational institution of prime moral importance.

Girls were taught to be gentler than boys and the literature written to assist this teaching was different in its tone and content. Charlotte Yonge celebrated the family, its place in cherishing children and the need for girls to adapt to the needs of their family, even to the extent on occasion of marrying against their wishes. W.H.G. Kingston told of boys leaving the family to make their way in the world at large, albeit in a Christian way and eventually to return to a loving and supportive mother or wife. Women were to be chaste and preserved from temptation; men must know the temptations of the world and even might yield to them, though their loving womenfolk would usually forgive them if they did succumb.

Children also had to obey their parents. Authority within the family at the time was unreasoning and unquestioned. All the power was on one side and sanctions existed to enforce parental, usualy paternal, authority. Thus, we know of and read about fathers threatening to disinherit their sons. A daughter who would not obey her father in marrying his choice of partner would end up without a dowry or married to a poor husband or as a governess. Normative sanctions were also used in that parents might appeal to a filial duty, often seen as divinely ordered. The final course open to a boy who would not obey his father was to run away from home, usually in novels with the aim of going to the USA or the colonies by stowing away on a ship or by working his passage. Girls were once again worse off in that this course was not open to them. The claustrophobic nature of Victorian family life has often been noted, but nowhere were its effects stronger than in its broad educational functions and particularly in relation to the passing on of the contemporary moral code.

Education

The family was an educational institution in the widest sense, but during the first half of the nineteenth century a switch had begun from educating children largely at home to sending them away to school. In saying this one is referring to the education of boys more than girls and to the middle and upper classes, because, since there were no schools provided by the state, the formal educational institutions then in existence were too expensive for the working class. When discussing formal education in the early Victorian era, therefore, people were either referring to preparatory and secondary schools for those who could afford that expense, or to elementary schools provided out of charity, offering a minimal curriculum, for members of the working class, often at the cost of a penny or so a week.

The demand for a public school education had increased since the 1830s and one index of this is the increase in the number of schools that later became acknowledged as public schools by the admission of their heads to the Head Masters' Conference (HMC). There are objections, as Honey (1977) has pointed out, to using this index, as many of the schools now seen as having high status then do not have it now and some now counted to be public schools were not then thought to have that status. However, if one uses the 1962 list of HMC schools, consisting at that date of some 200 schools, 3 were founded in the 1830s, 15 in the 1840s, 6 in the 1850s and 14 in the 1860s (Bamford, 1967: 270).

This increasing demand was obviously based on increased wealth or in an increased willingness to use existing wealth on the education of sons, but why was it channelled into the public schools – particularly at a time when there were also an increasing number of proprietary schools, based on the entrepreneurial activities of their capitalist heads? The question is an apt one in view of the acknowledged low repute of public schools around the turn of the century, believed, and rightly, to be characterised by immorality, sexual and other, and by violence, often leading to rebellions, far fiercer than any 'barring out', which on occasions had to be put down by the militia. The answer appears to be that the reforms carried out at Rugby during the period from 1828 to 1842 when Thomas Arnold was head convinced their potential users that these schools were not only closely linked to high status, but were once more places where what was seen as a sound education could be gained.

However, the influence of Arnold did not work in any simple way. Arnold's reforms were based on his assertion of the independence of a head from his governors in all matters of school discipline and routine; on the view that assistant masters were themselves of professional status and not mere ushers as had been true in the past in most public schools and was so then in most proprietary schools; on a belief that the school had a corporate identity that must be encouraged and maintained; on a ruthless policy of removing unsuitable pupils, regardless of loss of revenue; and, finally, on the use of the prefect system whereby much of the administration and even of minor organisational matters in the school, and hence of much of its educational effect, was handed to the senior boys (Newsome, 1961: 40-2). Furthermore, though Arnold claimed that his first priority in education was intellectual and though it is true that he put much more emphasis than was usual at the time upon academic work, nevertheless, in practice, and by his own admission, his priorities were well in tune with his times: '1st, religious and moral principle, 2ly, gentlemanly conduct, 3rdly, intellectual ability' (Stanley, 1844: 107). The oft-repeated phrase 'a Christian and a gentleman' was, indeeed, very much the aim of Arnold's Rugby.

The Arnold legend was largely the creation of his outstanding former pupil, A.P. Stanley, who two years after Arnold's early death in 1842, brought out *The Life and Correspondence of Thomas Arnold* in two volumes, a book that was very successful, much discussed and soon reprinted. In it Arnold's work was presented in a very favourable light, in Broad Church terms and with emphasis on the success of the organisation he established to run his school. In the late 1840s the expansion of numbers of public schools was largely, though not entirely, met by the creation of schools such as the Woodard schools, aimed not so much for the upper middle class as for the middle, and lower-middle classes and for farmers. In the 1850s/1860s new public schools, based on the reforms made by Arnold, were founded by his disciples, by heads who had been boys or masters under him, and by some others who had taken up his ideas. Thus, Arnold's reforms were influential on the direction of growth of the English public school system, but not in the simple imitative way in which the argument has in the past usually been presented (Honey, 1977: 46).

Arnold's name is also often associated with the cult for games. He himself, as noted above, put a much higher emphasis upon academic work and by his own actions did not either encourage or discourage games at Rugby in any definite way. Certainly, though he did try to control some of the unorganised forms of physical activity like boxing, fishing or shooting, especially where this would either give the opportunity for going to public houses or for other forms of 'immorality' or where the activity could lead to conflict with the local community, he did not himself or through his prefects actually encourage the highly organised systems of sport that later became common in these schools. Many of the leading schools of the period gave no real prominence to sports at all and these included Rugby, Harrow and Winchester (Newsome, 1961: 205). Furthermore, the preeminent public school Eton, was particularly unreceptive of the reforms of Arnold or of the earlier ones of Butler of Shrewsbury upon whose work Arnold had to some extent built. Under its eccentric but very powerful head, Hawtrey, Eton put less emphasis upon religion, continued to go its own way in games, to the extent of preserving its own form of football, and, finally, by retaining the tutorial system, avoided the need to adopt any prefect system of the Arnoldian type (Newsome, 1961: 85-6).

David Riesman used a telling phrase, 'the academic procession' (1956) about the wide scope of university level institutions in the USA, ranging at the top from Harvard or the University of California at Berkeley to local state agriculture or religious colleges, each of which under a capitalist system meets different parts of the complex existing market for tertiary education. Certainly at the secondary level there was an academic procession in England in the middle of the nineteenth century. At the top were the nine great public schools, later recognised as such because they were joined together for investigation by the Clarendon Commission which reported in 1864; these included Eton, Harrow, Rugby and the ancient day schools, Westminster and St Paul's. Next there was a host of new public schools, often old grammar schools, jostling to achieve a higher status under the impact of the ambitions, backed by fees, of the new middle class. At a lower level was an even greater number of entrepreneurial proprietary schools, sometimes having only a short life, some in towns and others in rural areas, apeing the classical curriculum of their higher status brethren. Below these were a wide range of commercial schools of one sort or another and these gradually merged into the better type of elementary schools. There was no state provision or control of schools at the secondary level, though since 1833 some government funds had started to flow into the elementary section through approved religious bodies either to assist the schools directly or to help in the training of teachers (Musgrave, 1968).

It was from this educational system that writers would draw their material for readers whose expectations were governed by their own experiences within it or when exercised on behalf of their sons were influenced either by their own education or by that which they hoped would enable their sons to achieve the higher status to which they aspired on their sons' behalf.

Conclusion

A writer in *Household Words* in the 1850s saw the members of the human race

> all advancing, some faster, some slower, to a better education, a better social condition, a better conception of the principles of art and commerce, and a clearer recognition of their rights and their duties, in a more cheering faith in the upward tendency of humanity (quoted Dalziel, 1957: 166)

Today we would criticise this passage as a prime example of the Whig view of history. Yet, as can be seen from the brief account given here of the salient parts of the social structure, it could represent an entirely believable account to readers at the time. The focus upon didacticism, the concern with the problems of change and above all the underlying religious tone were all expected of the literature of the time. Nowhere was this more true than in the literature offered to children, because this would influence future generations. Its readers were to be the generals and subalterns, the industrialists and professionals of the future, serving Britain at home or in the Empire, because this literature was aimed very largely at the middle class. The working class were in large part illiterate and though, of course, upward mobility was encouraged, this was to be achieved by rigid adherence to the qualities expected in the middle class. Though the literature of the times catered for both boys and girls, the one recent major change in the expected form of children's literature was in answer to the changing role of men in British society. This was the development of the boy's adventure story. School stories were very rare; boy's adventure stories were, however, becoming readily available.

These relations of expectations were supported by the contemporary British social structure and, more particularly, through a *laissez-faire* market for books. Those who published books were deeply imbued with a view of what would sell and also what should be offered to readers. They were mediators of the religious spirit of the times and were supportive of the crucial social, and even political, role of the patriarchal family. Yet they were as conscious as Arnold had been of the need for more realistic books for children, particularly for boys, and had encouraged the growth in the 1840/50s of the adventure story, a genre characterised by realism, but also by didacticism. This in brief was the situation in 1856/7 when Thomas Hughes was writing *Tom Brown's Schooldays*.

3

Tom Brown and *Eric*

As an introduction to this chapter, in which two of the major exemplars of what was to become a minor literary genre are to be examined, let us take three statements, all by respected writers, made over the last fifty or so years, and examine them. In 1933 Hicks produced the pioneering study of the place of the school in English – and German – fiction. He wrote, 'In England the school novel has no real literary ancestry. *Tom Brown* was a revoluionary phenomenon from which later school novels dated' (Hicks, 1933: 7). Clearly, after the evidence of the last chapter, one cannot really agree with that. Eight years later Mack in another pathbreaking study, making extensive use of school stories, claimed that Thomas Hughes 'single-handed . . . created a new literary genre' (Mack, 1941: 91). Partly for the same reason this too seems extreme, but it also ignores any influence of *Eric* and we shall see that this was great. Finally, in her 'Preface' to the Penguin edition of *Tom Brown* (1971) Naomi Lewis wrote, 'But not only did *Tom Brown* start a vast train of books about the wonderful myth of boarding school life it also influenced school life' (1971: 7). The argument to be developed here is that no 'vast train' of the nature of which Naomi Lewis hints followed. In this chapter the evidence will be set out about the writers, the contents and the reception of these two books, both extremely important in the ultimate development of the genre.

Tom Brown *and* Eric

Tom Brown's Schooldays

Thomas Hughes

Thomas Hughes was born in 1822 at Uffington in the Berkshire countryside, second son of John Hughes, who had been at Oriel College, Oxford, with Arnold and admired his character, but not his politics; they were too radical for a typical English country gentleman. Before he went to Arnold's Rugby Thomas Hughes was sent to a private school near Worcester where sports were given some emphasis. From 1833 to 1842 Tom was at Rugby, where he became captain of cricket and of football. He left to go to Oriel in the spring of 1842 a few months before Arnold died. He was at Oxford till 1845 where he played for Oxford at cricket and rowed for his college. He also became a skilled boxer and a tenacious cross-country runner.

After going down from Oxford he read for the bar, initially at Lincoln's Inn from 1845 to 1848. F.D. Maurice was chaplain to the Inn. In 1848 Hughes switched to the Inner Temple just before being called to the bar. In the same year he married and in 1851 moved to Wimbledon where he shared a house with John M. Ludlow, his great friend, also a barrister and a Christian Socialist. It was in this house that he wrote *Tom Brown's Schooldays*, mainly during 1856 in the summer law vacation. In some doubt as to its quality he showed it to Ludlow who said that it must be published and put him in touch with Alexander Macmillan who was so impressed that he immediately accepted the book. Hughes's much loved daughter, Evie, died of scarlet fever in the middle of his writing *Tom Brown* and many have attributed the apparent change in tone between Parts One and Two to this bereavement. *Tom Brown* was published anonymously, 'by an Old Boy', in 1857 and was an immediate success.

Hughes wrote one other similar book, *Tom Brown at Oxford* (1861) which was less successful though by no means a failure. Throughout his life he was interested in social reform, eventually using much of his own capital to set up a utopian community in Tennessee where he himself spent the period 1878 to 1882. On his return he was fortunate to be appointed a county court judge in Chester and he remained so until his death in 1896.

This brief biography (D.N.B.; Mack and Armytage, 1952) shows that Hughes was by no means the usual Victorian writer of books for boys. In the first place he had experience of Rugby, a school where much change had taken place and was known to have done so. More particularly, Rugby was not seen as a purely aristocratic school. It was a school where sons of aristocrats, of the upper middle class, professional and industrial, and of those in the new professions mixed together and worked out within the new organisational framework established by Arnold a compromise within which academic work was allowed some status. Games, if not organised, were beginning to be brought under some control (Dunning and Sheard, 1979: 73-8) and morals were much stressed so that the standards of behaviour there were thought to be much improved. There is, however, evidence to suggest that 'Arnold did not solve the problem of discipline at Rugby'; for the average boy life 'did not differ markedly from that before and after his time'. There certainly had been improvements from the bad days, but these took place around 1815 under Wooll and further changes did occur somewhat later after Arnold's time (Bamford, 1957).

The impetus to write *Tom Brown* came when Hughes was considering the impending departure of his eight-year-old son, Maurice, to school: 'Thinking over what I should like to say to him before he went to school I took to writing a story, as the easiest way of bringing out what I wanted' (quoted Mack and Armytage, 1952: 86). Therefore, not surprisingly in his preface to *Tom Brown* he wrote, 'My whole object in writing at all was to get the chance of preaching.' Internal evidence of this is also to be found within *Tom Brown* itself. On the stage coach on his way to Rugby during the long cold night Tom has gone back in his mind over 'his little past life' and

> he has been forward into the mysterious boy-future, speculating as to what sort of place Rugby is, and what they do there, and calling up all the stories of public schools which he had heard from boys in the holidays. (I. IV)

Hughes aimed to meet a lack of appropriate school stories, particularly about public schools, in order to try to prepare his son and others so that they gained what he felt they ought from the opportunity before them.

One difficulty was that Hughes knew Arnold's Rugby, not that of the 1850/60s, and as we have seen public schools were developing away from Arnold's original conceptions. Furthermore, his own career at Rugby had been oriented more towards games than towards work, whereas Arnold had put his priorities the other way round. Both had, however, in the words of Squire Brown, put moral qualities first:

> If he'll only turn out a brave, helpful, truth-telling Englishman, and a gentleman, and a Christian, that's all I want . . . and upon this view of the case framed his last words of advice to Tom (I. IV)

The order of these moral qualities is worth noting; courage first and Christianity last. In this we can see the influence of Hughes's close friend, Charles Kingsley, whose admiration of athletic Christians had earned for his views the sobriquet of 'muscular Christianity'. No one is quite certain who invented this term. Leslie Stephen thought that it was a writer in the *Saturday Review*, but by the time Hughes wrote *Tom Brown* the term was already being applied to the writing of both Charles Kingsley and his brother, Henry, much to the former's annoyance (Martin, 1959: 219). Another literary influence must have been Marryat who is referred to by Tom Brown when considering his plans for the time when he and his friend, East, would be given a study: 'every night from locking-up . . . they would be together, to talk about fishing, drink bottled-beer, read Marryat's novels, and sort bird's eggs' (II. I).

But above all, though thinking initially of his own son, Hughes was influenced by his potential readers. In the Preface to *Tom Brown at Oxford* he wrote:

> When I first resolved to write the book I tried to realise to myself what the commonest type of English boy of the upper middle class was, so far as my experience went; and to that type I have throughout adhered, trying simply to give a good specimen of that genus.

Tom Brown's Schooldays

Thomas Hughes introduced the book by setting Tom firmly within his family circle at home in the Berkshire countryside. He is brought up with love and care by his mother and family servants. He plays with the village children, learning their games including wrestling, fighting and such country pursuits as fishing and climbing trees. At the age of nine Tom was sent for a year to a private school. 'Tom imbibed a fair amount of Latin

and Greek at the school, but somehow it didn't suit him, or he it.'
Apart from Tom's tendency to be a dare-devil which caused
trouble 'the two ushers . . . were not gentlemen' and their
methods which included 'encouraging tale-bearing' and 'favouring
grossly the biggest boys' made Tom unhappy. When a fever
broke out in his third half year and he was sent home Squire
Brown arranged for him to go early to Rugby, meeting Tom's
greatest wish 'to send him at once to a public school' (I.
III).

Tom goes by stage coach through the night to Rugby and on
arriving at the school is met by East, whose aunt 'lived
somewhere down your way in Berkshire and . . . asked me to
give you a lift'. East like Tom was in School-house and they were
to become very close friends. East helped Tom to settle in,
showing him round the buildings, and took him after dinner to
watch School-house play the rest of the school at football. There
follows a spirited account of a game of rugby football, as played
in the early stages of its development. East plays a small, but
courageous part. Tom himself at the end joins the fray and earns
the praise of Old Brooke, the house captain, 'Well, he is a plucky
youngster, and will make a player'. Occasional authorial moral
comments are made; for example, 'as endless as are boys'
characters, so are their ways of facing or not facing a scrummage
at football' (I. V).

Tom soon settled to become a keen young Rugby boy, doing
what work was needed with the help of 'cribs' when preparing for
Latin and Greek translations, but playing hard at all sports
whether team games or unorganised activities like fishing or bird-
nesting. He has to earn his place in school by being a fag and by
overcoming the severe bullying. Tom and East stand up against
the bullying of seventeen-year-old Flashman, 'a formidable enemy
for small boys'. Ultimately because of Tom's refusal to part with
his tickets for the favourite in a Derby lottery, Flashman 'roasts'
Tom on the School-house fire. Tom, though 'badly scorched',
refused to tell how it happened. Hughes comments:

> I trust and believe that such scenes are not possible now at
> school, and that lotteries and betting-books have gone out;
> but I am writing of schools as they were in our time and
> must give the evil with the good. (I. VIII)

On his return to school after a couple of days in the sick-room
Tom took up his adventurous career again. He was now in the

upper school so that if he was discovered doing wrong he was 'sent up straight to the Doctor at once' and he met Dr Arnold on several occasions because of 'a series of scrapes into which [he] managed now to tumble'. He was flogged for fishing where he should not have done, for attending a fair in town when this was forbidden, and, ultimately, on the last but one day of the half he and East are called to see the Doctor. He spoke seriously to them of their future, ending,

> He should be sorry if they had to leave, as the School might do them both much good, and wishes them to think very seriously in the holidays over what he has said. Good night.

Dr Arnold believes that 'They don't feel that they have any duty or work to do in the school.' The master of their form, 'a model young master', in fact Cotton who was to become headmaster of Marlborough from 1852 to 1858 and then Bishop of Calcutta, suggests,

> 'I think if either of them had some little boy to take care of it would steady them. Brown is the most reckless of the two, I should say; East wouldn't get into so many scrapes without him.'

Part One ends with the Doctor promising 'I'll think of it' (I. XI).

Tom returns to Rugby, fully prepared to be in a study with Harry East. On arrival the matron tells him that he is to have a study with George Arthur, a new boy of thirteen, who is 'very delicate and has never been from home before'. He and Arthur are summoned to tea with Mrs Arnold where the Doctor cheerfully advises Tom that Arthur 'doesn't look as we should like to see him' and needs some 'Rugby air and cricket. And . . . some good long walks.' Despite great temptation, incuding such taunts as 'a queer chum for Tom Brown', Tom sticks to Arthur. Very soon the first major challenge comes, when Arthur kneels beside his bed to say his prayers. Sneers and a slipper from a big boy follow. 'Then Tom saw the whole, and the next moment the boot he had just pulled off flew straight at the head of the bully'. This chapter, entitled 'How the Tide Turned' carries at its head Lovell's lines

> Once to every man and nature comes the moment to decide,
> In the strife of Truth with falsehood, for the good or evil side;

Tom had met his first point of decision. Many more, some apparently trivial, followed. 'Several times he faltered for the devil showed him first, all his old friends calling him "Saint" and "Squaretoes", and a dozen hard names.' Tom took to saying his prayers in public. Others followed. He learnt 'the lesson that he who has conquered his own coward spirit has conquered the whole outward world' (II. I). The 'young master's' plan was beginning to be successful. Ultimately, Arthur becomes very friendly with Martin, an unusual boy who was 'quite out of place at a public school', not on grounds of social status, but because of his odd interests; he had 'a passion for birds, beasts and insects' and 'was also an experimental chemist'. With him Arthur becomes 'a bold thinker and a good runner' (II. III).

The next chapter contains the well-known account of Tom's fight with Slogger Williams, a much bigger boy. Tom took him on to defend Arthur, who offended Williams by breaking down while translating a particularly emotional passage in the *Iliad*. The fight was a hard one and Tom only began to win when he used a throw learnt from a skilful village friend in Berkshire. This caused some argument about whether wrestling was allowed. Young Brooke, Old Brooke's brother and now a member of the Sixth, ruled that certain holds were permissible. The fight began again, till the Doctor, who knew of it all along, emerged from his quarters. All scattered except Brooke. He arranges for Williams and Tom to shake hands which they did 'with great satisfaction and mutual respect'. The chapter concludes with an authorial comment, which starts with these words:

> Boys will quarrel, and when they quarrel will sometimes fight. Fighting with fists is the natural and English way for English boys to settle their quarrels. What substitution for it is there, amongst any nation under the sun? What would you like to see take its place? (II. V)

Two years pass and fever breaks out in the school. Some boys go home, but most stay:

> On the Saturday Thompson died, in the bright afternoon, while the cricket match was going on as usual on the big-side ground; the Doctor, coming from his death-bed, passed along the gravel-walk at the side of the close, but no one knew what had happened till the next day.

Arthur, however, had caught the fever and 'was reported worse each day' so that his mother, a widow, was summoned. 'But God had work for Arthur to do, the crisis passed'. Tom now spent much time talking with him to help his recovery. One evening Arthur said he wanted to talk to Tom 'very seriously'. He told him, 'Tom, I want you to give up using vulgus books and cribs.' Tom asks, 'Why, young'un?' 'Because you're the honestest boy in Rugby and that ain't honest.' Tom replies that he does not see how he can do all he wants at Rugby without resorting to such aids.

> I want to be A1 at cricket and football and all other games and to make my head keep my heart against any fellow, lout or gentleman. I want to get into the sixth form before I leave, and to please the Doctor; and I want to carry away just as much Latin and Greek as will take me through Oxford respectfully . . . I want to leave behind me the name of a fellow who never bullied a little boy, or turned his back on a big one.'

Arthur's mother comes in and thanks him for all he has done for her son. Tom leaves, having promised indirectly to do as Arthur has asked, and returns to his study to find there a fine new fishing rod and 'a splendidly bound Bible . . . on the title page of which was written – TOM BROWN from his affectionate and grateful friends, Frances Jane Arthur: George Arthur' (II. VI).

Tom explains to Harry East what he has promised and after much difficulty persuades him also 'to give the new plan a fair trial'. Their discussions over honesty lead East to want to be confirmed though he is somewhat older than usual for this. Tom advises him to see the Doctor who permits him to take Communion at school with Tom before confirmation and arranges for him to be confirmed at home in the holidays.

The book concludes Tom's career at Rugby with an account of 'Tom Brown's Last Match' against the MCC. He is now 'a praeposter and Captain of Cricket' and Arthur too is a member of the XI. The match ended with the school having nine runs to make with two wickets in hand, but, because time runs out and the MCC had scored more in the first innings, 'The Lord's men are declared the winners' (II. VIII). A brief chapter follows telling of how whilst on a walking and fishing tour in Skye Tom heard of Arnold's death. 'He felt completely carried off his moral and intellectual legs, as if he had lost his standing-point in the invisible world . . . . He felt an irresistable longing to get to Rugby . . . and travelled as fast as boat and railway could carry him to Rugby station.' He found Thomas, the school servant, who told his tale.

THE CONVERSATION DURING THE MATCH.

'Where is he buried, Thomas?' said he at last. 'Under the altar in the chapel, sir' answered Thomas. 'You'd like to have the key, I daresay.'

Tom went to the chapel, prayed and 'while the tears flowed down his cheeks, knelt humbly and hopefully, to lay down there his

TOM'S VISIT TO THE TOMB OF DR. ARNOLD.

share of a burden which had proved itself too heavy for him to bear in his own strength'. Hughes closes the book, commenting:

> it is only through our mysterious human relationships, through the love and tenderness and purity of mothers, and sisters, and wives, through the strength and courage and wisdom of fathers, and brothers, and teachers, that we can come to the knowledge of Him, in whom alone the love, and the tenderness, and the purity, and the strength, and the courage, and the wisdom of all these dwell for ever and ever in perfect fullness. (II. IX)

What, then, is the structure of feeling in this rich mix of games, fights, country pastimes, lessons, sickness and health, and Christianity? First, the family is an important focus, even though Hughes writes, 'It is not within the scope of my book, however, to speak of family relations' (I. III). Three of the eighteen chapters are mainly about Tom's home life. Although Tom's return to his family in holidays is never described in detail the final paragraph quoted above makes clear the important place of the family in the book. Yet it is the Victorian upper middle class to which the appeal is made. Women and men each have their separate spheres and even have different qualities of personality to learn. In the main body of the book women play a small part. Mrs Arnold gives boys tea and allocates studies. Mrs Arthur, a widow, nurses her son through his illness, but only appears once in person to talk to Tom. Tom's mother plays her part in the early chapters and so does Charity Lamb, Tom's old nurse. The school matron is mentioned too. But males dominate this world for all the implicitly acknowledged but largely taken-for-granted importance of women in the background.

Next, patriotism is important, but not in any excessively jingoistic way. The first four chapters are full of a feeling of the glorious superiority of rural England. Battle heroes and whole families are mentioned, though

> those noble families would be somewhat astounded if the accounts ever came to be fairly taken – to find how small their work for England has been by the side of the Browns. The great army of Browns . . . are scattered over the whole empire on which the sun never sets . . . whose general diffusion I take to be the chief cause of that empire's stability (I. I)

Fighting, as we have seen, is also related to Englishness. The evils of industrialisation are mentioned, because Arthur's father had been 'the clergyman of a parish in the Midland Counties', but

> There is no need to dwell upon such tales; the Englishman into whose soul they have not sunk deep is not worthy the name: you English boys for whom this book is meant . . . will learn it all soon enough. (II. III)

Yet it is the somewhat backward-looking patriotism, reminiscent of Cobbett, which pervades the spirit of the book. Rural England – Hughes is rude about 'Highlanders' – and rural pursuits of home and school, are lovingly described. Early in Chapter I Hughes tells that he is 'going to introduce' the reader to one 'English neighbourhood' and 'those who don't care for England in detail may skip the chapter' (I. I).

We have seen that Squire Brown set out his moral aims for Tom – to be a Christian and a gentleman. Christianity, as many of the quotations already cited show, permeates the whole book. There are, in addition, a number of set pieces that emphasise the place of Christianity. The first is a three page description of Sunday afternoon chapel and Tom's first sermon from the Doctor. Despite their worldly interests they

> listened, as all boys in their better moods will listen (aye and men too for the matter of that), to a man who [they] felt to be with all his heart and soul and strength striving against whatever was mean and unmanly and unrighteous in our little world. (I. VII)

Hughes, the Christian Socialist, here portrays Arnold, the Broad Churchman, urging his pupils to a moral, useful, purposeful and Christian life. The second set piece is another three-page passage where Arthur tells Tom how near he came to death and how he heard a voice say 'The vision is for an appointed time; though it tarry, wait for it, for in the end it shall speak and not lie, it shall surely come, it shall not tarry.' Arthur then speaks to Tom of his life's purpose: 'It will take me my life and longer . . . to find out what the work is' (II. VI). Finally, there is the brief concluding chapter, in which we leave Tom –

> where better could we leave him, than at the altar, before which he had first caught a glimpse of the glory of his birthright, and felt the drawing of the bond which links all living souls together in one brotherhood. (II. IX)

But this moral character has to be built amidst the many temptations of a public school, the bullying, the cribbing, the dangers of 'the small friend system' (II. II) and the great independence granted, that, for example, allowed boys with some ease to drink at public houses. Furthermore, 'In no place in the world has individual character more weight than at a public school.' A boy was shrewdly judged by his peers for what he was and could 'have more wide influence for good or evil on the society . . . than ever . . . again' (I. VIII). Individuality was exercised and learnt amongst others, in a society. Because of this team games assumed some importance. In conversation with the young master on his last evening at Rugby Tom says

> And that's why football and cricket, now one comes to think of it, are much better games than fives or hare-and-hounds, or any others where the object is to come in first or to win for oneself and not that one's side may win.

And from this same feeling comes the young master's differentiation between 'working to get your living' and 'doing some real good in the world' (II. VIII), encouraging a moral impulse which sustained many late nineteenth-century professionals and administrators.

Academic work had some place in all this, but as Squire Brown put it when trying to decide what to tell Tom when he went to Rugby:

> 'Shall I tell him to mind his work, and say he's sent to school to make himself a good scholar? Well, but he isn't sent to school for that – at any rate not for that mainly. I don't care a straw for Greek particles, or the digamma, no more does his mother.' (I. IV)

There are few descriptions of work in school or of preparing for school lessons, though no doubt academic work forms a ground base to the other more salient experiences involved in friendships and enmities and in games and other school activities.

The way in which the school was organised is a very important part of the setting of the book and embodies the structure of feeling so strongly that it becomes a part of that structure in its own right. The headmaster, the Doctor, who was also Tom's housemaster, is ever present in the background, especially for the older boys, whom he taught. But Tom only realises on his last night at school how despite all his teaching in the Sixth the great Head-Master had found time in those busy years to watch over the career of him, Tom Brown, and his particular friends . . . and all without taking the least credit to himself, or seeming to know, or let any one else know, that he ever thought particularly of any boy at all. (II. VIII)

He worked through the hierarchy he had established, through housemasters, form-masters and the members of the Sixth form.

The relationship between boys and masters was a crucial part of Arnold's scheme. Boys of all ages and types mixed together, boys easily could go astray, as Tom began to when 'the temptations of the lower fourth soon proved too strong for him' (I. VIII). Learning to survive in this society ruled by boys was an important part of Arnold's plan for development of character, both for the older and younger boys. Masters rarely intervened, certainly not in public schools, though as Hughes noted things were different in private schools (I. III), and the view held of masters at the time by boys below the Sixth is clearly presented by Tom when discussing with East Arthur's request to stop the use of cribs

'Only what one has always felt about the masters is, that it's a fair trial of skill and last between us and them – like a match at football, or a battle. We're natural enemies in school. That's the fact. We've got to learn so much Latin and Greek and do so many verses, and they've got to see we do it.' (II. VII)

Significantly Tom added, 'All's fair in war, but lying.'

The house was a vital part of Arnold's administrative machinery. There the boys lived with each other under a prefect and with a housemaster somewhere in the background. One of the set pieces in *Tom Brown* is Old Brooke's address to School-house after winning the great football game against the whole of the rest of the school. In it he said they had succeeded because

'We've more reliance on one another, more of a house feeling, more fellowship than the school can have. Each of us knows and can depend on his next hand man better – that's why we beat 'em today. We've union, they've division – that's the secret – (cheers).' (I. VI)

House spirit was so important that the house rather than the school could become more important to the boys, particularly those who were good games players.

Games, of course, were central to Hughes's book, if not to Arnold's vision of Rugby. Some were becoming highly organised. Football in *Tom Brown* was less so than cricket. For instance, there was no 'uniform of cap and jersey . . . except the School-house white trousers'. The members in teams were not fixed. Although these team games were important as much space is given by Hughes to descriptions of hare-and-hounds and of fishing and birds-nesting. Indeed, love for rural England is one of the abiding feelings left from reading this book.

In the social circumstances of the times, outlined at the end of the last chapter, the way in which this book would be read is clear. In brief, an upper middle-class boy, seen as one of us, after a sound upbringing in a family where the differentiated roles of male and female are taken for granted, goes to a public school to learn to be a gentleman and a Christian. Academic work has some importance, but is not as crucial as the moral lessons to be learnt. These lessons are largely learnt by mixing with other boys in house and school. The administrative structure of the school, established by the head, ensures that the games, the house and the relationships between master, prefects and boys play so crucial a role in the whole educational process that they in turn become a vital part of the whole structure of feeling embodied in the book.

Tom Brown's reception

Tom Brown's Schooldays was an instant success. It came out on 24 April 1857 and by the end of the year five impressions had been sold. By the year of Hughes's death in 1896 fifty editions had been published in Britain alone (Mack and Armytage, 1952: 90). It was run in abbreviated form in *Beeton's Boy's Own Magazine* in 1858. Reviews were widespread in serious newspapers and journals: *The Times* (1857); the *Edinburgh Review* (1858); the *(Melbourne) Argus* (1858); the *Quarterly Review* (1860) and together with *Tom Brown at Oxford* in the *Spectator* (1861). Despite its anonymous authorship its semi-biographical nature was recognised. By and large, despite some criticism at a very high level, *Tom Brown* was a critical and financial success. Readers wanted the book and Macmillans supplied them with it. In a letter to Hughes, dated 2 February 1858, G.G. Bradley wrote, 'It is only a very few I take it who kick at the preaching of the book.' Thirty years later Edward Salmon, an expert on children's literature, could still support the same position about its 'preaching':

Its sermons are of a particularly fascinating and spiritual
kind . . . . The incident seems to me to illustrate the
sermon, quite as much as the sermon to explain the
significance of the incident. (1888: 89)

Despite some objection, as Charles Kingsley had predicted, to the
'strong language', which readers today would be hard put to find,
Tom Brown was seen at the time, and even eighty years later, by
many as a 'fairly sober and authentic record' (Jenkinson,
1940: 18). In its review *The Times* wrote, 'We hail this little work
as the truest, liveliest and most sympathetic description of a
unique phase of English life that has yet been given to the public'
(*Times*, 1857). *The Times* believed that *Tom Brown* gave 'a most
faithful and interesting picture of our public schools', although
Dean Stanley whose book (1844) had been so influential in
creating the Arnoldian myth was appalled. 'It was an absolute
revelation to me, I was utterly ignorant' (quoted Bamford,
1957). In the twelfth edition of his *Life and Correspondence of
Thomas Arnold* he wrote,

> It is not too much to say that – at least as far as the school is
> concerned – a more vivid picture of Dr Arnold's career is
> conveyed in the occasional allusions and general tone of that
> charming book . . . than is given in the elaborate descrip-
> tions in this work.

The *Quarterly Review* admired 'the combination of moral and
physical force' implicit in the Arnoldian public school, but
thought 'it is impossible to raise the moral standard of the schools
above that of the great world of which they reflect the image'
(1860: 415-16). The review saw the need for 'no great change in
the ordinary method . . . , but merely to apply it with judgement, patience, and tact' (1860: 419). Fitzjames Stephen in the
Edinburgh Review, however, was more approving of the schools
and felt that 'every page in *Tom Brown's Schooldays*' showed that a
method of education had been evolved which encouraged in its
pupils simplicity, lightheartedness, honesty, purity and courage,
that by doing this 'it had solved a far more difficult problem than
is involved in the production of any amount of classical learning'
(1858: 176).

The Times thought *Tom Brown* 'the first book for boys about
boys in which the characters were really a collection of human
beings, all alive and all different, at a genuine school.' And,

indeed, boys were soon reading *Tom Brown*. Thus, for example, in a sermon in 1857 at Marlborough, Cotton referred to the fact that boys were already reading Hughes's book (cited Honey, 1977: 186). Yet *The Times* also began its review by noting, 'The tale before us belongs to a class written for boys, but intended to be read by men.' Fitzjames Stephen made the same point,

> Like old-fashioned sermons, the book is addressed to two descriptions of persons: boys and men. The part of the book which is addressed to boys is very simple, and we think it so good that hardly any praise can be too high for it. (1858: 172)

But, as anyone who has preached in a school chapel knows, to pull off success with both audiences is well-nigh impossible and Stephen continues, 'Passing from the story which is addressed to boys to the moral addressed to men, our praise of *Tom Brown's Schooldays* must be far more qualified' (1858: 176). Stephen expressed admiration for the character and construction of the English public schools and for Hughes's worship of Arnold, but in each case there were reservations. First, he was concerned for the peculiar boy, the genius or the oddity like Martin, who became Arthur's friend. Even Hughes had noted this point. 'If we knew how to use our boys, Martin would have been seized upon and educated as a natural philosopher' (II. III). But, as Stephen pointed out, when successful with such boys, public schools tended to turn them into prigs. Indeed, Stanley himself could be seen in this light. He went late to Rugby, never fagged, met Arnold almost immediately, as he quickly went into the Sixth and Rugby worked for him as an intellectual forcing house. *The Times* had noted the 'priggish nature of the model Rugby sixth form boys'. The *Quarterly*, too, was critical of an organisational point, the way in which Arnold took on the joint role of head and chaplain: 'it is a grievous mistake to establish too close a relationship between religious obligation and the routine business of a school' (1860: 405).

Yet the main religious point made by Stephen, *The Times* and the *Spectator*, concerned what Stephen called Hughes's tendency to see Arnold and Rugby through Kingsley's eyes. Kingsley's method was

> open to very grave objections. It consists of writing novels, the hero of which is almost always drawn in most glowing

colours, and intended to display the excellence of a single massive understanding united with the almost unconscious instinct to do good, and adorned, generally speaking, with every sort of athletic accomplishment. (1858: 891)

In his final paragraph Hughes might be said to have given a possible partial answer to this argument. 'Such stages have to be gone through, I believe, by all young and brave souls, who must win their way through hero-worship, to the worship of Him who is the King and Lord of heroes' (II. IX). The *Spectator* had a different quibble with Kingsley. It saw him as 'the first of the wrestling novelists':

It is not often that considerable literary power is found in connexion with the ethical instincts of a genuine wrestler [who] loves a struggle for its own sake, and is happier in it, and less likely to construct a deeper prejudice thereby, than is a life of rational sympathy and observation. (1861: 1288)

Kingsley's heroes, and Hughes's moral focus tended, the *Spectator* believed, to lead to lax argument. All these critics believed Kingsley's influence led Hughes to overemphasise games. Stephen wrote: 'A boy might really infer from *Tom Brown* that he was sent to school to play at football, and that the lessons were quite a secondary consideration' (1858: 893). Though this might be the truth, Squire Brown would have seen it as pointless criticism precisely because it was true. In this connection *The Times* took the opportunity to 'protest . . . against the short sighted plan of making games compulsory'. It did so not just 'because pleasure should not be tortured into pains', but because the system led to fake 'dodges and excuses' to avoid games.

Yet overall both *The Times* and Fitzjames Stephen in the *Edinburgh Review*, as were the other reviewers too, were impressed. *The Times* said:

It is an attempt, a very noble and successful attempt, to Christianise the society of our youth through the only practicable channel – a hearty and brotherly sympathy with their feelings. (1857)

Stephen concluded:

We heartily congratulate Mr Kingsley on a disciple who reproduces so vigorously many of his own great merits, and who sympathizes so ardently in feelings which we do not

entirely share, but which are generous even in their defects.
(1858: 893)

What is impressive is that such a barrage of formidable critical
opinion was brought to bear so quickly upon a story for boys
and, furthermore, that there was such approval, because those
words from Fitzjames Stephen were very high praise. Only
Kipling's *Stalky and Co.* and, perhaps, Waugh's *The Loom of
Youth*, of the books to be considered here, earned and stood up to
such an attack. What is more, the critical acclaim, as is not always
the case, did not die with the passing of time. In 1888 Salmon
could write that *Tom Brown's Schooldays* was 'unquestionably
entitled to the first place among this class of stories' (Salmon,
1888a: 84). And in 1940 Jenkinson could still speak of 'the
remarkable popularity of *Tom Brown's Schooldays*' (Jenkinson,
1940: 18).

Eric

Dean F.W. Farrar

Frederick William Farrar (D.N.B.) lived from 1831 to 1903. He
was born in Bombay where his father was a missionary. He
returned with his older brother to England at the age of three and
lived with two maiden aunts at Aylesbury. His parents came on
furlough for three years from 1839 to 1842 and took a house at
Castleton Bay in the Isle of Man. The boys were sent to King
William's College there, eventually as boarders in the headmaster's house. The head, Dr Dixon, was evangelical in religion
and not a great scholar. In 1847 Farrar's father came home to
become curate at St James, Clerkenwell. Farrar, who had become
head of school, went to King's College, London, where he came
under the influence of F.D. Maurice, gaining his BA in 1852.
Earlier in 1850 he had won a scholarship to Trinity College,
Cambridge, and he worked very hard there, playing no games
and being elected a member of the famous and highly intellectual
undergraduate club, 'The Apostles'. In 1854 he was placed equal
fourth in the Classical Tripos and a Junior Optime in the
Mathematics Tripos.

Before hearing these results he had accepted a mastership at
Marlborough under Cotton, who had been appointed to reorganise the school after the rebellion of 1851. It was to Cotton that

Farrar dedicated *Eric*. On Christmas Day, 1854 Farrar was ordained deacon, becoming a priest in 1857. He had moved in 1855 to Harrow. In this same year he was elected to a fellowship of Trinity. He soon became a housemaster at Harrow. Dr Butler who succeeded Vaughan as head in 1860 and was later to become Master of Trinity, wrote to Farrar in a letter saying, 'Your teaching and inspiring powers would throw life and thought into any form of any school in England.' One of Farrar's old pupils wrote of him in the *Cornhill Magazine*, 'The first characteristic . . . which struck the average school boy was his grandeur of manner'; he was 'positively tireless' and 'unconventional' as a 'disciplinarian' in using encouragement rather than force. 'He was as unlike in nature to the typical schoolboy as it was possible to be.' Consonant with this picture another former pupil recounted some of his humorous remarks which, as might have been expected, seem to us today rather heavy-handed: 'How many centuries have elapsed since your boots were last cleaned?' and 'Your ignorance is so profound that it ossifies the very powers of sense' (Farrar, 1904: 82, 84-6, 172-81).

In 1858 Farrar, aged twenty-seven, wrote *Eric or Little by Little*. If this was by no means the literary success that *Tom Brown* was it became very famous and ran through many impressions in Farrar's lifetime. Farrar wrote two more similar stories: *Julian Home, a Tale of College Life* (1859) and *St Winifred's, or The World of School* (1862). Both were popular at the time. Farrar wrote much else, particularly in the fields of theology and education. In 1867 he was editor of an influential collection, *Essays on a Liberal Education*, and on taking over at Marlborough one of his first acts was considered very radical, the appointment of a science master. In 1874 he published his best known theological book, *The Life of Christ* of which twelve impressions were published in its first year. He was a scholar of some repute and in 1866 was elected a Fellow of the Royal Society in recognition of his work in philology.

Farrar left Marlborough in 1876 to become Canon of Westminster where he was a successful preacher and did much to reorganise the Abbey and St Margaret's, the parish church of the House of Commons, whose Chaplain he became in 1890. In 1895 he became Dean of Canterbury and took a major part in restoring the Cathedral. In 1899 he developed muscular dystrophy, dying in 1903. Clearly Farrar had the qualities and achievements that earned men a bishopric in the last century. Probably he was too radical in theology to be seen as quite a safe enough choice. He certainly was in many ways an archetypal Victorian: something of a polymath, incredibly hard-working, innovatory in some matters, for instance, religion and education, but starkly conservative in others – morality in Farrar's case.

The question inevitably arises whether there was any link between the publication of *Tom Brown* in 1857 and *Eric* in 1858. In his rather laudatory biography Farrar's son, Reginald, really says nothing of this. The only slight clue could lie in one sentence about *Eric* and is unhelpful: 'The inner history of the book will never be fully given to the world' (1904: 73). We shall probably never know.

Eric or Little by Little

In his Preface to the New Illustrated Edition of 1889 Farrar wrote:

> The story of *Eric* was written with but one single object – the vivid inculcation of inward purity and moral purpose, by the history of a boy who, in spite of the inherent nobleness of his disposition falls into all folly and wickedness, until he has learnt to seek help from above.

Eric Williams was this inherently noble boy. Aged twelve he lived with his aunt, Mrs Trevor, and her daughter in the beautiful Vale of Ayrton. His parents were in India, but came home bringing their younger son, Vernon, and took a house in the Isle of Man, sending Eric to Roslyn School as a day boarder. Dr Rowlands, the headmaster, places Eric in the Fourth form, 'the lowest form of all' under the Rev. Henry Gordon, a strict master (I. II). Eric is bullied by Barker, but on one occasion, when his new friend, Russell, has come to his rescue, the incident is seen by Eric's father, who thrashes Barker. 'From that day Eric was never troubled with personal violence by Barker or any other boy.' Eric, however, could stand on his own feet and 'the other boys . . . liked his frankness, his mirth, his spirit and his cleverness' (I. III).

Eric was caught apparently cribbing, though he was in fact passing a crib to another boy. He would not 'sneak' and Mr Gordon gave him his first caning. Despite his difficulties with Mr Gordon he and his friend, Owen, gained equal first place in the end-of-term examinations and earned their remove into the Upper Fourth, still under Mr Gordon. 'The second term at school is

generally the great test of the strength of a boy's principles and resolutions.' Novelty has gone; sustained effort remains. As long as Eric was a day boarder his parents could support him. But 'his popularity was his fatal snare. He enjoyed and was proud of it.' So cribbing and the temptation to play games rather than work were hard for him to resist. With his friends, Dunn and Llewellyn, he was flogged by Dr Rowlands for laughing at the discomfort of a stout lady, a visitor to the school chapel, when an insect landed on her hat. He went home

and flinging himself on his bed, brooded alone over the remembrances of his disgrace. Still nursing a fierce resentment, he felt something hard at his heart, and, as he prayed neither for help nor forgiveness, it was pride and rebellion, not repentance, that made him miserable. (I. V)

Mrs Williams, 'was not unobservant of the gradual but steady falling off in Eric's character.' At the end of term Eric was eighth not first and his parents returned to India worried. Eric, very upset, said to his aunt, 'Oh, I *will* be a better boy, I *will* indeed', 'God helping you, dear', said his aunt (I. VI).

On the return to India of his parents Eric became a boarder and alone without his family faced all the temptations of life at Roslyn School. He was now in the Shell as were his friends Russell, Owen and Montague, under Mr Rose, 'a far truer and deeper Christian' than Mr Gordon was. He was 'taken up' by Russell's older cousin, Upton, who was a bad influence on him and he swore for the first time in Russell's company, calling Mr Gordon 'a surly devil'. In an authorial comment Farrar comments on 'the sinfulness of little sins' (I. VIII). In his dormitory a boy called Ball used foul language in the presence of a new boy. Eric knew he should speak out: 'Now, Eric, now or never! . . . Speak out, boy!', but he did not, ignoring Russell and Montague's advice to do so. Eventually he began himself to listen to Ball's foul stories: 'his curiosity was awakened; he no longer feigned indifference, and the poison of evil communication flowed deep into his veins' (I. II). After a rag in the dormitory Eric was caned again by Dr Rowlands. 'Mr Rose sadly remarked the failure of promise in his character and abilities' and talked with him seriously. Ultimately

> Boy and master knelt down humbly side by side, and, from a full heart, the young man poured out his fervent petitions for the child beside him . . . . and he loved him as a brother. He rose from his knees full of the strongest resolutions, and earnestly promised amendment for the future. (I. X)

Mr Gordon gave Eric an imposition of writing out the *Fourth Georgic* for repeated disobedience. On the Saturday upon which this was to be handed in a notice appears on the board, 'GORDON IS A SURLY DEVIL' (I. XI). Eric is suspected, denies his guilt but is put into coventry by the school except for Russell and a few friends. Dr Rowlands tells Avonley, the head of school, 'to have a regular trial and hear the evidence'. Barker is found guilty and expelled. Once again, Eric, when warned by Mr Rose of the 'no light battle to resist many kinds of temptation', replies with humility, 'Believe me, sir, I will try' (I. XII).

In the Easter holidays many boys stayed at school as going home from the Isle of Man was a long journey. Eric with others went one day to walk on the cliffs. He, following Upton's example, smoked, but the others persuaded him to stop. Eventually, forgetting the time, they were cut off by the tide on a rock. All except Russell escaped. Eric returned to stay with his friend who had been severely hurt trying to jump to safety. Eric stopped with him all night till the life boat could save them. Edwin Russell became very ill as a result of exposure and his injuries. Eric visited him daily, but ultimately he is near to death:

> A little before ten that night Eric was again summoned with Upton and Montague to Russell's bedside. He was sinking fast. . . . They came, and were amazed to see how bright, how beautiful the dying boy looked. They received his last farewells. . . . Sweetly he blessed them, and made them to promise to avoid all evil, and read the Bible, and pray to God. . . . He sighed very gently; there was a slight sound in his throat, and he was dead. (I. XIV)

Eric, Owen, Montague and Upton all determined to reform themselves. Eric achieved second place in his form. He went home for the summer holidays. Soon he received a letter from Upton, repenting his bad example to Eric, and saying he is leaving school to go to India. Vernon is to return after this holiday to school with Eric, who, worried about the temptations before him, wrote to Mr Rose. He replied that 'with God's help' (I. XV) Vernon will come through.

A year later, many changes had occurred. 'To Eric the changes were not for good.' Bad habits were resumed, though he was high in the form and captain of the school eleven. A new boy, expelled from another school, Brigson, now became Vernon's friend and Eric did nothing despite 'the deep intolerable, unfathomable flood of moral turpitude and iniquity which he bore with him' (II. I). Montague thrashed Brigson, but he regained his influence, largely, according to Farrar, because there was no prefect system at Roslyn. Eric next 'took up' a twelve-year-old, Wildney, who persuaded Eric and Dunn to go out at night to buy beer from Billy, landlord of the 'Jolly Herring'. Mr Rose caught Wildney, who was flogged, and saw another boy whom he suspects to be Eric, who said nothing when challenged.

Eric was invited on Wildney's instigation by the 'Anti-muffs' to a party at the 'Jolly Herring'. All except Eric and Wildney, but including Vernon, were caught. Later that day Eric refused an order from Mr Rose, who lost his temper 'and laid the cane sharply across his back'. Eric, slightly affected by drinking, snatched the cane, broke it and flung one piece on the fire and the other at Mr Rose (II. III). He was made to apologise publicly. Brigson, however, arranged for the juniors to 'crust' Mr

Rose – to throw bread crusts at him. Mr Rose discovered the instigator and flogged him. Brigson then asked his father to take him from Roslyn. Eric cuts him and on his last evening Brigson told him, 'You cut me, curse you; but, *never fear, I'll be revenged on you yet.*' 'Do your worst', answered Eric contemptuously; 'and never speak to me again' (II. IV).

Drinking, not only of beer, but of brandy, became common amongst Eric's group. After a noisy party Eric hit and fell out with his great friend, Montague, who by now was much concerned for him. Soon, however, Eric and Montague had a serious fight. This was stopped by Duncan, but without their shaking hands to make up their quarrel. A party was soon planned for Wildney's birthday. Wildney planned a raid on Mr Gordon's pigeon loft. Eric and Wildney took some pigeons, but were disturbed, though not discovered, in carrying out the raid. The ensuing party resulted in both Eric and Wildney becoming so drunk that Eric 'was too giddy with the fumes of drink to walk straight or act naturally' at roll call. They were noticed and Dr Rowlands publicly expelled them both. Eric appealed emotionally to the head, who relented largely because of Eric's bravery in trying to save Russell (II. VIII). They were flogged and gated. Eric now once again reforms 'and in the Easter examination came out high enough in the Upper Fifth to secure his remove into the Sixth after the holidays' (II. IX).

During the Easter holidays a sail was planned and Montague included in the group. Vernon and his new friend, Wright, who had been an influence for his good, could not go in the boat because of the numbers and so walked along the cliffs. In trying to reach a bird's nest Vernon slipped, fell and was killed, only to be found by Eric and his party in the boat on their way home. Time healed Eric's sorrow and he wrote to his aunt, 'I *must* be a better boy . . . I am laying aside, with all my might, idleness and all bad habits, and doing my very best to redeem the lost years.' At the very moment he wrote this Billy appeared at his study door claiming £6 for the dinner at the 'Jolly Herring', having been put up to this by Brigson. Eric went to Mr Rose for help, who advised him to tell his aunt the truth and ask her for the money. This Eric did and his aunt sent the £6 saying, 'she still has perfect confidence in the true heart of her dear boy' (II. X). But Billy now said that he knew who took the pigeons and that £5 reward had been offered for information. He demanded £5 from Eric who almost stole the cricket club money to pay Billy's claim. In fact by mistake in putting the money back into the box he did keep a sovereign in his pocket.

Billy now stole the cricket money whilst Eric was out playing cricket. His interest had returned and he was playing well. When the theft was discovered Eric was suspected since his need is known to some. He told Montague the whole truth. Dr Rowlands, who had been told of the suspicion, locked Eric in his room, 'half contemplating the possibility' of his running way. However, Eric used his sheets to escape from his room and managed to find a berth as a cabin-boy on a small ship, the 'Stormy Petrel', that sailed the next morning. He suffered a terrible trip to Corunna and back to Liverpool where he escaped and was just able to reach his aunt's home, though his physique had been undermined by his experiences at sea. Despite good nursing he gradually wasted away. Montague and Wildney came to see him and told him that his name had been cleared, because Billy had been discovered to be the thief. A letter then came from India to say his mother was dying.

> 'Oh, I have killed her, I have killed my mother!' said Eric, in a hollow voice, when he came to himself. 'Oh, God, forgive me, forgive me!' (II. XIII)

A few minutes later Eric died. The final chapter tells of the fates of the others in the story and of Mr Rose's sermon in chapel at the start of the next term:

> 'Many a time have I mourned for him in past days, when I marked how widely he went astray – but I do not mourn now, for after his fiery trials he died penitent and happy, and at least his sorrows are over forever . . . and for all eternity the young soul is in the presence of its God. Let none of you think that his life has been wasted.' (II. XIV)

In much the same way as Hughes used his school experiences to write *Tom Brown* Farrar used his time on the Isle of Man at King William's College to form the basis for *Eric*. Yet the tone of each book is clearly different. The most apt short description of *Eric* is that it is 'a moral cliffhanger' (Townsend, 1971: 10), whereas in *Tom Brown* the emphasis is on achieving good rather than avoiding sin. Much of the difference in tone is due to two factors. The first is Farrar's style which constantly emphasised morality and was earnest in the extreme. The second is that King William's was a very different school from Rugby; the head was no Arnold and, as Farrar on several occasions points out, there was no prefect system, so that 'evil' could flourish more easily. Yet the structure within which these differences were contained can be seen to be rather similar to that found in *Tom Brown*.

The family is given much emphasis. Eric's upbringing at home is described in approving terms, both with his parents when he was a 'day boarder', and with his aunt from whom he learnt 'to be truthful, to be honest, to be kind, to be brave' and 'the sense . . . of a present loving God, of a tender and long-suffering Father' (I. I). Women are again in the background. Eric's mother and aunt are set apart and seen as good; Dr Rowland's wife is kind and less important to the story even than Mrs Arnold in *Tom Brown*. The tone of feeling about the family is well expressed in the stanza by Farrar himself that heads the last chapter of Part One:

> O, far beyond the waters,
> The fickle feet may roam,
> But they find no light so pure and bright
> As the one fair star of home:
> The star of tender hearts, lady,
> That glows in an English home. (I. XV)

Eric's family and home are haven from the storms of the world, Tom Brown's a base from which to venture forth into the world. Eric does not play or fight with the local children, though we are told that attending the village school taught him 'practically to despise the accidental and nominal differences which separate man from man' (I. I). We do not need to be told this of Tom Brown; we know it.

As with Tom Brown 'Nature – wisest, gentlest, holiest of teachers – was with [Eric] in his childhood' (I. I) and on occasions he goes out from Roslyn school on excursions in the country, but these descriptions are not made the covert vehicle of patriotism as in *Tom Brown*. Wildney and Upton end up as 'fine and manly officers' (II. XIV), but there is no mention of Britain or the Empire in this connection.

The main emphasis, as must have been made palpably clear, is on the religious and moral aims of the school. *Eric* is about the development of character with, an unusual focus, the direction of development being 'little by little' for the worse. Farrar writes not just of 'the sinfulness of small sins', but of the growing difficulty of withstanding temptation as each small sin is committed. The end was described by Mrs Trevor, Eric's aunt, 'Vernon dead, and Eric, she feared not dead, but worse than dead, guilty, stained and dishonoured' (II. XIII). The school had to teach the ability to withstand temptation and for this experience of at least the presence of evil, if not its exercise, was essential. Mr Rose told Eric in his letter calming his fears for Vernon as a new boy at Roslyn, 'The innocence of mere ignorance is a poor thing; it *cannot* under any circumstances, be permanent, nor is it at all valuable as a foundation of character' (I. XV).

The conduct approved of is the same as in *Tom Brown*, but the approval is often given with great emphasis. Even the fact that Montague had a 'naturally noble and chivalrous bearing' (I. III) would have been conveyed by Hughes in action and dialogue. Furthermore, Hughes could never have shown his belief in telling the truth as did Farrar; Mr Rose told Brigson who had lied to him over the 'crusting' incident, 'You have told me a lie!' . . . 'No words can express my loathing for your false and dishonourable conduct.' Wildney, a little later, calls for 'Three groans, hoots, and hisses for a liar and a coward' (II. IV). 'Sneaking' is not approved of, even in the case of bullying: 'It is a far better and braver thing to bear bullying with such a mixture of spirit and good humour, as in time to disarm it' (I. III). Of excess drinking we know Hughes disapproved; the bully, Flashman, is described as taking too much, but not in such violent language as Dr Rowlands used to the whole school when expelling Eric: 'the brutalising and fearful character of this most ruinous vice' . . . 'a sin most disgraceful and most dangerous'. School work may seem to be more central to *Eric*, but in reality it is always seen as one important vehicle in the story for the development of character. Competition in class, cribbing and ragging masters are all described not in relation to academic worth, but to the achievement of a more worthy character. Those moral qualities that were to govern behaviour were all rooted in belief in God. There are constant references to His saving grace. Prayer is often mentioned. Eric prays in repentence for forgiveness and strength in future temptation. Mr Rose prays, lies awake at night asking for guidance in his dealings with the boys. Though one of Eric's earliest misdemeanours occurs in the school chapel there are no religious set pieces as in *Tom Brown*. The same function is fulfilled in *Eric* by the death scenes. Three of the main characters die – Edwin Russell after his accident on the rocks, Vernon by falling from the cliffs and Eric himself on his return to his aunt after his trials in the 'Stormy Petrel'. Particularly in the first and last cases much is made of these scenes, of which *Tom Brown* had but one equivalent, Arthur's near death from fever. Farrar's heroes repented, but died; Hughes's hero with God's help recovered to live a useful life.

There is less emphasis in *Eric* on the formal organisation through which the moral qualities desired can be encouraged. This is largely because Roslyn was so differently organised to Rugby. There were no prefects so that 'brute force had the unlimited authority' (II. I) and games were not organised even to the level found then at Rugby. Though Dr Rowlands was not so charismatic a figure as Dr Arnold he nevertheless was a strong head in the mid-nineteenth-century mould. His masters dealt more directly than at Rugby with all the facets of the school and we hear more of them, particularly of Mr Gordon and Mr Rose, the latter of whom was clearly seen by Farrar as a model master, much as Hughes's 'young master' had been in *Tom Brown* – and here we should remember that *Eric* was dedicated to Cotton, himself the model for Hughes's 'young master'. Farrar's views on the need to provide more structure than Roslyn did within which boys may develop are seen in one comment about Mr Gordon's lack of organisation of his class during examinations:

> Mr Gordon was fresh at his work, and had not yet learnt the practical lesson (which cost him many a qualm of sorrow and disgust), that to trust young boys to any great extent is really to increase their temptations. (I. IV)

In many ways this is a revealing passage, not only because it shows Farrar's belief in the need to plan the details of schools and their organisation carefully, but also because it demonstrates his profound pessimism expressed here less emphatically than often, about human, especially boy, nature. Hughes was very much more optimistic.

Eric's reception

Between initial publication in 1858 and Farrar's death in 1902 *Eric* went through thirty-six editions. *Julian Home* (1860) was in its eighteenth and *St Winifred's* its twenty-sixth edition when Farrar died (Farrar, 1904: xiii-xiv). There were, however, constant criticisms of *Eric* and in a letter, written in 1858, to Professor C.S. Beesly, Farrar himself admitted to the fault most often attributed to his book, 'The lacrimosity is, I know, too much, and arises from the state of mind in which I wrote it' (Farrar, 1904: 75).

The first major notice of *Eric* was in the *Quarterly* in 1860 when it was reviewed with five other books on education, three of which were school stories and two non-fiction works. The stories were seen as 'purpose' novels and the comment made that there was an 'attentive and sensitive audience' for works about education. 'The anxious mother, who has hitherto sighed in vain to pierce the veil which shrouds school life from her view, devours with eager and credulous interest the narrative which professes to reveal its mysteries' (*Quarterly Review*, 1860: 38-8). Yet the *Quarterly* was as scathing about the reality of the picture drawn in *Eric* as *The Times* had been congratulatory of that in *Tom Brown*. 'The picture of school life which [these books] present is neither faithful nor edifying' (ibid., 388) and particularly commented on Farrar – 'the ill-managed Pandemonium of his tale' (ibid., 391). The reviewer thought that the boys were ill-drawn, some mere 'caricatures', the masters unrealistic – Mr Gordon was too 'idealistic' and Mr Rose showed 'ecstatic fervour', and Dr Rowlands an unlikely head in allowing 'disorder in his own house' (ibid., 392-5). 'The tragic events of Mr Farrar's tale are powerfully and graphically narrated, but they are quite inadmissible, each individually, and still more collectively, as a series, in a picture of school life.' What was worrying was that, though the masters were so excellent, they failed in 'the objects of education' and despite Eric's noble disposition he rushed into disaster and disgrace almost without major temptations. What, the reviewer asked, would happen to average masters and average boys? (ibid., 399-400). The problem was that the book was 'full of exaggerations'. Dr Butler, Farrar's headmaster at Harrow, where he was a master when he wrote *Eric*, had also spoken of 'his rooted tendency to exaggerate' (Farrar, 1904: 88).

Some twenty years later criticisms of the same type were still being made. In an article on 'Boys' in the *Saturday Review* in 1882 the writer felt that 'The original and amusing character of boys has been too little studied'. Schoolmasters had missed their chance.

Canon Farrar was a schoolmaster when he wrote *Eric*, and a number of other maudlin fables about boys who were vicious, boys who were sentimental, but never about boys as they are with their gross barbaric view of life and their inability to recognise any but their own code of customs.

Farrar's boys were 'sots or saints, or an unpleasant mixture of both characters'. The *Saturday Review* also referred to an essay on 'Tales of School Life' in *Amoeba*, the magazine of Woburn School, in which 'Canon Farrar's stories are reviewed with the same acerbity'. The presumably boy reviewer wrote of these stories thus: 'They leave behind a sickly flavour of little but feeble morals and questionable fact. . . . There is far too much conversation of the "goody-goody" type, tolerable only, if tolerable at all, on a wet Sunday in the nursery.' The *Saturday Review* noted that *Tom Brown* was not mentioned: 'perhaps Tom is out of date' (*Saturday Review*, 1882: 496). Almost twenty years later in *Stalky and Co.*, published in 1899, Kipling made McTurk, one of his three boy heroes, proclaim similar feelings, 'Besides we ain't going to have any beastly Erickin' (Kipling, 1899: 137).

A number of experts in children's literature wrote on *Eric*. In 1888 Edward Salmon summed up his views, 'No single book for boys presents so many difficulties to the mind of the critic as *Eric*.' Its mood changed rapidly from good to bad, yet despite some 'poetic touches', to his mind 'keeping in view the public to whom it is addressed, it is profoundly gloomy. . . . Mr Farrar has focussed within one school the besetting sins of many.' The major difficulty was, however, as in *Julian Home*, theological. Farrar

> declares that 'without temptation there can be no real virtue or tried strength'. To say that knowledge of sin is ruin, and continuance in it hell is a terrible danger. *Eric* holds out to those who have erred no hope whatever of being forgiven and reinstated in the world and God's favour. (Salmon, 1888a: 89-92)

This is, perhaps, an overdrawn picture, but the element of truth in it emphasises the importance to its readers, especially thirty years later when Salmon wrote, of its theological position.

Another expert on children's literature, Charlotte Yonge, contributed a series of three articles on 'Children's Literature of the Last Century' to *Macmillan's Magazine* in 1867; the third was entitled 'Class Literature of the Last Thirty Years'. She commented on 'the prodigious amount of what may be called class literature. Everyone writes books *for* some one; books for children, books for servants, books for poor men, poor women, poor boys and poor girls.' She did not note a class of school stories. But in discussing two books for girls, *Fanny Brown* and *The Lost Brooch* by Harriet Mozeley, Cardinal Newman's eldest sister, she noted their lack of 'any distinctively High Church doctrines'; 'yet there can be no doubt that they did their part toward the Church movement by manifesting the unloveliness and unsatisfactoriness of this particular phase of suburban Evangelicism.' There had been a recent growth of such books – 'books for the young, standing between the child's story and the full-grown novel' (Yonge, 1867: 449). *Eric* falls into this 'class' and, furthermore, can be seen to be Evangelical in tone, appealing very much to the new rising middle classes in the suburbs as a work to give to their sons. Many of the second-hand copies available in shops today have hand-written dedications showing them either to have been gifts at Christmas or birthdays from near relatives or given as prizes at schools or Sunday schools. The many quotations from classical authors, not in translation, throughout the book show that Farrar had a middle-class reader in his mind, a boy who knew some Latin and Greek – and French too.

Farrar's son acknowledged the criticisms, especially of *Eric*, in his biography, published the year after his father's death. He noted that it was often compared with *Tom Brown*, but 'for the discerning critic these books, each admirable in its own *genre*, no more challenge comparison than do the works of Fra Angelico and Frith'. Hughes as 'a realist, [giving] an incomparable picture of the average public-school boy . . . yet healthy and excellent as is [his] tone, we are not profoundly touched to finer issues by it.' Farrar was 'an idealist, and . . . never wrote without a definite moral purpose' (Farrar, 1904: 71-3). Hughes would have claimed the same of himself. Farrar's son continued,

> Hardly a week ever passed since *Eric* was first published without my father receiving from all parts of the English speaking world – from India, from the colonies, and from America – letters from earnest men who were not ashamed to write with gratitude that the reading of *Eric* had marked a turning point in their lives. (ibid., 74)

One of the examples he gives was a letter, dated 1901, from the curate of Hunslet, an industrial suburb of Leeds, who had also worked in East London.

> I have tried to do something by way of getting boys to read books of a healthy sort. And I have repeatedly noticed that both among the very poor of London, and among the better

sort of working folk here, boys have always been enthusiastic in praise of *Eric* and *St. Winifred's.* (ibid., 79-80)

This surprised him as he felt that these stories were not written for
that audience. This letter conflicts somewhat with the earlier
quoted essay from Woburn School and all we can conclude is that
boys of many kinds and social classes were still reading *Eric*, some
with disdain, but some reportedly with gratitude.

Farrar himself in the Preface to the New Illustrated Edition of
1889 emphasised the moral purpose of *Eric* and wrote, 'I am
deeply thankful to know – from testimony public and private,
anonymous and acknowledged – that this object has, by God's
blessing, been fulfilled.' *Eric* did go out of print in this century,
though republished in 1971. In 1958 a historian of children's
literature reported that *Eric* had been broadcast on the British
radio and described the book as 'a kind of immoveable moral
jelly-fish left behind by the tide' (Dainton, 1958: 309). It was a
considerable enough achievement to receive the same type,
though not the same quantity, of high level criticism as *Tom
Brown* and to survive, despite a severe mauling at the hands of
these critics, almost as well as Hughes had done.

Conclusion

Tom Brown and *Eric* were received on their publication as
important works. Few books written for boys have ever been
given such critical treatment. They touched a sensitive nerve of
mid-Victorian England. Education and schooling, particularly
that for middle-class boys, was a topic then, as now, of perceived
importance and of great interest. Hughes and Farrar were read as
authors providing books for the young about character development, their pioneering writing provided an innovatory model
within the existing relations of expectations from which further
innovation was possible.

Each writer had somewhat different intentions for and points
of view within their overall moral didacticism. Hughes wanted to
provide a political and patriotic framework within which rural
and industrial England could find unity before the changes
implicit in industrialisation irretrievably divided it. Farrar aimed
to emphasise the way in which Christianity should govern
morality amongst the middle class. Both quite soon achieved a

wider audience who would read these authors from their own standpoints. In much the same way Stanley had found *Tom Brown* a revelation, and not a pleasant one, whilst Charles Kingsley had welcomed its emphasis on the physical with delight. The heroes Hughes and Farrar created matched heroes their readers knew about – potential gentlemen, soldiers and sailors, and professionals and others who would help to run the expanding Imperial economy.

Though there were at the time critics of Farrar's – to use his own word – 'lacrimosity', and particularly of his deathbed scenes, we must remember that such accounts were to be found in other novels of that and a slightly earlier era, both for adults and for young people. Dickens wrote such scenes and there is a well-known chapter in Charlotte Yonge's *The Heir of Redclyffe* telling of the death of one of her heroes. Yet Farrar does, perhaps, outdo them all in his greater apparent sentimentality. The religious lessons to be learnt from a Christian death are almost offset by such remarks as that of Eric to Montague and Wildney whilst at home wasting away and nearing death, 'What a perfectly delicious evening. It's almost enough to make me wish to live' (II. XIV). Evangelicals might have wanted Christians to use death for redemption, but they did not, therefore, encourage believers, particularly, the young to wish to die.

This is one more example of the greater realism of *Tom Brown* than of *Eric*. As the *Quarterly Review* put it, there is no 'event disproportionate to the microcosm where the scene is laid' (*Quarterly Review*, 1860: 390). Hughes seemed able to place high spirits in a middle ground between purity and impurity or innocence and depravity. For Farrar the problem was not one of, say, purity *and* impurity, but of purity *or* impurity. His tendency to exaggerate drove him to this position. Their main focal themes were different. In technical terms it was the difference between a dichotomy and a continuous scale. Hughes was tracing a growth from thoughtlessness to responsibility, whilst Farrar was showing how exposure to good and evil could, not did, lead to a Christian maturity. To some extent these different themes dictated the standpoints from which they told their stories, Hughes from Tom's viewpoint, Farrar from the point of view of the writer.

Paradoxically *Tom Brown* was read as if it told of the Rugby of Arnold who, because of Stanley's book, was seen as an almost mythical figure. Yet Hughes did not portray Arnold's Rugby despite his first-hand experiences of it. He saw it through spectacles borrowed from Kingsley, already being labelled with the nick-name of 'muscular Christian'. Only one character, Arthur, an intellectual and earnest boy, who was, despite his cricket, not really an athlete, is a truly Arnoldian figure. Farrar, on the other hand, did look back to the introspective, morally striving boys that Arnold encouraged and that *The Times* condemned as priggish and precocious.

Despite this both writers were near to many English readers – or those who prescribed for them – of the times. Hughes tapped the spirit of the Broad Church movement which fitted the patriotism associated with the growing Empire and the need for social reform in a rapidly industrialising society. Farrar built on the still strong Evangelical spirit, which had much support amongst the rising industrial middle class and aspiring new professionals, though religion itself was increasingly in question under the impact of the discussions following Darwin's *Origin of the Species* (1859). To use Newsome's (1961: 36-7) terms, *Eric* looked back to 'godliness and good learning', *Tom Brown* forward to 'godliness and manliness' and to a changed view of manliness – of muscular manliness, not of earnest, moral manliness.

4

The 1860s to the early 1880s

Works for adults

The novel might be said to have been at a high point during these years. Trollope, George Eliot and Meredith were at the height of their reputations and were writing for a large readership which expected their novels to be in the form of the 'three decker' and which in large part read these and many other less famous novelists by subscribing to such circulating libraries as Mudie's. Often novels were brought out initially in periodicals as serials following the method popularised earlier by Dickens. Readers were beginning to hold a somewhat different opinion of the purpose of the novel. One view was that novels had a moral function and should be read with this in mind. For example, Trollope, writing in the *Nineteenth Century* in 1879 (January) in an article on 'Novel-Reading' felt that the novel had become 'the former of our morals, the code by which we rule ourselves, the mirror in which we dress ourselves.' But somewhat earlier a writer in the *Pall Mall Gazette* in 1869 (17 April) discussing 'the Literary Profession', admitted that some novels were works of art and that it was, therefore, possible that 'the reading of a novel is perhaps as near an approach to complete idleness of mind and body as can possibly be attained by a waking man'.

Whatever their purpose in writing, some of the great novelists put children into their work and either implicitly or explicitly expressed a view about their places in society and their upbringing. George Eliot's account of the development of Maggie Tulliver and her brother, Tom, in *The Mill on the Floss* (1860), is a fine example of the implicit presentation of a position, whilst

George Meredith in a number of his novels, for example, *The Egoist* (1879), has characters express ideas on schooling. This was the period of the great fame of Samuel Smiles's *Self-Help* (1859) and a number of novels were published in the genre, later named success literature (Harrison, 1957). A fine example was Mrs G. Linnaeus Banks's *The Manchester Man* (1872), the story of Jabez Clegg, an orphan, who received his schooling as a blue-coat boy at Chetham's College and by strength of character rose to become a master in his own right in early nineteenth-century Manchester when cotton was becoming king.

Two out of forty-seven chapters in Mrs Banks's book were about Jabez's scholing at Chetham's. Only two novelists of any stature at this time appear to have written whole novels about schools. These were Trollope and Mrs Henry Wood. Trollope wrote *Dr Wortle's School* in 1881. This novel is about a very good private school, called Bowick School, run by Dr Jeffrey Wortle, a clergyman, where 'No doubt a good deal was done to make the externals of the place alluring to those parents who love to think that their boys shall be made happy at school'. (I). Trollope refers to this schooling as part of 'the old prescribed form of education for British aristocrats [which] must be followed – a t'other school, namely, then Eton, and then Oxford'. A new master, Mr Peacock, is appointed who was a clergyman; as Trollope says 'an assistant school master is not often in orders, and sometimes not a gentleman' (II). This master, however, refuses to take services or in any way to act as a clergyman and keeps his wife very much in the background, declining to enter local society. Despite his success as a teacher doubts arise concerning himself and his wife. The truth ultimately comes out that there is some doubt about whether his wife's first husband, whom she had married in the USA, is really dead. Although in the end he finds that he is not a bigamist he has to leave Dr Wortle's school. Although one or two boys are mentioned, the plot really focuses on the adults and their affairs. It is not a story about a school, although it is set in one. Furthermore, this novel has never, at the time or since, been considered one of Trollope's best novels. He himself makes no mention of it in his autobiography.

Mrs Henry Wood was a successful popular novelist of the period, though her stature was not then and is not now rated equal to Trollope's. In 1867 Bentley's published her novel *Orville College*, in three volumes. There was some emphasis in the plot of this novel on the boys at Dr Brabazon's private school, but once again the main focus was upon a master, Mr Henry, whose real name was Arthur Henry Paradine. His father had died in gaol of a heart attack at a time when he was accused of fraud. Mr Henry came from Germany to be a master, teaching French and German, at Orville College, within easy distance of London, where he found the sons of his father's former partners, Loftus and Trace, were pupils. His young brother was also there, living with his mother nearby. The two sons of his father's old partners recognised George Paradine. Dr Brabazon was told of the matter, supported Mr Henry and asked that it be kept quiet. However, Loftus and Trace organised the persecution of George and of Mr Henry despite all the good qualities that both showed. Eventually the truth was discoverd that Trace's father committed the fraud, but by this time Mr Henry had sickened and at the end of the novel himself died of a heart attack. Mrs Wood was a strictly orthodox church-woman and a conservative (D.N.B.) and throughout the book there are religious references and authorial asides addressed to 'My Boys'. The novel seems to have been addressed to a dual readership of boys and adults. It was not, however, a great success, gaining no mentions in works about Mrs Wood, though in 1899 Macmillan published an impression in which they indicate that 38,000 copies had been sold.

One other work for adults that was certainly about a school, Winchester, must be mentioned. Winchester has apparently escaped the fate of almost all other major public schools in that no story has been written about it, but R.B. Mansfield, a family friend of Thomas Hughes, did write an illustrated factual account of Winchester and its customs, called *School Life and Winchester College or The Reminiscences of a Winchester Junior*. This was first published soon after *Tom Brown* in 1860; a second edition was published in 1870 and this was reprinted in 1893.

There were a number of authors who clearly wrote with dual readership in mind: two of these need only a brief mention. R.D. Blackmore wrote her West Country story, *Lorna Doone*, in 1867, in which Chapter I, 'Elements of Education' tells of Jan Ridd's time at Blundell's School in Devon, and Rider Haggard in the 1880s wrote a number of adventure stories which became very popular with young persons. The best known is *King Solomon's Mines*, published in 1885. However, a third novel, Anstey's *Vice Versa*, published in 1882 must be considered more fully, primarily because it was the first novel in which the schoolmaster is seen as a nincompoop. Reviewers, as will be seen, read this book as a criticism of private schools.

Thomas Anstey Guthrie was born in 1856, son of a successful London tailor. He was at a private boarding school until 1872, when he became a day boy at King's College in the Strand. In 1875 he went to Trinity Hall, Cambridge, to read Law. While an undergraduate in 1877 he wrote a school story 'Turned Tables' for an abortive journal, the *Cambridge Tatler*, with the idea of 'sending a father back to school in place of his son'. The journal collapsed so that the story was not published. In 1880-1 whilst reading for the Bar, Anstey rewrote this tale as a short novel. It was refused by two journals as a serial. Bentley's commented in their refusal note for *Temple Bar* that 'the story itself is not one to find favour with grown-up people so much as with younger readers'. Anstey had written it with adults in mind. Despite some doubts Smith, Elder's accepted the novel, now re-named *Vice Versa or a Lesson to Fathers*, and it was published in 1882 to become an instant success (Anstey, 1936). The new spirit abroad in regard to novels is seen clearly in Anstey's Preface to *Vice Versa*:

> The author. . . . feels that in these days of philosophical fiction, metaphysical romance, and novels with a purpose, some apology may perhaps be needed for a tale which has the unambitious and frivolous aim of mere amusement.

In *Vice Versa* Paul Bultitude, a widower, with two sons and a daughter, who is a colonial merchant in London, whilst wishing 'good-bye' to his elder son, Dick, on his return to school, says that he wishes he could change places with Dick. He is holding the Garuda Stone, an Indian relic, and no sooner wished than he does become Dick and Dick is transformed into his father. Mr Bultitude goes in Dick's place to Dr Grimston's Crichton House, modelled on Anstey's own old private school. His problem is that

> he was an ardent believer in the Good Boy of a certain order of school tales – the boy who is seized with a sudden conviction of the intrinsic baseness of boyhood, and does all in his power to get rid of the horrible taint; the boy who renounces his old comrades and his natural tastes . . . to don a panoply of priggishness which is too often kick-proof. (I)

Dick, on the other hand, was a high spirited boy who was involved in much mischief at school. Not unexpectedly Mr Bultitude does many things in his role as Dick that cause much surprise and difficulty for himself. Eventually he runs away from school and arrives home to find Dick, slightly drunk, holding a huge party. The Garuda Stone is lost, but his younger son, Roly, finds it and under his father's supervision uses his one wish to return things to normal. Dick goes back to Crichton House, but knowing that he is to go to Harrow next term, and Mr Bultitude returns to Mincing Lane to straighten out his business affairs which Dick had allowed to deteriorate.

Vice Versa was an instant success and was well reviewed. There was a leader in the *Daily News* and a generous review by Andrew Lang in the *Saturday Review* of 15 July. Lang questioned whether such a private school still existed 'where City merchants in good position send their sons'. He recommended this book

> very earnestly to all fathers, in the first instance, and their
> sons, nephews, uncles and male cousins next. We are afraid
> that with the other sex it will not find equal favour, but that
> is to be expected from the nature of the work.

After this success Anstey gave up his intention to pursue a career at the Bar and did what he had initially wanted to do; he became a professional writer, having a long and prosperous career as a novelist and dramatist, lasting well into the inter-war years.

Certainly there was no flood of adult stories during this period. One or two novelists seem to have tried this type of novel, though using the setting for a tale about an adult hero, rather than telling a story of boys at school for such a readership as Hughes and Farrar had done. Furthermore, the stories produced were not about public schools and one, written for adults, but in the end gaining dual readership, namely Anstey's *Vice Versa*, was implicitly critical of schoolmasters and private schools, which could not be said of *Tom Brown* and *Eric*.

Developments in children's literature

There was one major difference between stories for children or young persons and those for adults. They were usually much shorter. But other differences were emerging, some of which had been prefigured earlier in the century. The first, and most decidedly new, development was the coming of stories for children that were marked by an element of fantasy or of magic. The most famous of these was Lewis Carroll's *Alice's Adventures in*

From George MacDonald *At the Back of the North Wind*

Wonderland (1865) and its sequel, *Through the Looking Glass* (1871). There was another new quality about these books in that the heroine was motivated by curiosity, not a quality greatly encouraged by nineteenth-century parents or teachers.

Magic previously was most represented in fairy stories, although in passing note might be taken of the fact that even Anstey in *Vice Versa* introduced the Garuda Stone as a crucial factor in his plot. Gillian Avery (1965: 124-5) has noted that fairy tales of three types were created at this time: known tales were refashioned for contemporary children – Andrew Lang did much rewriting of this type in, for example, his *Red* and *Blue Books*; new tales were invented – Ruskin's *The King of the Golden River* (1841), written somewhat earlier, is a fine example; or the traditional world of fairy tales was romanticised to contrast it with the real world – Kingsley's *Water Babies* (1843) fits this last category, though it also had some other noteworthy characteristics. It was, in addition, a mixture of Christian preaching and the presentation of some simple science. Throughout the book Kingsley constantly returned to the way a child learns to be good and particularly the need for punishment to ensure that valued character traits are learnt. A further development of this tendency is seen in the work of George MacDonald, a Congregational minister, who wrote a number of fairy tales intended to show children how to grow up to be good. The most famous were *At the Back of the North Wind* (1870), *The Princess and the Goblin* (1871) and its sequel, *The Princess and Curdie* (1872).

Many of these fairy tales were linked to reality. In *The Water Babies* Tom, the hero, is a chimney sweep. *At the Back of the North Wind* is set in part in working-class London. There was a similar tendency to set stories that were factual in nature in working-class settings. The most famous writer working in this way was Hesba Stretton who published in 1867 *Jessica's First Prayer*, a very successful, but lachrymose book. This story was published by the Religious Tract Society and has been said to have founded 'a school of writing, the Sunday school story of the street arab, the homeless waif – rescued by crusading clergymen or benevolent ladies, to be translated either from a hospital to a home in the skies, or via the Liverpool emigrant packet to a Canadian Eden' (Bratton, 1981: 85). In 1868 she next wrote *Little Meg's Children*, in which she set a book for children in the slums, made fairly obvious the profession of one character, Kitty, and made clear that Meg herself was likely to suffer the same fate, though in the end her innocence wins through. What is becoming clear is that there was a short step between presenting material of this nature and being critical about the way in which society was then organised. Indeed, in 1879 Hesba Stretton did write *In Prison and Out*, a story about two boys who became recidivists. This book was an open attack on the prison system, especially of the way in which it influenced young prisoners and in it the writer compared the working-class child gaoled for stealing food with boys whose often illegal escapades are described in *Tom Brown*, wondering what would now be the state of some of the latter had they, as the former were, been committed to penal servitude.

These books were for somewhat younger children rather than for adolescents, but a similar critical spirit had begun to affect books written for the older age range. Two will be discussed here. The first was by Mrs Ewing, whose output consisted in the main of domestic tales. It is, therefore, the more startling that in *We and the World* (1878) she should write a tale for young persons in which she was quite openly critical of private schools and of a father's handling of his two sons. Jack and Jem are sent by their father to Grayshaw's, a school about which there were 'rumours of undue severity, of discomforts, of bad teaching and worse manners' (I. IX). A boy died of the physical effects and there were also serious moral effects; sneaking, bullying and 'terror of uncertainty' (I. X). Both boys ran away, but, though Jem was removed and sent to a private school and thence to a public school, Jack was sent back to Grayshaw's, but his character was saved by the beneficial influence of his home. The school was in the end broken up. Jack wished to go to sea, but his father put him into his brother's office as an articled clerk. He did not do well there and soon ran away to sea. The whole of the second part of the book describes his adventures at sea, where he led a Christian life amidst many temptations. His hard work and honesty saved him so that he returned home to a father who had by now appreciated his error, particularly as Jem had amongst other things run into debt at his public school.

The second novel is by Flora Shaw, a less well known novelist. Flora Shaw herself had a fascinating career, becoming head of the Colonial Department of *The Times* and in 1902 marrying Lord Lugard who became a well-known colonial administrator in West Africa (D.N.B.). In *Castle Blair* (1878) four children return from India to their uncle's house, Castle Blair in Ireland. There they, though fundamentally of good character, run wild; their uncle wishes them to settle down before going away to school. Murtagh, about twelve years old, plans for the factor of the estate to be killed, because of his 'cruelty' to the tenants, because he had shot his sister's dog, and, finally, because he had burnt down the children's play hut on an island on the river. The factor was very critical of the children's wild behaviour. Murtagh stole a gun and gave it to the son of a grieved tenant. In the nick of time he repented and in saving the factor was himself shot by him, though not seriously. All ends well as the factor realises his own harshness. However, once again there is an implicit criticism of a mode of bringing up children, though here there is also a revelation of the savagery of which children are capable.

There was one previous exemplar of this criticism of the family, though it was in an old and respected classic and probably not read in this way by most readers, particularly children. This was *Gulliver's Travels* (1726). In part IV Swift had described family life amongst the Houyhnhnms. Children were brought up according to a parody of the English aristocratic system. A child was removed at twenty months from his parents and entrusted to a public boarding school. Parents were allowed to see their children twice yearly for an hour at a time. However, an admitted and open parody of a children's book was published in 1872 and that was *The New History of Sandford and Merton*, though it achieved the success neither of *Gulliver* nor of Day's original book.

The final development on which comment will be made is also a continuation of an earlier growth, the adventure story. The boy's adventure story continued to develop strongly from the foundations laid by Marryat. The best known writer of this period was W.H.G. Kingston. His stories were set in many lands and were usually exciting, but they are forgotten whereas neither his predecessor, Marryat, nor his successors are. Henty is probably his most direct successor whose many books began to flow onto the market from about 1880. Rider Haggard has already been mentioned. Reference must be made here to one other writer, though he also began to achieve fame late in this period, that is, in the 1880s, namely Robert Louis Stevenson. In 1883 his most loved adventure tale, *Treasure Island*, was published. After the dedication are two stanzas 'To the Hesitating Purchaser'; in part, the lines run as follows:

> If studious youth no longer crave,
> His ancient appetites forgot,

Kingston, or Ballantyne the brave,
Or Cooper of the wood and wave;
So be it, also! And may I
And all my pirates share the grave
Where these and their creations be!

Stevenson's book was, and is, a 'good read' and 'a fine yarn'. It is not explicitly didactic, either in offering scientific or other facts as part of the story – not that one may not learn something of sailing ships – or in preaching Christianity. Indeed, Long John Silver, one of the main characters, escapes death and possible future hanging for having been a pirate by playing along with both sides and by building up moral credits and debits with his 'betters'. A very different lesson might be drawn from this behaviour than from, for example, the Christian straightforwardness of Kingston's tales of adventures which by the evidence of the verse quoted apparently Stevenson himself admired.

Children's literature was becoming more entertaining. Its range was growing wider, perhaps because more of its writers were now men to whom contemporary norms then permitted a wider range of interest and action. Yet the underlying morally didactic aim, particularly of a Christian nature, still loomed large and in mid-Victorian social circumstances this Christian spirit easily spread into criticism of much that then was allowed to happen, not just in the wider society, but to children in the family and at school.

Boys' school stories

In past discussion of the development of school stories there is one major gap and that concerns what happened to this type of book in the 1860s and 1870s, that is, between the publication of *Tom Brown* and *Eric* and the start of the *Boy's Own Paper* and the coming of the school of writers, particularly Talbot Baines Reed, associated with it (see, for example, Quigley, 1982: 43). In this chapter we must trace what was written of relevance during these years. First, two school stories by W.H.G. Kingston will be examined. Next, the three important writers of school stories in this period, H.C. Adams, T.S. Millington and A.R. Hope, will be discussed. Finally, a work by one woman, Ethel C. Kenyon, will be described.

The 1860s to the early 1880s

W.H.G. Kingston

Kingston was, as has been made clear, a well-established adventure story writer. In 1860 he published two books, one of which, *Digby Heathcote or The Early Days of a Country Gentleman's Son and Heir*, was in part about a school and the other, *Ernest Bracebridge*, was wholly about a school. In *Digby Heathcote* eight of the seventeen chapters are about Digby's time at Grangewood House, 'Mr Sanford's Academy for young gentlemen' (XI). The first nine chapters describe Digby's time, mainly under a governess, at his family home, Bloxholme Hall. Before going to Grangewood House he had boarded for a short time at his uncle's, Mr Nugent's, small private school some five miles from his home with five other boys. On his departure to school his father advised him in words very like Squire Brown's to Tom, 'But there is one thing I must charge you, never forget that you are a Christian, and a gentleman' (XI). On his arrival at Grangewood House Digby was teased because the other boys had heard John Pratt, Mr Heathcote's servant, deliver him to the school using the words 'son and heir'. Digby stood up well to this and to the other initial cruel treatment from the school bully, Scarborough. Mr Sanford, the head, was ill so that the school administration was lax. As one boy put it,

> 'And do you know, Heathcote, I really do believe that an usher at a school like this, when no one is exactly master, and the big boys have it much their own way, has a good deal to put up with.'

A boy called Julian Langley, whom Digby had known before coming to school and who had led him into trouble at home, now arrived. Despite Digby giving him a good start Julian soon fell in with a bad group. When their Saturday leave was cancelled for an unexplained reason Julian told how he 'had read of some fellows at a large school getting up a grand rebellion, barring out the masters, and standing a siege of several days till their terms were complied with' (XIV). The idea caught on and they collected supplies. The big playroom was the site for the barring-out which began on Monday. Scarborough and his group drank and smoked in a corner whilst the other boys manned the barricades, but no one besieged them. By Thursday their supplies had run out and Digby led a truce party out. They found a new head, Dr Graham, and a new staff except for one of the old masters, Mr Moore. All

93

were forgiven except Scarborough who was expelled. Digby soon did so well at the reorganised school that he stayed till he went to Cambridge rather than first going to Eton.

Despite the fact that *Digby Heathcote* was written so soon after *Tom Brown* it has little that parallels Hughes's book except the advice given to Digby on leaving for school and the potential readership which by the evidence of such passages as the following must have been upper middle-class:

> Digby felt somewhat like a fly in the grasp of a spider, for there was little of the *suaviter in modo*, however much these might have been of the *fortiter in re*, in Mr Twyman's proceedings. (XI)

Ernest Bracebridge or Schoolboy Days is also a mixture of similarities to and dissimilarities from either *Tom Brown* or *Eric*. Ernest is sent to Grafton Hall, a small private school, for three years prior to working with a tutor for entry to the Indian Service. School work is very rarely mentioned in the book. Games are described in great detail. These games are more various than were available to Tom Brown at Rugby and more of them were unorganised. There were: hare hunt, kite racing, military exercise, fishing, golf, hockey and football, cricket and skating. Kingston comments

> However, I am not writing an account of the lesson hours of my schoolboy days, but rather of the play hours. At the same time, I believe that they are more connected, and the importance of the latter is greater than some people are apt to suppose. (VIII)

There is a morally didactic strain in the book, though it is not overtly Christian. Of Blackall, a bully, Kingston writes,

> as his character is so odious I hold him up as a warning to some not to imitate him, and to others to avoid, and on no account to trust to or form any friendship with such a person when they meet them. (XI)

And in rather the spirit later expressed by Mr Bultitude, but mocked by Anstey, Ernest and his friends were crusaders,

> They did their utmost to put a stop to swearing or to the use of bad language. They at once and with the exertion of their utmost energy put down all indecent conversation; and if they found any boy employing it, they held him up to the

reprobation and contempt of their companions. Falsehood of every description, either black lying or white lying, they exhibited in its true colours, as they did all dishonest or mean practices, indeed, they did their utmost to show the faults and the weak points of what is now generally looked on as schoolboy morality. The system of fudging tasks, cribbing lessons, deception of every sort they endeavoured to overthrow. (XVI)

Yet the head, Dr Carr, was not like Farrar, a believer in human perfection:

The Doctor, however, knew the world, and that in no human institution can perfection be attained – nor can it be expected that [boys] should be without faults; but he knew also that by care and attention those faults may be decreased, if not altogether got rid of, and he did not despair. (XI)

The boys in this private school were definitely aspirants for higher social status. A point is made of Ernest visiting Eton to see a friend's brother and the 'big fellows' made a plan to have a system of fags, 'Oh, don't you know?' exclaimed Dawson, 'It's a plan we have got up for becoming a public school' (IX). Despite the interest roused at the time by *Tom Brown* and *Eric* neither *Digby Heathcote* nor *Ernest Bracebridge* seem to have sold well, as they seem not to have been reprinted. Kingston did not repeat his attempts to write school stories; his adventure stories were more successful financially and were adequate vehicles for expressing the moral lessons that he wanted to pass on to adolescent boys. Others did, however, do so with greater success, though their work was, as will be seen, more in the tradition of Farrar than of Hughes and, as has been shown here, Kingston himself was no slavish imitator of Thomas Hughes.

Three successful early writers of boys' school stories

Two of these writers were clergyman and one was a schoolmaster. The Reverend Henry Cadwallader Adams had been a Fellow of Magdalen College, Oxford and Chaplain of Bromley College, before he became Vicar first of Dry Sandford with Cothill in Berkshire and then of Old Shoreham, Sussex. He wrote on the Greek testament and on Church history, produced Latin exercises and poems, as well as writing a number of school stories

95

between the 1860s and 1880s (*Crockford's*, 1882). Adams's first school story, entitled *The First of June or Schoolboy Rivalry*, was written in about 1857 (Salmon, 1888a: 98). After this he wrote a string of such stories. By 1874 these included four stories, each about one hundred and fifty pages long, about Charlton School under Dr Young, which were entitled: *The First of June*, *The Cherry Stones*, *The Doctor's Birthday* and *Walter's Friend*. Charlton School was a smallish private school, but Adams wrote one long school story for boys about a public school and it is this book, *Schoolboy Honour. A Tale of Halminister College* (1861) which will mainly be discussed here.

Adams's book is a long and rather complicated story, marked by a number of sub-plots, about a public school in a country town and it has many of the characteristics of *Tom Brown*. The story starts with two friends, Cole and Austen, who have known each other since childhood, discussing honour. One asks, 'Why don't they set the police on us, or have ushers always with us, as they do at private schools?' (I). This was quite a common sentiment in the stories of this type at the time. Indeed, Kingston, in *Digby Heathcote*, in an authorial aside, puts the reverse point of view: boys in private schools have an advantage in that 'If they wish to study during school hours they can do so, under the eye of the master without fear of interruption' (XII), whilst the system of studies in public school leads to idleness. Cole has a bet with O'Grady about which of their guns is the better. After this, though sub-plots deal with matters of honour in class in relation to, for example, cribbing, and in general in relation to, for instance, betting on horse racing, the main plot relates to the attempts to organise a shooting match to settle their bet. This is ultimately held in the country near a public house known to some of the boys. After the shooting match, on the way back to the boat in which they came, the two boys fire at some rabbits and this brings them into conflict with a gamekeeper, Greenwood, from whom they run away, though he is hurt by tripping during the pursuit. He sees enough of one of them to be able to identify him later. The culprits do not own up at school but the gamekeeper recognises Austen, one of the party, whilst he is coxing an eight in the school's annual regatta. Austen, though knowing much, is not the real culprit, but is thrashed because he will not 'sneak' by naming the true culprits in this and some other matters. Meanwhile, Cole, who was involved in the bet, but not in the other matters, has been summoned to his mother's bedside since she is believed to be dying after an accident to a coach though she recovers. He returns to school in time to clarify all the tangled skeins of the plots. He is judged to have suffered enough, but two others are expelled.

There are some references to homes and families, but not as many as in *Tom Brown* or *Eric*. Nor is the family or school seen as a patriotic institution. Adams puts the main focus in *Schoolboy Honour* on the values inculcated by the school. Even the organisation of the school, though clearly somewhat like Rugby, is given minor emphasis. Therefore, comparison with *Eric* is more appropriate than with *Tom Brown* and from the examples now to be quoted to indicate the notions of honour presented in the book the style and tone will be seen to be more like that of Farrar than Hughes. For example, in discussing betting Austen says,

> 'It is true that a fellow who acted upon honour would not lie or cheat, but it does not seem to me to prevent him from doing other things – flying into a passion, for instance, or cursing or swearing, or getting drunk, or that sort of thing'
> (I)

When Cole and Austen arrived as new boys, Mr Holdford, the master who helped them much, advised them, first, to read the Bible daily, but not to talk of it to others unless sure that they care for it, and second, to come for help if need be; 'I don't mean come and tell tales of the other boys, that is mean and cowardly; what I never encourage or allow' (IV). They acknowledge 'the schoolboy's grand moral principle – vis. "stand up for your schoolfellows through thick and thin; first and chiefest against the masters, and after this against all mankind" ' (XVII). Two masters, Mr Holdford and Mr Singleton, also discuss honour, Mr Holdford saying,

> 'I did not object to *dealing* with boys upon honour, but to *putting* them upon honour. Arnold did the first, but never the second . . . to *put* [a boy] upon honour is to teach him that, if on certain specified occasions he will act up to a high and right standard, he may on all ordinary matters adopt a low one.' (VII)

How the school was run, in other words, governed what was learnt, but 'despite a house system and prefects unlike in *Eric*' we hear very little of the details of how the school was run. The tone or culture of the school, however, is emphasised. There is a three-page discussion of vice in the school which ends:

> There is in large schools . . . a certain number of boys in every generation who become the centre of vice received from their forerunners, and who hand this on to their successors in the same unholy priesthood. The mantle worn by these evil prophets is often handed on in the manner above described in the initiates in sin taking to themselves younger companions whom they enrol in the brotherhood, rendering them fit to exercise the same detestable ministry, when they themselves shall have departed from the scene. (VII)

Austen is 'taken up' by a 'blood' called Howard who is later expelled, though Austen's basically sound character sees him through the temptations involved. At one point Austen has a major personal struggle over lying which is described thus by Adams:

> Do not think lightly of this trial, reader. . . . It may be that there have been martyrs, to whom it was a less exertion of faith and courage to defy the cross or the stake, than it was to Robert Austen to renounce the good will of his companions and resist the entreaties of his friends, rather than to give up that which in his heart of hearts he felt to be his duty. (XII)

Cole, too, arriving home at his mother's supposed death-bed, asks himself, 'Was this heavy blow the chastisement due to his falsehood? Had he really provoked God to visit his sin by taking his mother from him?' (XXI). This he does because he had told a lie at about the time his mother had been thrown from the carriage and hurt severely. He prays and his mother returns to consciousness at the very moment at which he decides to tell all he knows. Later Mr Holdford explains to him that, 'You must not expect that He will always be pleased to answer your prayers so directly and promptly; but you need not doubt that He did so answer them on this occasion.'

At the dénouement Dr Campbell, the head, says in public,

> 'I trust that the occurrences of the last few weeks will impress on you, and on all the difference between true and false HONOUR – the latter of which is so often the base of a schoolboy's life. Your [Cole's] great mistake has been in

believing that you could be false to duty in your actions and yet truthful in your words.' (XXIV)

Schoolboy Honour can be seen to be a story about a public school, marked by great seriousness, emphasising values, raising difficult moral and theological issues and doing this more within an Evangelical than a Broad Church framework. Adams's other stories are either about Charlton School or in *The Chief of the School or Schoolboy Ambition* (1874), about Nethercourt. They are set in private schools. One of the Charlton series, *The Doctor's Birthday*, will be briefly mentioned. In it there is rivalry between Charlton and 'a large middle class school for the benefit of the neighbourhood' whose boys are called 'half breeds' by the Charlton boys (II). The plot concerns the boys' main winter 'game', which is not organised by the school and is based on much reading of the Waverley Novels, involving an assault and siege of a castle, built by the boys. Once again, for unexplained reasons their game is stopped by Dr Young, the head, and a boy, John Houghton, plans a rebellion. He locked the master, Mr White, in a cupboard with another boy who escaped and released Mr White. Houghton was, of course, expelled. These books are shorter, less moralistic, and rather straightforward tales of private schools in which games are both various and largely unorganised. For example, at Nethercourt in *The Chief of the School* there is mention of hare and hounds, cricket, rounders, marbles, fives, football, hockey and top.

The second writer to be considered here is the Reverend Thomas Street Millington who after working in parishes in the Isle of Man and in Northampton became in 1853 Vicar of Woodhouse Eaves in Leicestershire. He wrote religious books as well as school stories (*Crockford's*, 1882). The latter included *Straight to the Mark* (1883), published by the Religious Tract Society, and *Some of Our Fellows* (1886). In his Preface to the first of these books Millington wrote,

> The subject of the following story is TRUTH. . . . Yet his first object was to produce an entertaining book for the amusement of a leisure hour . . . And with this in view he has not hesitated to use fiction.

The story was about Abbotscliffe, 'an old foundation school with a modern development, [which] generally went by the name of the College . . . intended by its founders as a day school for the benefit of the town, the pupils now consisted almost exclusively of boarders' (VIII). Yet Abbotscliffe sounds more like a private than a public school for all the social ambitions of its head, Dr Piercy, and many of the boys. The book, as title and Preface make clear, is about truth at a number of levels – between boys, between masters and boys, between parents and their children at home and between adults at home and at work. Except that there is a major sub-plot concerning a local inhabitant, a boat builder, there is nothing unexpected in this book, whereas the other work by Millington mentioned here, *Some of our Fellows*, introduces a number of typical new themes to which no reference has yet been made and reinforces some other developments already introduced to the argument.

Some of our Fellows is about North Cray, a small private school, supposedly limited to forty boys, though, when pressed hard, Mr Lightfoot, the head, admits one or two extra pupils. 'It was not what could be called a public school, though where the limits began and where they ended nobody could tell' (II). Two new boys were admitted at the start of the story; one Pierre Le Brun, a shipwrecked orphan, apparently French, befriended by a local doctor, who was a friend of Mr Lightfoot, the other, Moreton Pougher, the son of a wealthy merchant, a boy with social aspirations. In many of the school stories of the time that are about private schools there is found a character who hopes to use the school to help in his own or his parents' social ambitions. A clear example was William Dixon in Adams's *Walter's Friend*, who

> was the son of a man of small means, gaining his living as a surgeon among the poor in the East End of London. He had often impressed on his son the necessity of getting on in the world, by the help of such connections as he could contrive to make. (I)

Pierre Le Brun has many difficulties at school and also suffers from lapses of memory. Pougher throws his and his father's money about freely; his father pays for a cricket professional, named Duck, and for the erection of a flagstaff on his son's request. Pierre is very good with the ropes and signal flags that are connected to the flagstaff, but is suspected of cutting some of the ropes, because he is found mending them after someone else has damaged them. The true culprit is later discovered to be a local small farmer who has a quarrel with the school over boys apparently taking apples from his orchard. Pierre runs away taking five pounds, not to steal it, but to buy some plants for the school gardens. Pierre has in fact suffered from a lapse of memory and when it returns he is found to have been a member of the crew of a 'coffin' ship owned by Pougher's father. This introduction of material relating to a contemporary social campaign, namely that over the Plimsoll line in the 1870s, is worth noting and parallels Hesba Stretton's emphasis on recidivism in *In Prison and Out* (1879).

Throughout *Some of Our Fellows* the most obvious new attitude introduced by Millington, whether to exorcise it or not is unclear, though, as will be seen, if this was the intention, his method was too naive to achieve this aim, was xenophobia. One key character was Meyer who 'was German, a sort of half pupil . . . [who] had to talk German with the boys' (IV). Meyer is not liked. The narrator, a boy in his last year at school, says,

> 'Of course there is nothing really in Germany that can be compared with Great Britain, though I shall never think of saying it to a foreigner, and if I did he would not agree with me. He would not be worth much if he did. Still, Rule Britannia – God Save the Queen – Home Sweet Home – them's my sentiments; and all the boys at our school were of the same opinion, except Meyer.'

After a row with Meyer, Sergeant, a monitor says, 'I hate all those foreigners. They ought not to be admitted into English schools', though Mr Merivale, a master replies, 'Meyer is none the worse for being a foreigner. That has nothing to do with it. He is a bad specimen, that's all' (XI). Another boy, Jervis, 'was conscious of having a prejudice against Pierre, he scarcely knew why. It was a feeling which prevailed more or less among many of the fellows. We none of us liked foreigners. They are so odd to say the least of it' (XIII). The boot boy who found Pierre trying to repair the ropes of the flagstaff said, 'Caught in the very act, and wants to throw it on someone else . . . Ah, them furriners! them furriners' (XIV). This distrust of and mocking at the French and Germans can be found in other school stories, in the form of making them, particularly when Modern Language masters, stereotypical and ridiculous figures. In *The Doctor's Birthday*, Adams has the boy, Houghton, say of Mr White who has come from Germany, 'Yes; he gives me the idea of having lived among foreigners, and doesn't understand how to deal with Englishmen at all' (I). This rather jingoistical xenophobia also extended on occasions into anti-Semitism. In Mrs Ewing's *We and the World* (1878) one important minor character is 'Moses Benson, the Jew clerk' in the office where Jack is unsuccessfully articled. He has 'a very big nose', odd speech, black curly hair and is subservient in demeanour, but very ambitious in fact (I. XII). Such rather obvious anti-Semitic feeling is to be found in school stories of a somewhat later era, though odd traces of it are also to be found in this period. In *The Doctor's Birthday* Adams comments on a knife which one boy owned; an old aunt 'bought it I believe, off a Jew in London' (III) – seemingly a gratuitous comment.

The third writer of school stories during this period to be discussed here is A.R. Hope, whose real name was R. Hope Moncrieff. He was a schoolmaster educated at Edinburgh University who retired in 1868 to take up full-time writing. His serial 'At the Masthead' was included in the first volume of the *Boy's Own Paper* and he wrote a number of short stories about schools which were published as single volumes. He began in 1868 with *A Book about Boys* and followed this in 1869 with *A Book about Dominies*. One of his books, *My Schoolfellows* (1870) was seen as a classic (Lofts and Adley, 1970: 248). This book was a collection of twenty stories with titles based on most of the letters in the alphabet, for example, '*A*lexander the Great', and '*E*mily'. In 'Alexander the Great' the author explains that he had been 'a pupil in several schools of different kinds. . . . Thus, a juvenile Ulysses, I made the acquaintance of many boys and had much varied experience of scholastic manners.' In this tale, 'Alexander announced his intention of giving a prize at Christmas to the master whose record came out highest on his list.' The writing master won a second-hand copy of an 'odd volume of British essayists'. 'Emily' was about a French boy in an English school – Hope also wrote an account of French lycées. 'This was a school of much loftier pretensions than the one I have just been telling about – a real public school, full of 'sound' English ways and prejudices.' There is something rather odd about a Scot, an offspring of the 'auld alliance', first writing about public schools and, second, poking faint fun at the French in the way in which Hope did in this story.

In *Stories of Whitminister* (1873) Hope included eight stories having common characters under such titles as 'The Favourite', 'Cupboard Love', and 'Little Monkeys'. In his Preface Hope wrote that these were very ordinary stories of ordinary boys at an ordinary school, and contain nothing but ordinary incidents and reflections, which, nevertheless, may be thought worthy of more than the ordinary attention bestowed on such matters.

He made a point that 'if my tales cannot make themselves understood they do not deserve any explanation of what was intended as their purport'. In other words these books were a series of stories about different kinds of boys and of schools. They were not really about schools so much as about boys at schools, but there was, nevertheless, no very strong development of a story or of the characters involved – this was difficult since each was so short. Finally, there were morals to the stories, but they were not specifically Christian and were obvious, as Hope himself promised in the Preface to *Stories of Whitminister* and, indeed, were often merely trivial, as was the case with two stories in *My Schoolfellows*, entitled 'Guzzly Gus' and 'Lazy Laurence'. Lest the impression be given that these tales were mere knock-about stuff reference will be made to one, 'A History of Hampers', in which the idea is presented, in terms of Conservatives, Whigs and Nonconformists, that much national history parallels school history. The point that will be built on later is that Hope was publishing collections of school stories about schools or on occasion about one school.

Ethel C. Kenyon

Ethel Kenyon wrote *Jack's Heroism. A Story of School Boy Life* in 1883. In view of the earlier preeminence of women in writing for children and young persons it is of interest to note that Ethel Kenyon is the first to be discussed here in connection with the development of boys' school stories in these two decades, although it must be admitted her story does seem to be aimed at younger rather than older adolescents.

Two brothers, Ralph and Jack Waring, are left at Dr Grant's small private school by their father – their mother died five years earlier – on his return to China as a missionary. Jack tells Ralph of his father's parting advice,

'He said I was to try to become a brave, good man. He said life was for every one something like a battle; but all were not heroes. Ralph, he told me to be a hero, and I mean to be one too.' (I. I)

Ralph will not tell Jack what their father told him. Their father had summed his sons up shrewdly and given different advice to each. Jack quickly fits in well with the others at school

> His greatest failing – pride – was strengthening rapidly from day to day. Ah! boys, boys, remember who said, 'Woe unto you when all men shall speak well of you.' (I. II)

Jack is soon in trouble and Dr Grant promises to write to his father, telling of his misdemeanour. Jack is tempted to steal the letter from the head's study,

> Should he go in and take the letter? He trembled at the temerity of the idea. No one would see him. Ah Jack! you forget the Eye that is ever present. (I. IV)

He did steal and burn the letter, but later confessed to Dr Grant. They knelt and prayed together. Then they returned to the school room where Dr Grant reported his confession, continuing, 'Waring being deeply penitent, I have forgiven him' (I. IV). He was soon again in trouble and punished once more, being sent to his room, whence he escaped to a friend's house, where there was a large gas balloon. One boy cut it loose and they drifted away. Even then, during the cold hours of the night, one boy was comforted 'to think our Father is watching over us all the time' (I. VI). They landed by a wonderful coincidence in the Doctor's garden. Jack's next major escapade occurred during a paper chase during which another boy, Dent, was sent up a cottage chimney, where a fire was lit. Once back at school Jack went to apologise to Dent who refused to accept his apology, but promised to avenge himself. After the holidays Jack was given a bicycle and Dent knocked him off this. Jack successfully overcame the temptation to fight back – 'a valiant fight . . . between good and evil, the powers of light and darkness' (II. V). Then a fire broke out at the school at night. Dr Grant believed his daughter, Mabel, to be at a friend's house, but unbeknown to him, she had returned and the Doctor, seeing her trying to escape, fainted, but Jack saved her, though he died as a result of serious burns. Ralph says to Jack on his death-bed,

> 'Anyway, you're a hero now Jack.'
> 'You know – I always failed when trying to be a hero before – but you, Ralph, told me to begin in the right way and, thank God, I did – it was just – thinking of Jesus –

praying to him about everything – that is the way to win – tell father – He's with me now.' (II. VII)

A little before Jack had befriended and saved two pauper children from starvation. At his death he commended them to his aunt who adopted them.

Ethel Kenyon's tale was well-known at the time. It appears to use the by now popular school tale as a vehicle for the rather overt teaching of Christian moral principles. It is near to Farrar's theology in that Christianity is seen to be applicable at every level of action at school and in life. The school is a small private school and once again there is rivalry with the local grammar school, whose pupils are seen as inferior by those at Dr Grant's school. In this book, the family, albeit a single-parent one, is seen as important. There are no patriotic sentiments and little attention is given to school work or school organisation. The main focus is moral didacticism.

Some conclusions are possible from this consideration of these writers of the period from 1860 to the early 1880s. There were more school stories written than there had been beforehand, but except for odd details they by no means showed any very close connection to *Tom Brown's Schooldays*, their previously supposed progenitor. They had little of the patriotic but non-jingoistic love of England expressed by Thomas Hughes. They were mainly about small private schools rather than big public schools. They emphasised the values to be taught, but not the administrative mechanisms set up to teach the lessons that were made explicit or were implicit in them. Indeed, because the schools were small, they were administratively more simple than a big public school. In particular games were not usually well organised and were played among individuals rather than in teams. Furthermore, the values emphasised were far more evangelical in spirit than those recommended by Thomas Hughes; they were nearer in tone and content to those demonstrated by Farrar. In fact, if these school stories had any common ancestor it seems to have been *Eric* rather than *Tom Brown*.

The middlemen

In the end pages of many books of this period the publisher bound a catalogue of his books considered relevant to the readers of each class of his works. At the back of a 'juvenile' book would be found his current catalogue of books for juveniles. These were substantial lists, running in the case of such major publishers as Nelson or Routledge to many pages. We have already seen that Charlotte Yonge in 1867 thought that 'everyone writes books *for* some one.' How did the publishers sustain these separate markets? In 1874 the Nelson catalogue included as categories 'stories with a purpose'; 'present and prize books', and 'books of travel and adventure for boys'. The extreme differentiation of the market can be seen by laying out all the categories used in Routledge's catalogue for the same year:

Juvenile Books: 7/6d, 6/–
5/– books:
5/– Juvenile Books
    (included H.C. Adams)
1/6d Juvenile Books
Bowman's Juvenile Books 3/6d
3/6d Reward Books
3/6d Juvenile Books (majority
    of boys stories)
British Poets 3/6d
Standard Library 3/6d
3/– Juvenile Books
One Syllable Series
Half Crown Juveniles
Books for Young Readers 2/–

2/– Gift Books
The Hans Anderson Library 1/6d
Eighteen penny Juvenile
1/– Song Books
The Master Jack Series
1/– Juvenile Books
Christmas Book 1/–
9d Juvenile Books
6d Story Books
Miniature Library 6d
6d Songs
6d Handbooks
4d Juvenile Book
Little Ladders in Learning 6d

There was also a Catalogue of Nursery literature:

3d Toy Books
6d Toy Books
Coloured Picture Books 3/6d

New Series of 1/– Toy Books
5/– Books
3/6d Books

Finally, a notice was included advertising the *Young Gentlewoman's Magazine*; amongst the contributors was H.C. Adams. The catalogues of Mudie's and other circulating libraries were also divided into categories rather similar to those used by publishers in their catalogues. Clearly the market for children's literature was now both large and well differentiated. A close examination of the catalogues shows that publishers catered specifically for boys and for girls, and for children of differing ages. There is room for much discussion as to whether this finer division of the market was created by publishers, writers or parents, or others buying books for children. Probably the pressure came from all those involved and in the order indicated at the end of the last sentence.

However, the point to notice is that these divisions now existed and were sustained by a public demand that kept the publishers profitably in business.

The Religious Tract Society has already appeared as one important publisher in the field of children's fiction as well as of religious tracts for juveniles. In 1863 the Sixth Annual Report of the Society contained its view of the 'essential rules for healthful fiction'. Stories were to be:

1. *Moral* – no vice being investigated with interest;
2. *Natural* – true both to nature and to fact, free from false representations of life and exaggerations of character;
3. *Unexciting* – leaving the spirit calm and the passions not unduly moved.

These rules would seem to us today to exclude Farrar's *Eric* for publication by the Society, but they were in line with the views of many at that time.

Thus, in the *Quarterly Review* in 1867 B.J. Johns wrote an article on 'Books of Fiction for Children' in which some of the same views, although in a less blunt form, were expressed. There was still a residue of the feeling common earlier in the century against fiction for children. Johns wanted to show that fiction was a better vehicle than 'history' in which he included all factual accounts, to teach moral lessons to children, because the latter was so full of bad examples. He quoted *Tom Brown* as providing some bad examples, particularly the 'historical' descriptions of fighting. He thought that rather than using such 'history', 'a good fairy story takes up the cause of right against wrong, of good against evil' (61). He was opposed to the exaggerated didacticism of books like *The Fairchild Family*:

We can only trust that these books which have had a run in their day gradually cease to mar the well-being of thousands of innocent children. The race of hypocrites and maw-worms is large enough already, without adding to their number by specimens of the same genus Fairchild. (71)

Furthermore, he was fully aware of the problems that all publishers, and not just a body like the Religious Tract Society, had to circumvent in the matter of religious viewpoint: 'A sound, healthy, honest, story, containing a fair picture of life, though it have no party odour, no special air or views, may yet teach a wise and good lesson' (86). Using this question-begging recipe he provided one example – The Parables. Yet, though we may be snide about Johns's prescription, his was representative of a wider view of fiction for children.

The opinions on such matters of a better known 'expert', Charlotte Yonge, are to be found in a series of three articles in *Macmillans Magazine* for 1867. These were entitled: I 'Nursery Books of the Eighteenth Century'; II 'Didactic Fiction'; III 'Class Literature of the Last Thirty Years'. Charlotte Yonge, herself a relatively High Churchwoman who had known and been influenced by Keble in her youth, was also opposed to an exaggerated focus on religion in didactic works:

> But a 'religious tale', overloaded with controversy and with a forced moral, should be carefully distinguished from a tale constructed on a strong basis of religious principle, which attempts to give a picture of life as is really seen by Christian eyes. (1867: 310)

Though she had some minor criticisms she praised Maria Edgeworth's *Parents' Assistant*, a work first published as long ago as 1796, for its approach to moral matters and for a reason which is very unexpected in an earnest High Churchwoman. Charlotte Yonge pointed out that Maria Edgeworth took for granted 'the minor morals of life' and 'the good sense . . . and expediency of life are the theme':

> It is high-minded expediency, the best side of Epicureanism. Honesty *is* the best policy, but policy it always is: success is always the object and the reward, but it is not a strong, gaudy gratification of vanity, although it may be pride. (1867: 303)

The rebellion in 'The Barring Out' was defeated by honest negotiation, by the use of expedient reason. Her criticism concerned inaccuracies and those about Eton in 'Ad Montem' are explicitly mentioned.

In her third article Charlotte Yonge dealt with 'Class Literature' as she called it, though, as we have seen, this was now an accepted term, used in at least one publisher's catalogue. She bluntly stated that 'Exaggeration is the great error of the books that are written avowedly for boy-taste.' This led to 'loss of sensation'. She had 'little liking for "books for boys" ', believing that parents and others should 'bring children as soon as possible to stretch up to books above them, provided those books are noble and good'. She did, however, have some comments on a number of the authors mentioned here. 'The unapproachable Tom Brown' was compared with 'that morbid dismal tale, "Eric's School-days" '. An older tale, Harriet Martineau's *The Crofton Boys*, 'is full of life and cleverness . . . [and] Hugh, a truly boyish little hero'. Finally, 'Perhaps, Mr Hope's "Stories of School Life" is more a book for masters than boys' (1867: 448-56). We may conclude from Charlotte Yonge's articles that boys' books were now definitely seen as a separate category, that moral didacticism was an approved mode, though not in any exaggerated form, and that the restriction on fiction as reading material for children had now turned into suspicion rather than proscription.

The work of one other 'expert' will be quoted. In 1888 E. Salmon's *Juvenile Literature as it is* was published. This date is a few years beyond the end of the period under discussion, but we have no other source of such richness for views of writing for children nearer to the early 1880s. Furthermore, Salmon included in his book the results of a survey undertaken in 1884 by a Charles Welsh, in which he sent out 'a circular containing several questions such as "What is your favourite book and why do you like it best?" ' to 'numerous schools for boys and girls' (1888a: 12-13). He received about 2000 replies from boys and girls as well as from 'masters and mistresses'; 790 were from boys. Their first five favourite authors were: (1) Charles Dickens (223 choices); (2) W.H.G. Kingston (179); (3) Sir Walter Scott (129); (4) Jules Verne (114); (5) Captain Marryat (102). Thomas Hughes was not mentioned as an author. The individual books chosen were: (1) *Robinson Crusoe* (43); (2) *Swiss Family Robinson* (24); (3) *Pickwick Papers* (22); (4) *Ivanhoe* (2); (5) *The Boy's Own Annual* (17); (6) *The Bible* (15); (7) *Tom Brown's Schooldays* (15); . . . (9) *Vice Versa* (12); (10) *St Winifred's* (11); . . . (24) *Eric* (6). For girls the list of favourite authors was: (1) Charles Dickens (355); (2) Sir Walter Scott (248); (3) Charles Kingsley (103); (4) Charlotte Yonge (100); (5) Shakespeare (75). W.H.G. Kingston had 19, Marryat 5, and Anstey 5 choices. Most popular individual book was *Westward Ho!* (34 choices). Charlotte Yonge's *The Heir of Redclyffe* was 11th (12 choices) and Farrar's *Eric* and *St Winifred's* were equal 22nd (8 choices each).

Salmon thought 'boys' literature . . . admits divisions into several distinct classes' (1888a: 52) and without specifying any criteria he allocated a chapter each to: stories marked by 'the love of exciting exploits', in which he considered Marryat, Mayne

Reid, Verne, Kingston and Ballantyne; 'historical romances'; 'pictures of school life'; and, lastly, 'ordinary adventures' or 'romance and general adventures'. Here we find school stories emerging as a definitely separate category. In his chapter on school stories Salmon dealt with Thomas Hughes (5 pages), Archdeacon Farrar (2), T.S. Millington (2), A.R. Hope (2), H.C. Adams (1) and Talbot Baines Reid, the subject of the next chapter (2). We have noted in the last chapter his views on Hughes and Farrar. In Adams's books he found 'one defect' – they were 'diffuse . . . unimportant incidents are needlessly elaborated'. This is certainly true for a modern reader of *Schoolboy Honour*. However, Salmon thought that 'his books are among the best for boys' (1888a: 98-9). Millington was praised because there was 'nothing pessimistic in his pages' and he was 'graphic and readable when dealing with physical and moral crises'. Millington was 'always prepared to stand up for strict honour and truth, [was] not a sentimentalist, and censure[d] only wilful deception' (1888a: 93-5). These remarks had followed soon after Salmon's critiques of Farrar and, perhaps, literally mirrored his views on *Eric* and *St Winifred's*. A.R. Hope was seen by Salmon as 'probably the highest authority in Great Britain on the thoughts and lives, the joys and the troubles of schoolmaster and pupil'. Because of the nature of his books, collections of short stories, Salmon clearly saw that his appeal might be somewhat limited. Yet 'the purity of his tone, his keen appreciation of humour, and the general excellence of his subject and form are to be commended' (1888a: 96-8).

In 1869 Charlotte Yonge had proclaimed that 'Schoolboy literature is . . . more read by mothers, sisters, and little boys longing to be at school, than by the boys themselves.' We have internal evidence in the books themeselves that mothers and little boys read school stories and the survey, carried out by Welsh in 1884 and quoted by Salmon, shows that girls were reading, for instance, Farrar's books. Yet Salmon also shows, both from the survey and by the scale and tenor of his critical remarks, that a category of boys' school stories was now recognised which was read by the boys for whom it was intended. Certainly publishers appeared to be finding it a profitable market in which to operate, as these stories were advertised regularly, at different prices and in several impressions. Indeed, because of this there is some difficulty in discovering the date of first publication and even the initial title of some of the books in this category.

Conclusion

Since in the next chapter the argument will be that the minor literary genre, the boys' school story, was created in the 1880s largely through the publication of the work of Talbot Baines Reed there is a need to outline the situation immediately prior to this decade. In this chapter we have seen that by 1880, publishers, readers and 'experts' were using a category 'school stories' and had expectations of what material should be included by writers in such books. The intended readership was middle-class boys, but girls and women and some members of other classes did read these books. The schools in which the stories were situated, and this was also true of the few adult stories that had been written, were in the main small private schools. Although by this date entertainment was seen as a legitimate aim of novel reading, the stories were usually openly didactic, a word used at the time in relation to children's literature, and were mostly better described as being Evangelical rather than Broad Church in tone. Anstey spoke in his Preface to *Vice Versa* of 'these days of philosophical fiction, metaphysical romance, and novels with a purpose'. School stories were nearer in their spirit to Farrar than to Hughes. The family was still given some space and seen as the source of the approved moral values upon which schools later built. However, patriotism was either ignored, as Farrar had done, or was dealt with in a jingoistic manner rather than in the matter-of-fact way in which Hughes had displayed his love of England. One common element in the plots of these books, which was found in neither *Tom Brown* nor *Eric*, concerned rebellion against the head and the masters and this can be traced at least back to Maria Edgeworth's 'The Barring Out' (1796), that is, well before the 1850s. However, there was one new and recent element in some children's literature, namely a critical spirit. Though this was not yet found in school stories specifically written for boys, in Anstey's *Vice Versa* (1882) there was severe criticism of contemporary schools. Furthermore, this book was read by literary critics in this way. It was into this social situation that Talbot Baines Reed was to move during the next decade.

5

Talbot Baines Reed:
the genre defined

In this chapter the starting point must be the birth of the *Boy's Own Paper* or *BOP*, as it was from the beginning popularly known, because it was for that journal as a serial that Reed wrote *The Fifth Form at St Dominic's* (1881/2). This and the other school stories that he wrote before his early death in 1893 very soon defined readers' expectations of what a school story should be.

The birth of the *BOP*

Throughout the 1860s and 1870s there was a growth in the publication of cheap periodicals. There had been some quality periodicals for boys, apart from purely religious journals, before 1860. Thus, *Beeton's Boy's Annual* began in 1855, but during these two decades there was a great increase in what Salmon called 'the print of the Gutter' (Salmon, 1888a: 9) and what a reviewer in the *Quarterly* termed 'the literature of rascaldom' (*Quarterly Review*, 1890: 152). These 'Penny Dreadfuls', as they were even then known, often included a school story, featuring a wide variety of schools from charity schools to public schools. The stories were in some ways modelled on *Tom Brown* in that they were in the main about schools hierarchically organised on Arnoldian principles, but they omitted any trace of Hughes's didacticism. They were often tales of cruelty, of bullying and of flogging (James, 1973: 92-3).

Many commentators were worried about what these periodicals did to their readers. Salmon gave examples of 'the disastrous effects of the "dreadfuls" on the minds of our boys and girls': a boy shot his father after reading one tale; another made fireworks after reading a 'dreadful' and a bad explosion resulted; finally, a third read about Ned Kelly and immediately stole a horse from a Clapham stable and by riding bareback at night caused much danger (Salmon, 1888a: 189–91). The *Quarterly* pointed out that,

> This foul and filthy trash circulates by thousands and tens of thousands amongst lads who are at the most impressionable period of their lives, and whom the modern system of purely secular education has left without ballast or guidance. (1890: 154)

There could, then, be no surprise that 'the authorities have to lament the prevalence of juvenile crime'.

There was a well-accepted tradition of periodicals for boys and, indeed, as has been noted earlier, *Tom Brown's Schooldays* had appeared after its initial publication as a serial in *Beeton's Boy's Annual*; some of A.R. Hope's stories were published in this same journal. Both *Tom Brown at Oxford* and *The Water Babies* had also been run as serials in *Macmillan's Magazine*. The real concern at this time was with the new and very cheap type of periodicals. Their progenitor was an entrepreneurial publisher named E.J. Brett (1828–95). In the mid-1860s he was manager of The Newsagent's Company in Fleet Street which became so notorious for the violent nature of its publications that in 1871 the police raided its offices. Brett had, however, moved by then to another office in Fleet Street and was running *Boys of England*, begun in 1866, which sparked off other competitors, for example, the *Young Englishman's Journal* (1867). But by the 1870s the estimated sales of Brett's *Boys of England* were about a quarter of a million copies per week. In 1871 this journal began to present a series called *Jack Harkaway's Schooldays*, written by an old Etonian, Bracebridge Hemyng, in fact an unsuccessful barrister. This series was modelled on a previous series about Tom Wildrake in the *Sons of Britannia*, started a few months earlier. Both portrayed extrovert youths, happy at school, who were caught up in slapstick escapades and eventually left school to live adventurously overseas, sometimes, as was true of Wildrake, in the army (James, 1973).

The *Quarterly* criticised these publications for their 'weakness and curiously "second-hand" air. . . . The best that can be said of them is, that they are comparatively harmless; the worst, that no boy is likely to be the better for reading them' (*Quarterly Review*,

1890: 156). We know that they were read during this decade at Westward Ho!, Kipling's school, because he is reported as objecting strongly to them. His friend, G.L. Beresford, who appears as 'McTurk' in *Stalky and Co.*, says in his memoirs:

> It really got on his nerves that they should keep on reading *Jack Harkaway* and the cheap paper-backed novels that were to be had in such plenty in those days, and which Gigger [Kipling] seemed to take as an infliction aimed especially at himself. (1936: 33)

One of the important bodies which focused much of this concern was the Religious Tract Society, a body founded in 1799 with a long history of publication of children's books. The Society's catalogue for 1849 advertised 'more than three hundred' titles for children 'and their annual circulation had for some years averaged about five millions'. In 1871 in an attempt to offset the effect of 'Penny Dreadfuls' and other such literature the Society began 'the issue of a monthly shilling volume for the "younger members of Christian families" '. One contributor was W.H.G. Kingston. Yet, despite some success, by the end of the decade the Society knew that it had not solved the problem of supplying what it called 'wholesome periodical literature for boys and girls', partly because its own monthly was so expensive. In the Report for 1879 the Society reported its decision in this matter:

> The Committee, fully admitting the terrible necessity of a publication which might to some extent supplant those of a mischievous tendency, yet hesitated to enter upon the task. To have made it obtrusively or largely religious in its teaching would have been to defeat the object in view. Yet it did not come within the scope of the Society's operation if this was not the case. . . . [There was also] the risk of pecuniary loss which such a publication seemed to threaten. . . . It was thus forced upon the Committee to attempt an enterprise from which others shrank.

The Society determined to begin a weekly paper for boys. In order to try to throw off the connection with the Society which it felt many readers would see as a guarantee of sanctimonious material the decision was taken not to use the Society's name on the new journal. It was published under the imprint of 'Leisure Hour'. The first number of the *BOP* appeared on 18 January 1879 and 'Success was as immediate as it was unexpected' (Green, 1899: 49, 78-9, 127).

The Society appointed Dr James Macaulay, the General Secretary of the Society, as editor and Mr Andrew G. Hutchison as his assistant. Hutchison had been editor of the *Social Science Review*, *Sunday School World* and the *Baptist* (Warner, 1976: 1-2). However, after the first volume Hutchison became the editor and remained so until his death in 1914. Hutchison was a strict Baptist, but he adhered rigidly to the Society's policy, hinted at in the quotation above from the 1879 Report, that religion, particularly that of any one denomination, should not be pushed in the *BOP*. The motto of the *BOP* was, appropriately for its era, in Latin: 'Quisquid agunt pueri nostri libelli farrago' – 'Whatever boys do makes up the mixture of our little book'. The *BOP* contained stories and articles of all types, and queries were answered from a wide range of readers. Within three months the circulation amounted to about 200,000 and Macauley estimated a readership of 'over 600,000'. This was possible because the weekly sixteen illustrated pages, $8\frac{1}{4}$ by $11\frac{3}{4}$, stitched in an orange paper cover, cost only a penny, or the price then of a dozen boxes of matches. There was also a monthly version containing the weekly editions together with a special frontispiece. The *BOP* remained a weekly until 1914 when it became a monthly, the price rising to a shilling from 1918 to 1939, until its demise in 1967, ostensibly because it could no longer attract advertising (Warner, 1976: 171).

One of Hutchison's greatest attributes was his ability to select and encourage appropriate and attractive writers for the *BOP*. The following well-known writers were all at one time or another contributors: Jules Verne, R.M. Ballantyne, G.A. Henty, Conan Doyle, Algernon Blackwood and W.H.G. Kingston. The payment was at the time a flat rate to all contributors of a guinea a page. In 1887 Hutchison contributed a Preface to T.B. Reed's *The Fifth Form at St Dominic's* when this former *BOP* serial appeared as a book. In this 'Preface' Hutchison clearly indicated his policy. Referring to the boys portrayed in this book he wrote:

> Such boys stand at the antipodes alike of an effeminate sentimentality – the paragons who prate platitudes and die young – and of the morbid specimens of youthful infamy only too frequently paraded by the unreal sensationalism of today to meet the cravings of a vitiated taste.

The writers mentioned all fit easily into this category of the healthy adventure story. In addition, Hutchison had to include a number of writers of school stories, since this was expected by purchasers of these periodicals. He selected, amongst others, the three writers considered in the last chapter: Adams, Millington and Hope, whose serial 'At the Masthead' appeared in Volume I. Writers like Adams and Millington could be relied upon to include the religious element that the Society's field of operations demanded. Indeed, Hutchison, as editor, had no doubt to make sure with such writers that this element, though present, was not too obtrusive.

From our point of view and, indeed, for his own success Hutchison's happiest choice was Talbot Baines Reed. Reed's older brother, Charles Edward, was on the committee which investigated the problem of children's literature for the Society and as a result Reed himself who, as we shall see, was already regularly contributing to various journals, was asked to write for the *BOP*. The first number opened with a half-page picture of a game of rugby football, illustrating an article 'My First Football Match by an Old Boy'. This was by Reed, but, before examining Reed's background, for the sake of completeness mention must be made of the *Girl's Own Paper*.

The sister paper began in January 1880, a year after the *BOP* when the latter's success had already become clear. It ran until 1956. The *Girl's Own Paper* had some problem of defining its readership. All agreed that boys would be boys and that many men would go on behaving as boys when of adult years, so that the *BOP* could cater for boys, knowing that it had a wide readership for boys' interests. In late Victorian times, however, girls had to become women, so that the *Girl's Own* was never quite sure whether to address itself only to girls or also to young women (Cadogan and Craig, 1976: 73-4). At a later date this ambiguity did help the *Girl's Own* to gain advertising revenue during the Edwardian era at a time when the *BOP* was beginning to lose some of its initial success.

Talbot Baines Reed

'Tibby' Reed, as he was known at home, was born in 1854, the third son of Sir Charles Reed. His mother was the youngest daughter of Edward Baines, the well-known and influential proprietor of the *Leeds Mercury*. Reed's grandfather was a Congregational minister and Sir Charles was a keen Congregationalist who in the 1850s and 1860s, was active in educational politics against state aid. He became an MP, first for Hackney and then for St Ives (Cornwall). After the 1870 Education Act Sir Charles became a member of and ultimately chairman of the London School Board. In 1841 he founded what became a prosperous printing firm (Morrison, 1960).

At the age of ten Reed was sent to the City of London School, then as now a day school, and was a contemporary there of H.H. Asquith, later to become Prime Minister. He was popular at school and successful at games. He was a half-back at rugby, and a school friend said of him, 'Here his strength of muscle, length of limb, boldness of attack, absolute fearlessness and perfection of nerve, always made him conspicuous.' He left school at seventeen and entered the family business. Whilst on holiday in Ireland at this time he won a Royal Humane Society medal for saving a cousin from drowning. In 1878 he married Elizabeth Greer, the daughter of a county judge and Irish MP. What has to be remembered about Reed is that for the rest of his relatively short life – he died in 1893, apparently of consumption – he was fundamentally a businessman. His father died in 1881 and Reed then became the managing director of the family business. He remained a deacon of the Congregational Church, but he was able to keep his religion a private matter and continued to read widely – we know he read Oscar Wilde's *Dorian Grey*; he was also a member of both the Reform and Saville Clubs.

Reed's earliest printed effort appeared in 1875 in a magazine for young people, called the *Morning of Life* and was entitled 'Camping Out', an account of a boating expedition on the Thames, but, as well as the considerable number of articles, stories and books for boys that will be discussed here, he wrote a well-respected book in his own professional field, *A History of the Old English Letter Foundaries* (1887). He also edited and completed his friend, William Blade's *The Pentateuch of Printing*. These activities meant that he was involved in and, despite his poor health at the time, became the first Secretary of the Bibliographical Society on its foundation in 1892.

For many years he wrote a non–political leading article each week in the *Leeds Mercury*. He was a life-long Liberal, though he disagreed with Gladstone's eventual policy on Ireland (Sime, 1895: *xx-xxi*). On 16 August 1884, for example, he wrote on 'Penny Dreadfuls'. These, he felt, had become 'a literary institution' because 'a taste, more or less disguised, for the terrible, is inborn in most of us'. Writers had to sell to live and, therefore, such periodicals were written and sold. He described the poor illustrations and poor text, encouraging a taste for bloody adventure and luxurious living, and concluded that 'it is melancholy to have to admit it, in these days of School Boards . . ., but it is nevertheless a fact that the popular literature of the streets is still the Penny Dreadful.' Reed entered the family printing business in 1869, the year before the 1870 Education Act. He grew to maturity at a time when literacy was growing, but when in his view the reading matter available for children was inadequate. There were 'Penny Dreadfuls' for the working class and for the middle class there was *Eric* together with very little else. He gave his views about *Eric* in the *Leeds Mercury*. It was a narrowly disguised religious tract by a writer who did not understand boys. He spoke of Farrar's use of the 'powder-in-jam' formula and added that this was one method that he carefully avoided in his own writing. What he wanted for his sons was 'manly reading' (Morrison, 1960: 9-10). His own Christian moral philosophy was briefly and accurately stated, both in content and in tone, in a message he sent to a Boys' Club in Manchester on the occasion of its opening:

> The strong fellows should look after the weak, the active must look after the lazy, the merry should cheer up the dull, the sharp must lend a helping hand to the duffer. Pull together in all your learning and praying. (Morrison, 1960: 72)

Before Reed's work appeared in print in the *BOP* he had completed two books 'solely for his wife's amusement and interest'. One was called *Dunluce* and contained material that was later included in his Elizabethan adventure tale, *Sir Ludar* (1888). Reed's last book was also a historical adventure story, *Kilgorman. A Story of Ireland in 1798* (1895), which was written during his final illness and not quite completed at his death.

However, despite this wide range of writing Reed was best known in the 1880s and afterwards for his boys' stories, usually about schools in whole or in part, in the *BOP*. In the third number there appeared the first of his series 'Boys of English History' and in March Reed reported the Boat Race, as he did yearly thereafter. In August on Hutchison's suggestion his first serial story began; this was *The Adventures of a Three Guinea Watch*. Simultaneously he contributed a series of character sketches, 'Boys We Have Known'. In 1881 *The Fifth Form at St*

Dominic's began. Hutchison then suggested to him that as his previous books and articles had been about public schools he should write about a 'lower middle class school' and also build upon his business experience. This Reed did in *My Friend Smith* (1882) which told of the career of a boy first at a school, compared by Hutchison to Dotheboys Hall, and then in an apprenticeship in printing (*BOP*, 1894: 346). There followed a succession of stories for boys, largely, but not entirely, about public schools.

When Hutchison suggested that Reed write a serial school story he produced *The Adventures of a Three Guinea Watch* which was only in part about boys at school. *St Dominic's* was, however, entirely about a school. Reed wrote five other stories entirely about public schools: *The Willoughby Captains* (1883); *The Master of the Shell* (1887); *Follow My Leader* (1887); *The Cock House at Fellsgarth* (1891); and *Tom, Dick and Harry* (as a serial named *Tom, Harry and Dick*, (1892). In addition to these books and his two historical adventures, Reed wrote two other books mainly about tutors: *Roger Ingleton Minor* (1886) and *A Dog with a Bad Name* (1886).

All this writing was done by Reed for pleasure whilst at the same time he pursued an active and successful business career, fulfilled his religious and philanthropical obligations, and gave time to bringing up his own family. Perhaps not surprisingly the healthy youth of the City of London School days was an overworked adult unable to throw off illness and died at the age of thirty-nine. His books were republished many times after his death, indicating their great popularity with boys, certainly into the 1930s. Here his writings other than his six major school stories will be considered first before passing on to an examination in some detail of *The Fifth Form at St Dominic's*, the most successful of his school stories, though some attention will also be given to the five other stories about public schools that Reed wrote.

Reed's writings other than major school stories

Many of Reed's early stories and articles for the *BOP* were collected and published in 1905 with an introduction by Hutchison under the title *Parkhurst Boys*. The name Reed had given to the school in 'My First Football Match', the first article in the first number of the *BOP*, was Parkhurst. There were three parts to this collection, the first of whch was entitled 'Parkhurst

Sketches', containing seven simply told stories, each in length some 3500/4000 words. Five stories were about some organised game – a football match, a paper chase, a boat race, a cricket game, an athletics meeting – and two were about unorganised activities – a boating adventure and a 'swimming reminiscence'. Simple morals were implicit in the stories; success was not automatic – the sixteen-year-old in the cricket game made a duck in the first innings. But sometimes fairly explicit moral points are made; before the football game the captain advised the sixteen-year-old Adams, playing his first game for the school, 'All you've got to take care of is to keep cool, and never let your eyes go off the ball.' A comment is made when describing the paper chase, 'Altogether it is to be doubted if a real meet of hounds to hunt real hares – a cruel and not very manly sport after all – could be much more exciting than this is' – oddly, though, an authorial aside admitted to hunting by horseback.

Part Two was entitled, 'Boys We Have Known' and was a series of brief articles of 1800/2000 words in length about, for example, 'The Sneak', 'The Sulky Boy', 'The Boy who is "Never Wrong" ', 'The Untidy Boy', 'The Unorganised Boy', 'The Grouch', 'The Dandy' and 'The Bully'. Each is related to the type of adult the boy will become and each has a school tale to illustrate the moral involved. Bullies are, for example, classified into 'amateurs' and 'professionals'. Bob Bangs in the story is an example of the latter. Spite and 'cruelty of heart' drive such boys and for some also 'power becomes a ruling passion'. Finally, 'A gentleman cannot be a bully, and a bully cannot be a gentleman.' A gentleman is defined as 'a man (or boy) of honour, kindliness, modesty and sense'. The moral in 'The Grouch', simply expressed, as in all these short articles, is, 'When you catch yourself grumbling, make sure the grievance is a real one.' 'The Sneak' is an interesting tale because throughout Reed's stories and, indeed, throughout the history of English school stories 'sneaking' is universally abhorred. The sneak is seen to be driven by 'many detestable qualities' – cowardice, jealousy, falsehood, ingratitude, malice, officiousness, hypocrisy and self-conceit. Near the end this warning is given:

> Boys cannot be too early on their guard against sneaking habits. No truly English boy, we are glad to think, is likely to fall into them . . . . Every disease has its cure. Be honest, be brave, be kind and have a good conscience, and you *cannot* be a sneak.

The third part of *Parkhurst Boys* was entitled 'Boys of English History' and included twelve stories of boys in English history; examples were: 'Richard the Second the Boy who Quelled a Tumult'; 'Lambert Simnel, the Baker's Boy who Pretended to be King', and 'Edward VI, the Good King of England'. Also included in this collection was Reed's first school story, 'The Troubles of a Dawdler', in two chapters, written in 1879. The hero dawdles from childhood and when he goes to school always puts off work so that he fails exams. When he leaves, he misses the first job he applies for because he is an hour late for the interview. Eventually on hearing that his father is seriously ill he misses the train to find his father dead on arriving home. The concluding words are, 'Boys, I am an old man now; but, believe me, since that awful moment I have never, to my knowledge, dawdled again!'

Reed wrote two other early short school stories, both of which were in the same vein of a simple plot and an obvious moral. Both were published in *The School Ghost and Boycotted and Other Stories*. In 'Boycotted' Browne is expelled for a crime about which no one at Draven's knows. The narrator is cut by the whole school because he is believed to have told the head of this crime. The error is discovered by someone writing to Browne, but just as the boys are about to apologise the narrator collapses from the mental and physical strain. One other story in this collection, 'The Poetry Club', is worth mentioning because it betrays a certain air of anti-intellectualism. 'A serious epidemic has broken out at the school; medical authorities are incapable before it.' It is 'writing poetry', and 'one poet in a school is bad enough'.

From an examination of Reed's collected short tales an impression of naivety of plot, simple characterisation, moralistic writing and laboured wit may have emerged, but the long stories, all of which, except his final historical tale, *Kilgorman*, were first published as serials in the *BOP*, are very different and, as will be seen, are much more complex in their construction. The first was *The Adventures of a Three Guinea Watch* (1880). The 'prefatory note' in the 1891 edition states, 'This book is eminently suitable for parents to place in the hands of their boys when first leaving home, whether for school, or the larger, sterner training ground of the world.' In it Charles Newcome's father gives him a three guinea watch on his first going away to school, but he is later given another and better watch when he is older. So he gives the first one to Tom Drift and from him the watch goes off on travels round the world and away from school. The popular success of this tale led to Reed writing *The Fifth Form at St Dominic's*, after which Hutchison asked him, as noted earlier, to write about a 'lower middle class school' and to build on his business experience.

Reed, therefore, wrote *My Friend Smith* (1882). The hero, Frederick Batchelor, is an orphan, brought up by his uncle, Mr Jakeman at Brownstoke, a small country town. By the age of twelve Frederick is constantly in fights, together with the other boys at the local grammar school where he is a pupil, against the village boys. His uncle sends him away to Stonebridge House, an 'Academy for Backward and Troublesome Gentlemen'. Before leaving, Mrs Hudson, his old nurse, in the midst of giving him instructions on using his own comb and clothes, tells Frederick to 'say your prayers regularly night and day, won't you?' (II). At the school, the housekeeper, Mrs Henneker, who is very cruel, is all-powerful and has Mr Ladislaw the head, Mr Hasleford the master, and Hawkesbury the usher, under her thumb. Frederick is in much trouble and a wide range of punishments is used against him and the other boys, including a 'flogging administered to one helpless boy by the whole body of his schoolfellows, two of whom firmly held the victim, while each of the others in turn flogged him' (IV) for talking in the dormitory at night; locking Frederick and his friend, Jack Smith, in 'a small and perfectly empty garret', wearing only his nightshirt and knickerbockers for a whole night with no light on (V); 'strict silence'; impositions; eating only bread and water; and confiscation of belongings. Letters were censored and even stopped. A year after Frederick went to this 'Dotheboy's Hall' one afternoon when Mrs Henneker was out Jack Smith as leader organises the boys to rebel. The staff are all locked and screwed into their rooms, whilst the boys take over the school. In the end Smith releases the staff and is expelled. Frederick stays one year longer before leaving, having gained little beyond the three Rs, but 'a good deal wilder' (IX). Frederick goes to work in an office in London where Jack Smith also works. Jack tells Frederick his mystery: he is the son of a convict. Frederick accidentally revealed this secret so that, when money is stolen from the office, Jack is blamed. In the end, of course, honesty wins and all turns out well for Jack and Frederick.

Apart from his two historical tales *Sir Ludar* (1888) and *Kilgorman* (1895) Reed wrote three other long stories, the first of which, *Reginald Cruden* (1885), began with two brothers, Reginald and Horace, at a public school, Wilderham, which

> was not exactly an aristocratic school, but it was a school
> where money was thought less of than 'good style', as the
> boys called it, and where poverty was far less of a disgrace
> than even a remote connection with a 'shop'. (II)

As Reginald put it, 'It's not pleasant to have the fellow who cuts
your waistcoat coming over you in class' (I). The boys' father dies
and is found to everybody's amazement to be almost bankrupt.
The boys have to leave school and start work as apprentices at 18s
a week at The Rocket Newspaper Company Ltd. Reginald finds
this degradation hard to bear and soon leaves to become secretary
of what turns out to be a fraudulent company in Liverpool.
Horace endures the difficulties and begins to earn money on the
side as a journalist, meanwhile helping to uncover the foreman's
fraudulent actions to further his betting activities. Reginald
realises too late the nature of the business in which he is involved,
but is arrested, though eventually released from gaol as innocent.
Then Reginald and his mother both fall seriously ill. However,
Mr Cruden is discovered to have had one investment in the USA
which now suddenly becomes profitable. So once again Horace's
steadfast honesty and Reginald's repentance are rewarded.

Reed's two other long stories were both about tutors, though
schools are mentioned in both. In *Roger Ingleton Minor* (1886)
Frank Armstrong, Roger's tutor, becomes his guardian and a
trustee of his father's estate on his death. There is a long struggle
with the other male executors to gain control of the estate – Frank
defending Roger, and Edward Oliphant, Roger's cousin, a rather
disreputable former Indian Army Officer, attempting to defraud
him. Frank has a secret: he is Roger's lost half-brother and,
ultimately, this is revealed. The plot is complicated, involving a
love interest, trips to Paris to search for various of Frank's lost
relatives, and battles over legal and financial matters. At the
conclusion Roger gains full control of his estate on his twenty-
first birthday and Frank is revealed not merely as a caring tutor,
guardian and friend, but as one of the family.

When Reed began to write *A Dog with a Bad Name* in May 1886
he wrote to Hutchison, describing in outline the plot:

> The story shall begin at a public school, and following the
> hero as usher in a little boy's school, and afterwards as a
> private tutor in a mansion, till it leaves him with the temper,

which was once his infirmity, in subjection, and the bad name which has dogged him, lived down. (Hutchison, 1897: xvii–xviii)

John Jeffreys, an orphan, is at Bolsover College which, in a term common at the time, has 'dry rot':

Years ago it had dropped out of the race with the other public schools. Its name had disappeared from the pass list of the University and Civil Service candidates. Scarcely a human being knew the name of its head-master; and no assistant master was ever known to make Bolsover a stepping stone to pedagogic promotion. The athletic world knew nothing of a Bolsover Eleven or Fifteen; and worse still no Bolsover boy was ever found who was proud either of his school or himself. (I)

A new head, Mr Frampton, arrives and makes football and cold baths compulsory. In a game Jeffreys, in scoring a try, seriously hurts Forester who tried to stop him. Forester becomes an invalid, Jeffreys is ostracised by his fellows who believe he did this on purpose because of a previous argument. Jeffreys runs away to his guardian, Mr Halgrove, in York, who casts him off. Mr Halgrove claims that the investments that he holds for John have turned out badly. Jeffreys first teaches at a small boys' school near York, but he has to leave when his secret is discovered. Mr Frampton helps him with money and advice. By chance Jeffreys saves a boy, Percy Rimbolt, from kidnapping and is appointed by Mr Rimbolt, an MP and bibliophile, as his librarian at his country home, Wildtree Towers in Westmoreland. Mr Rimbolt had been at Oxford with Mr Frampton.

Percy is about fifteen and

The year he has spent at Rugby has redeemed him from being a lout, but it is uncertain whether it has done anything more. The master of his house had been heard to predict that the boy would either live to be hanged or to become a great man. (XI)

Percy takes to Jeffreys and gradually Jeffreys becomes as much his tutor as the librarian. Mrs Rimbolt unfortunately does not like Jeffreys, who has come to feel great affection for Raby, Percy's older sister. After some time Jeffreys is recognised by a visiting former fellow pupil, who also falls in love with Raby. Jeffreys tells his secret to Mr Rimbolt, who puts even more trust in him and makes him his secretary when he is in London with the task of helping him prepare for his parliamentary work. However, his rival for Raby tells Mrs Rimbolt of Jeffrey's secret and she dismisses him when Mr Rimbolt is away from home. John Jeffreys now goes through a very bleak period, working as a casual labourer in London and earning a little extra from his sketches. Raby and John, by coincidence, come into contact again because of her philanthropic work in a slum where he is living. At this moment news comes that his investments in trust with Mr Halgrove have turned out well. With Mr Rimbolt's help he becomes librarian 'of a great library in the North' (XXIX) and at the end of the book is planning to marry Raby. John Jeffreys has also heard from Mr Frampton at Bolsover College 'of how it was at last begining to recover from dry rot' (XX). The football team is beginning to make a name for itself; prospects for cricket are good; and recently two Oxford scholarships were won.

Both these 'tutor' tales have one other element in common to which passing mention was made in discussing H.C. Adams's *The Doctor's Birthday*. They both have references to chivalry. Roger Ingleton, setting off for France to look for his brother, is described in the following words: 'Like a knight of old, set down to a desperate task, the fighting blood rose joyously within him' (XX). When John Jeffreys is considering what to do about his feelings for Raby, Reed writes, 'Had he been an errant knight of course his horse could have settled the question' (XI). Forrester, the boy John had hurt and whose late father had been in the Indian Army, enters the story again later, and keeps his father's sword 'by [his] couch like a Knight Templar' (XXIX). Similar references occur from time to time in Reed's school stories.

These boys' stories that were not exclusively about public schools can be seen to be more subtle in characterisation, more complex in plot and less overtly moralistic than the short stories and articles which were described earlier. Nearly all, except the two historical tales, give schools a place in the plot and the schools, partly because Hutchison wanted this, were not exclusively public schools, but it was in his tales about this latter type of school that Reed made his major impact at this time and on later generations of boys.

School stories

Of Reed's six boys' school stories the first and the most popular, at the time and afterwards, was *The Fifth Form at St Dominic's* which initially appeared as a serial in the *BOP* between October 1881 and June 1882 and was published as a book in 1885, remaining in print till 1948. It was reprinted in a new edition in 1971 (Alderson, 1971). These stories are all, though with perhaps some doubts in the case of *Tom, Dick and Harry* (1892), set in schools that can clearly be described as public schools. The realistic nature of Reed's settings and writings about such schools is remarkable since he himself was at the City of London School, a day school, which at the time Reed was a pupil, was fighting hard for the full status of a public school to which it soon undoubtedly attained and which it has ever since retained.

In *The Fifth Form at St Dominic's* Reed tells of the first year at school of Stephen Greenfield, of the adventures during the same year of his older brother, Oliver, in the Fifth form, and of the moral decline of Loman, a Sixth former, whose fag Stephen was. Stephen had arrived full of hopes and very green to join his brother. His naivety was soon unlearned and he became avidly involved in the life of the 'fourth junior class' in which he was placed (V) and in the struggles between the Tadpoles and Guinea Pigs, 'the names given to two combinations or clubs in the clannish Junior School' (I). He himself became a Guinea-pig. Stephen quickly took to using cribs in class and 'was in fact settling down into the slough of idleness, and would have become an accomplished dunce in time, had not Mr Rastle [his form-master] come to the rescue.' Mr Rastle told him,

> School will not be without its temptations and you will find it hard always to do your duty. Yet you have, I hope, learnt the power of prayer; . . . At school, my boy, as elsewhere, it is a safe rule, whenever one is in doubt, to avoid everything, no matter who may be the tempter, of which one cannot fearlessly speak to one's father or mother, and above all to our Heavenly Father. (X)

Stephen became a central figure by the end of term in a strike organised by all the fags against their fagmaster, started because one of their numbers was not allowed time off to attend a Junior School cricket feast. Loman, Stephen's fagmaster, did in fact in a cowardly fashion thrash Stephen because he would not fag for him, but Stephen, despite pressure from Mr Rastle, did not sneak. After the holidays the fags all returned to their tasks as if the strike had never occurred.

Oliver Greenfield was a good games player and a promising scholar, but he did not seek popularity and remained somewhat apart from the rest of the Fifth. He had one very close friend, Wraysford. In a quarrel he was suddenly and unaccountably struck by Loman, but failed to hit back. The Fifth all took this to show that he was really a coward. Later, after another insult from Loman, this time on the cricket field, Oliver told Wraysford the real reason for his restraint: 'I've been trying feebly to turn over a new leaf this term. . . . And one of the things I wanted to keep out of was losing my temper, which you know is not a good one.' Reed comments that Oliver's self-restraint 'was not altogether an unmanly act' (IX). By the end of term Oliver told Wraysford, 'I've been off my luck completely this term', to which his friend pointed out that he had won the English prize and got into the XI. Oliver answered that he had not helped Stephen enough, had been called a coward because he did not fight Loman and had been 'a worse Christian since [he] began to try to be one'. Furthermore, he was sure that he would not do well in 'the Nightingale', a school scholarship of £50 for three years, upon which his future hopes of going to Cambridge depended. There were three candidates for this scholarship: Oliver and Wraysford, both in the Fifth, and Loman in the Sixth. Oliver succeeded in the examination brilliantly, but was seen the night before, coming out of the head's study where he had been to try to tell Dr Senior of Stephen's misdemeanours, largely under Loman's influence. Oliver also met Loman in the passage outside the study. The school decided that Oliver had cheated and put him in coventry, even hissing him when he received the prize on Prize Day. Even Wraysford lost his confidence in Oliver's innocence and for a time they refused to speak to each other.

Loman was 'a comparatively new boy', having been only for some eighteen months at St. Dominic's. He was 'agreeable',but 'never popular' (VI). Mr Cripps, publican of 'The Cockchafer', tried to sell a fishing rod to him at an extortionate price. Loman broke it and sent Stephen, his fag, to return it. Cripps did sell a poor cricket bat to Stephen, again at a high price, but Stephen was helped by Oliver to pay and, as explained above, was removed from Loman's influence with the help of the Head. Eventually he became Wraysford's fag. Mr Cripps offered Loman a way out of paying for the rod by backing a certainty in the Derby. The horse, as might be expected, did not win and Loman's debt reached £30. He entered the Nightingale in the hope of paying Cripps what he thought he owed him. There is much that is reminiscent of *Eric* in Loman's gradual downfall. He had to see Cripps when he should have been playing for the Sixth at cricket, so he pretended that he had sprained his wrist: 'so easy is the downward path when once entered on – a lie had become an easy thing to utter' (XIII). Then, when some of his misfortunes seemed to have been, if not overcome, at least postponed, 'Things altogether were looking up with Loman. Cheating, lying and gambling looked as if they would pay off after all' (XXVIII). Later Reed comments Loman 'was to be pitied, wasn't he? He hadn't been naturally a vicious boy, or a cowardly boy, or a stupid boy, but he had become all three' (XXXI).

Oliver now entered for another scholarship to show to the school that he had won the Nightingale honestly. Once again he was first, Wraysford second and Loman a very bad third. The school now realised that they had misjudged Oliver; Wraysford and Oliver were reunited. For Loman now all seemed lost and he asked Oliver and Wraysford for money to pay some of the debts. They loaned money to him in a spirit of forgiveness. However, the missing exam paper, which Dr Senior had replaced with a different set of questions, thereby unknowingly foiling Loman's theft, now publicly turned up in Loman's copy of Horace. He denied any knowledge of how it came to be there, but, fearing his guilt would be revealed, he ran away. Despite much searching he could not be found, till Oliver discovered him in a barn and managed to persuade him to return. Loman now tells the whole truth to Oliver. They are out all night in a terrible storm and on their return Loman is in bed for four weeks recovering before he

> left St Dominic's a convalescent, and, better still, truly penitent, looking away from self and his own poor efforts to Him, the World's Greatest Burden Bearer, whose blood 'cleanseth us from all sin'. (XXXVII)

In a final chapter the positions of the main characters are briefly told some five years later. Stephen is captain of the XI; the Guinea Pigs and Tadpoles have become Buttercups and Daisies; Oliver has rowed in the Cambridge VIII and has been called to the Bar; Wraysford is a fellow of his college; and Loman after 'four or five years' farming and knocking about in Australia' is coming home to go into his father's law office. Oliver tells Wraysford, 'When he does, I tell you what: we must all make up a jolly party and come down together and help him through with it' (XXXVIII). Oliver's spirit of forgiveness is displayed once again.

Elsewhere (Musgrave, 1982b) the characteristics of boys' school stories as a minor literary genre have been enumerated. They are four: the plot is seen from the boys' point of view; the school is seen as an organisation; the character of the hero or heroes develops during the story; and, last, there is a morally didactic element in the story. Each of these characteristics was present to a greater or lesser extent in *Tom Brown* and *Eric*, though two other characteristics were also present in those books. In both of these earlier stories there was far more emphasis on the family of the heroes, but in *The Fifth Form* this emphasis has largely disappeared. Mrs Greenfield – once again the heroes' mother was a widow – is hardly mentioned. On one occasion a letter from her is discussed by Oliver and Stephen. In the chapter concerning their holiday almost all the action concerns a boating trip with Wraysford on the Thames. The only real mention is when Stephen tells of his scrapes at school 'till the good lady's hair nearly stood on end, and she began to think a public school was a terrible place to send a small boy to' (XVIII). Other members of the family or old retainers earn no mention. The second missing characteristic in comparison with *Tom Brown* is any pronounced spirit of patriotism. Despite the one mention of what is right for 'English boys' to do, the emphasis, both overt and latent in *Tom Brown* – particularly in Hughes's descriptions of the country-side – is not present in Reed's book. The other four characteristics, found in Hughes and Farrar's books, will now be discussed in relation to *The Fifth Form at St Dominic's*.

The plot is seen essentially from the boys' point of view. Dr Senior and Mr Rastle play some part in the plot; one or two other masters are mentioned; and the college servant, Roach, appears once. The main action concerns the boys and is described as it affects them. There are occasional authorial asides, particularly of a didactic nature, but even the moral lessons are often stated by the boys themselves or are expressed implicitly because of what befalls them.

However, this action occurs within the framework of the school. Public schools were seen to be by now much more structured places and this was certainly true when they were compared with the small private schools described in the works of, for example, W.H.G. Kingston or H.C. Adams or, for that matter, in Reed's *My Friend Smith*. There was an Arnoldian organisation, hierarchical in nature. The head, 'the Doctor', stood at the top with form masters and house masters under him. The boys were beneath them with prefects and/or monitors at the summit of this part of the hierarchy with a middle school and at the base the fags. The boys' hierarchy was complicated by the existence of different, but parallel, status systems for games and for work. This private world of the boys was a crucial part of the school organisation and was so seen by the staff. Thus, when Oliver Greenfield was in coventry, his health is discussed by the staff. Dr Senior thought that he might be ill from overwork. Mr Rastle replied

> 'I don't know what crime he has committed, but the tribunal of his class have been very severe on him, I fancy.'
> The Doctor laughed.
> 'Boys will be boys! . . . We have no right to interfere with these boyish freaks, as long as they are not mischievous. But you might keep an eye on the little comedy, Jellicott. It would be a pity for it to go too far.' (XXIX)

The hierarchy of the boys was seen as part of the structure which helped boys to develop. They learnt, as they moved up it, to obey and then to give orders. The story, like *Tom Brown* and *Eric*, is about development, but, unlike them and several of Reed's other boys' school stories, *The Fifth Form* does not trace the whole of a boy's career at school. Except for the last chapter the time involved is one year, but Reed solves the problem of showing the complete cycle of growth from early to late adolescence by the device of focusing upon two brothers, so that almost the whole school career can be covered by examining a year in the school life of Stephen and Oliver Greenfield.

Young people develop in a definite direction and it was the aim of the Religious Tract Society to influence the direction in which young English boys grew up. Reed had, therefore, to present a moral position. This he does, though not so obviously as either Farrar – certainly – or Hughes did. One point should be made before outlining the moral position displayed by Reed in *The Fifth Form*. There is far less didactic writing in this and Reed's other books than in the earlier works to which reference has been made in previous chapters. This may not appear to be so, because in making a case here the relevant portions of text have to be pulled out of their context. In Reed's books often one comment has to be taken from a long and otherwise innocuous series of exchanges about games, lessons, or play activities. His writing, though moralistic, particularly perhaps to a late twentieth-century reader, is very different in style and tone from that of Farrar or Hughes. We shall be concerned with the main elements of Reed's moral code, though there are the occasional, almost throw-away, remarks to which attention should be drawn. One of these occurs on the second page of the book where Bullinger, a fifth former, teases a third-form boy who is wondering whether to enter for the Nightingale scholarship and calls him 'you avaricious young Jew'. Even Reed seems to have been prone to, possibly slight, anti-Semitism.

Enough quotations have already been cited to show that, despite the Religious Tract Society's policy of not making religion too obtrusive, Christianity was none the less one of the key elements in the code of values to be taught to boys. It was the basis for the code of morality supported. There are, however, no large set-piece expositions of Christianity as in *Tom Brown*; nor is religion so all-intrusive as in *Eric*. Dr Senior does give a sermon and Stephen, as a new boy who has recently been pardoned for wrong-doing, is deeply influenced

In the few simple words in which he urged his hearers to lay the past, with all its burdens, and disappointments, and shame, upon Him in whom alone forgiveness is to be found, Stephen drank in new courage and hope for the future, and in the thankfulness and penitence of his heart resolved to commit his way more honestly than ever to the best of all keeping, compared with which even a brother's love is powerless. (XXII)

But religious principles have to be worked out in personal life with others. Dr Senior on one occasion found the work and behaviour of the Lower Fourth well below his expectations. He told them:

'the best way for little boys to get on is not by giving themselves ridiculous airs, but by doing their duty steadily in class, and living at peace with one another, submitting quickly to the discipline of the school.'

This is the obvious view that a headmaster would take – work hard and play hard within the rules of the school. The boys themselves, just because of the power given to them to run much of the administration of the school themselves, could evolve or support their own personal code of behaviour and, as we have seen, the staff let this happen as long as the resulting code fell within their range of tolerance.

This boys' code of behaviour is summed up well at one point.

> For it must be said of the Dominicans – and I think it may be said of a good many English public schoolboys besides – that, however foolish they may have been in other respects, however riotous, however jealous of one another, however well satisfied with themselves, a point of honour was a point which they all took seriously to heart. They could forgive a schoolfellow for doing a disobedient act sometimes, or perhaps even a vicious act, but a cowardly and dishonourable action was a thing which nothing would excuse, and which they felt not only a disgrace to the boy perpetrating it, but a disgrace put upon themselves. (XXIII)

'Sneaking' and lying were all subsumed under dishonourable behaviour; cribbing was not and one could try to beat masters by using such aids, but should never lie if caught. Furthermore, examples of dishonourable behaviour reflected upon the whole school, not merely upon the individual concerned. The school, or any affected part of it, used strong sanctions to deal with those who were seen to have offended against the code. Thus, Oliver was sent to coventry by his peers.

This corporate aspect of morality fits well with the emphasis upon team games in *The Fifth Form*. There are set piece descriptions of two cricket matches and a football game. Oliver, and even Loman, is a good games player. Stephen, too, is keen to do well in games. The fifth form paper, 'The Dominican', an important aspect of the tale, is run by a lame and witty boy, Pemberton; in it there are references to forthcoming games and to the teams chosen. Yet games at St Dominic's do not seem to have been compulsory, though they were important in the minds of the boys. Much is made of the difficulties of the captain of a team. Stansfield, the captain of St Dominic's rugby team

> was a model football captain. However worried and worrying and crabby he was in his ordinary clothes, in his football togs and on the field of battle he was the coolest, quickest, readiest, and cunningest general you could desire.

He said no more than he could help, and never scolded his
men while play was going on, and best of all, worked like a
horse himself in the thick of the fight, and looked to every
one able to do the same. (XXVIII)

Those at the top of the school had to set an example whether on
the games field or in life so that all might achieve a code of morals
based on Christianity, marked by unity, honour and deference to
those in proper authority.

The next boys' school story that Reed wrote was *The
Willoughby Captains*, serialised in the *BOP* during 1883/4. At
Willoughby, Wyndham is both School Captain, that is, head of
the Sixth, a post dependent upon academic merit, and captain of
games. Traditionally this had been so. When Wyndham leaves
there is no one with high achievements in both fields and Dr
Patrick ('Paddy') appoints Riddell, the head of the Sixth, but a bad
athlete, to be School Captain. The best athlete, Bloomfield, is a
poor classic, but feels that by rights he should have been the new
School Captain. He has support, even amongst a majority of the
masters, who ask Dr Patrick to reconsider his decision. But he is
firm. Already the juniors of Parrett's house have raided Welch's
house to settle an old score, rightly anticipating punishment from
Riddell. Bloomfield is elected Speaker of the School Parliament,
again against tradition, as the School Captain has previously
always held this office. A running battle for power develops
between Riddell and Bloomfield, the former using subtle
persuasion and avoiding physical punishment, whilst the latter
prefers the traditional, usually crude, methods. A school boat race
takes place and Parrett's eight – Bloomfield was in Parrett's –
loses, because a rudder string breaks. The rope is found to have
been cut. A big fight follows. Dr Patrick now asked Riddell to
move to Welch's house which is in a bad state of discipline and
'not pulling together' in order to bring this house up to standard.
After some self-doubts Riddell agreed and began to use his
persuasive methods there by, for example, encouraging the
juniors in their cricket. By this time Riddell had himself been
chosen to play in the XI because of his improved play. His main
concern was still to try to discover who cut the rope in the boat
race. He carried on this detective work quietly whilst his methods
in Welch's house resulted in the Junior XI easily beating Parrett's
by an innings and 29 runs. Now the culprit who cut the rope is
discovered – as usual the suspected boy turns out to be innocent.

Bloomfield and Riddell are brought together. The former resigns as Speaker and Riddell is elected, as the school has come to realise that he is a good and strong Captain – and by now he is in the XI!

The expected emphases are all present in *The Willoughby Captains*. The tale is told from the boys' view-point. Indeed, the only women mentioned in relation to the school were 'Mrs Patrick and . . . Mrs Patrick's sister, and before these awful personages the boldest Willoughbite quailed and trembled' (IV). The school organisation is emphasised and is hierarchical in the usual public school fashion, administered through houses and largely by the boys themselves:

> The discipline of Willoughby . . . was left almost entirely in the hands of the monitors, who with the captain, their head, were responsible as a body to the headmaster for the order of the school. It was very rarely that a case had to go beyond the monitors, whose authority was usually sufficient to enable them to deal summarily with all ordinary offenders. (II)

Riddell develops through the year, as Dr Patrick had believed would happen, into a fine School Captain. The code of values is the usual one except that Riddell is initially not a successful athlete. Yet games are important in the book. There are set-piece descriptions of the boat race, a school cricket match versus the county and a house cricket match – 'was not Willoughby one of the crack athletic schools of the country, boasting of an endless succession of fine runners and rowers and cricketers?' (I).

Riddell is an interesting character. He was 'reputed "pi" – as the more irreverent . . . were wont to stigmatise any fellow who made a profession of goodness' (III). He agrees to be School Captain, feeling that 'after all he might be shirking a duty he ought to undertake' (IV). When he considers one difficult decision about the punishment to give to a boy who has broken bounds he says to himself 'God help me!':

> Is the reader astonished that the captain of a great public school should so far forget himself as to utter a secret prayer in his own study about such a matter as the correction of a young scapegrace? . . . I am not quite sure that Riddell was committing such an absurdity as some persons might think. . . . What do you think? It is worth thinking over when you have time. (X)

A modern reader must remember that this phrase would have been read then as a prayer. Once Riddell had learnt to stand up to opposition his main problem was the difficult one of restoring the unity of the school whilst at the same time building up the morale of one house, Welch's. He sets about this task quite openly. A debate is held in the School Parliament on the motion that 'Willoughby is degenerate'. The proposer's intention was to discomfort Riddell, but he won a moral victory. He summed his position up with these words:

> 'And if each house pulls itself up, not at the expense of a rival house . . . but for the glory of the school – we shan't have to complain of Willoughby being degenerate much longer.' (XIX)

All the usual facets of the boys' code are emphasised, but the main emphasis is undoubtedly put upon Riddell's ability to stand out alone against the majority for what he sees as right. This was an inherent and central element in the contemporary definition of 'manliness'. Oliver Greenfield had to put up with being sent to coventry, despite his innocence, and this quality can be found emphasised in many later boys' school stories.

Three of Reed's subsequent school stories will be dealt with briefly. *The Cock House at Fellsgarth* (1891), almost by its title, proclaims its easy fit into the genre. Houses, inter-house rivalry – on and off the games field, a set-piece cricket game, a fag's strike, and so on, are all part of the plot. *The Master of the Shell* (1887) has all the usual characteristics, but by its title raises the suspicion that the story is told from the point of view of the masters, not the boys. This is not the case. A new and young master, Mark Railsford, a fine games player who has rowed for his university, is appointed to Grandcourt School as Master of the Shell. He is engaged to the sister of Arthur Herapath, a boy at Grandcourt. This circumstance is merely one element in the plot which, as expected in the genre, turns very largely on the doings of the boys seen from their viewpoint. *Follow My Leader* (1887) traces the careers of three boys as they move from Mountjoy Preparatory School to Templeton School, their doings as fags, on the games field, as spectators or players, and in the classroom. One of them, Coote by name, is wrongly suspected of the theft of a pencil from a local stationer's, but, despite some difficulties for the three over a boat which they have allowed to go out to sea, all turns out well and they become solid members of Templeton,

"WHAT'S THIS?" HE DEMANDED, LIFTING UP FISHER II.

137

"His Grace the Duke of Somewhere, and the Ladies Marigold." – *Page 206.*

where the school Captain, Pontifex, could describe the actions of some juniors in these words:

> And Ponty, as he lay . . . blinking in the sun, moralised on the matter, and came to the conclusion that there is hope for a boy as long as he loves to don his flannels and roll up his shirt sleeves, and stand up, with his head in the air, to face his rival like a man. (XIII)

Reed's last boys' school story. *Tom, Dick and Harry* (1892) has two new elements in its plot; the school is for both day boys and boarders, though Low Heath is described as 'a crack public school' (I), and, one master, Mr Jarman, is painted in a poor light, perhaps because he was the Physical Education master – games, as opposed to PE, were supervised by amateurs. Yet the book, as will be seen, falls well within the genre. The new boys in Sharpe's House establish a Philosophical Conversation Club and, pursuing its aims, go for a picnic by boat to a spot which they find to be already taken by the 'Urbans' or Day Boys. There is almost a fight, but a senior boy, Harry Tempest, arrives and after settling the quarrel organises a tug-of-war.

Tempest has written to his friend, Tom Jones, at his home that at Low Heath there is 'as much cricket as you like, and a river, a gymnasium, and all sorts of sprees' (III). Tom, an orphan, after being expelled from a private school for sneaking – an offence his friends believe him incapable of – was put by his guardian to work in his office, but sent for coaching locally to Miss Housfield's girls' school, where one mistress, Miss Steele, persuades him to enter for an exhibition to Low Heath. After a year's hard work, during which he is caught using a crib and burns it to win back Miss Steele's favour, he wins the exhibition. In a passage that is a satire on the rules and dress of public schools Tempest persuades Jones to arrive at Low Heath in tan boots, yellow gloves, and a square-topped hat. He also tells Jones 'to forget you're an exhibitioner . . . it's the sort of thing to be lived down here' (VIII).

Mr Jarman 'lags' all the boarders in Sharpe's for returning late from their picnic, giving them all extra drill and lines to write. A guy resembling him is made for Guy Fawkes Day and stored under the gym, but it explodes before November 5th. Tempest is suspected, though probably a cigarette end dropped by Mr Jarman caused the explosion. A magistrate has to intervene, but Jones and some others go along and tell the truth that they made it. Later

Mr Jarman is disobeyed when he tries to take the names of some members of Sharpe's House for disorderly behaviour. This matter is tied back to Tempest, who apologises, but at this time he is also discovered to be in debt through revelations by Crofton who becomes head of house in place of Tempest and offers through Jones to pay Tempest's debts of £5. As a result Tempest and Jones fall out. Under Tempest Sharpe's had become very slack. Bad behaviour was

> in fashion. And all of us were slack because our betters set us the example. It needs no little courage for a single boy to attempt to stem the drift of slackness in a school house.

Dr England, the headmaster, had to step in.

> 'This is not the first occasion this term on which this house has been reported, but I have previously refrained from interfering, in the hope that the good feeling of the boys themselves would assert itself and make any action of mine unnecessary.' (XIX)

It is the end of term and Tempest goes home for the holidays in low spirits:

> And the hopes of the wonderful term had been disappointed. I was a recognised dunce and idler at Low Heath. . . . My self-respect was at a low ebb. . . . The worst of it was, I could not get it out of my head yet that I was rather a fine young fellow if only people knew it, and that my misfortunes were more to blame for the failure of the term than my fault. (XXI)

The second term of the story starts with Crofton well installed as head of Sharpe's, but the house is badly burnt as a result of Mr Jarman carelessly putting a lit cigar butt into Mr Sharpe's wastepaper basket. Tempest saves Jones whose friendship he had so recently lost, from his dormitory, but Jones is seriously ill for a week from the effects of the fire. His mother comes to nurse him and before going home she

> urged me to show my gratitude for my escape, by seeking to follow more closely in the footsteps of that Saviour to whom she had so often taught me to look for hope and guidance. (XXIV)

Very soon the school sports day is held. This is highly organised into heats; all starts are efficiently organised and from blocks; there is much rubbing of calves. Redwood, the head of school and an Urban, is entered in the mile and runs successfully despite a badly burnt hand, about which he tells no one. This leads to a severe illness for him. Before the end of term examinations take place. Tempest does well, as do his two friends, Tom and Dick, the latter of whom plays a somewhat minor role in the story. It will be remembered in the *BOP* Reed named this tale, *Tom, Harry and Dick*.

In this last boys' school story Reed showed Tempest's development through adversity to a better character within a school with the organisation of a public school despite the presence of day boys. The code of behaviour described in his earlier books was again set forth with the usual occasional references to the Christian religion. The nature of Mr Jarman's character is novel in Reed's work, though Anstey would not have blinked an eyelid at it. Reed had by this time written five boys' school stories within the genre which he had himself firmed up in *The Fifth Form at St Dominic's*. The new emphases in *Tom, Dick and Harry* may have been due to a growing sense of the narrowness of the limits of the genre that he had defined. Hutchison himself implicitly, though not in any critical way, commented on the restricted range of activities in Reed's books, 'dealing as they do very largely with the dormitory and study life of the boys' (Hutchison, 1897: xviii). The spirit of this remark is true, although oddly he omits many sites of important action in these books, particularly the games field. No one else at the time had written so many of these stories and when they became more common in another twenty years or so, this narrowness would, as we shall see, be cause for comment.

Reception

Between March and June 1882, *Punch* ran a series of five humorous articles by 'Our Boys' Novelist. Being Stories of Wild Sport and Stirring Adventures for the Amusement and Instruction of the Youth of All Nations'. One of these was entitled 'Wet Bob or the Adventures of a Little Eton Boy amongst the Hotwhata Cannibals'. In England, if not Scotland, there is probably no greater accolade than to be taken humorously by *Punch*. The boys' adventure story, and even its newly developing near-relation the boys' school story, was coming to be recognised at the highest level!

The Religious Tract Society had no doubts by the 1890s about what had happened. In the catalogue of its series 'The Boys' Library of Adventure and Heroism' a work about the Boys' Brigade, Frederick Gibbon's *Comrades Under Canvas*, was compared with *Tom Brown* and *The Fifth Form* and described as likely to be 'the classic story of Boys' Brigade Life'. By the end of his life, when writing *Tom, Dick and Harry*, Reed was also certain enough of the public's view to have Tom Jones read the *BOP* in the train on the way to school, as did another Low Heath boy in the same compartment (V). We have already seen that against all its expectations the Religious Tract Society reported that within a year the demand for the *BOP* was very great. As the editor commented in the Correspondence column: 'We print 200,000 weekly, and nearly every copy has probably two or three readers' (14 February 1880). Who were these readers?

Correspondents wrote to the *BOP* of the nature of its readership. In 1879 a letter came from a branch of the Technical Department of the Post Office in Scotland, saying that out of 84 lads on the staff 63 took the *BOP* weekly and 5 monthly. At a Birmingham Grammar School 'quite half the boys' took the *BOP* and at a private school in Folkestone, 'Some fifty copies came into my school – by no means a large one – every week' (13 December 1879). One letter came from Wellington College, telling of the good reception of the *BOP* there. Thus, as well as school boys at all types of secondary schools, apprentices were reading this paper. In addition, the Correspondence column showed that Post Office message boys and boys in Australia and New Zealand were reading the *BOP*. Adults, too, wrote in to tell how they enjoyed it, for example, a sergeant in the Royal Engineers and a clergyman in Norfolk. The announcement of the winners of the weekly competition showed that the age range of readers ranged mainly from thirteen to nineteen, but also that it very soon included girls as well as boys. One letter came from a girl in Victoria, who wrote that 'not only boys, but a great number of girls out here read the *Boys' Own Paper*, and, I believe, especially the stories of Mr T.B. Reed'. By 1881 the editor commented that the *BOP* was being 'used as a reading book in many schools'. Furthermore, the *BOP* was 'so well thought of in high places that the fourth volume was dedicated by special permission to two of its readers, Prince Edward and Prince

George of Wales'. In the same year the headmaster of an Essex school wrote 'to ask if it is intended to publish [*The Three Guinea Watch*] in a separate form, as I believe there are many masters who would like to get it as a prize-book for their pupils' (1 October 1881). He was right. Not only had the Religious Tract Society begun a best-selling journal, they had also found a market for their serials as books, especially as Christmas presents, school prizes and Sunday School rewards.

Salmon's *Juvenile Literature as it is* (1888a) has been mentioned already. Salmon was very critical of 'Penny Dreadfuls' and thought that

> The only real antidote for these poisonous sheets . . . is the *Boys' Own Paper*, because the *Boy's Own Paper* is the only first-class journal of its kind which has found its way into the slums as well as into the best homes.

This was also the view of the *Quarterly Review*. It thought that the Religious Tract Society had been wise in its policy of publishing the *BOP* and the *Girls' Own Paper* 'without the imprint of the Society', which would have frightened many readers away (*Quarterly*, 1890: 168-9). So successful in this respect had the *Boys' Own Paper* been that 'the proprietors of penny dreadfuls try to induce booksellers to insert advertisement slips of their own rubbish into copies sold of *The Boys' Own Paper*. This nuisance has at times been so great that legal action has had to be threatened' (Salmon, 1888a: 185-7). The success of the *BOP* was attributed to its 'interest' and the number of 'adventures' it contained. Also there was 'no slang' and 'no sentimental tales' (ibid.: 17-18). The fact that girls read the *BOP* was, Salmon thought, because 'they can get in boys' books what they seldom get in their own – a stirring plot and lively movement' (ibid.: 28). Furthermore, no longer did those writing in this field write down to their readers. Salmon gave two pages to a consideration of Reed's work up to that date. In discussing *The Three Guinea Watch* he wrote:

> There should be a considerable future before him in the line he has adopted. He tells a story well and naturally, and is thoroughly conversant with every phase of school life. . . . The undertone of his work is not so deep as that of *Tom Brown's Schooldays*, and there are no little lectures, but the general tendency of the two stories is the same. (ibid.: 99-100)

One of Salmon's conclusions was that 'the whole body of successful boys' literature cannot be more concisely described than as a vast system of hero-worship' (ibid.: 217). However true this may be, and it seems an exaggeration, Salmon himself said nothing against the types of hero that, for example, Reed presented.

In the year before Salmon's book came out Charlotte Yonge (1887) produced a little work, published by the National Society's Depository, called *What Books to Lend and What to Give*. This was an annotated list of books, arranged under various headings, one of which was 'Boys'. In her introduction she wrote that 'wholesome and amusing literature has become almost a necessity among the appliances of parish work . . .; where . . . it is to be had, there is much less disposition to prey upon garbage' (Yonge, 1887: 5). She omitted some books from her list because they were not 'beyond censure'. For example, '*King Solomon's Mines* was', she felt, 'marred by the falsehoods told to the natives and . . . by the constant reference to bad language on the part of the naval lieutenant' (ibid.: 30). Reed's *Follow My Leader* was included as being 'Another public school story, sound and spirited, and likely to interest. People sometimes learn best from what does not profess to be about their own life' (32). *Tom Brown* was also included on the same grounds: 'though the sphere is so different from that of the elementary school boy, his tone may be raised by it' (31). In 1895, soon after Reed's death, Sime concluded that 'in the Little Library of boys' books which left his pen he has done as much as any writer of our day to raise the standards of boys' literature.' And he had not followed the 'powder-in-jam' principle. 'His boys are of flesh and blood'; his books had a 'wholeness of tone' and a 'breezy freshness' (Sime, 1895: vii–viii). But twenty years later critics were putting another viewpoint. Thomas Seecombe, in his Introduction to the first edition of Alec Waugh's *The Loom of Youth*, wrote of 'the calculated falsity of Talbot Baines Reed'. Later again, Frank Eyre wrote that in books like *The Fifth Form* Reed 'brought the type to a perfection of unreality that later writers would only copy' (Eyre, 1971: 82). When Hamish Hamilton reissued this book in 1971 Brian Alderson in his 'Postscript' whilst admitting such possible faults, highlighted as positive virtues its focus on personal relationship and 'the moral education involved in them' (Alderson, 1971: 305–6). Different ages inevitably read Reed differently.

From the beginning the Religious Tract Society had a

profitable enterprise on its hands. The minutes of its Finance Committee show that Volume I of the *BOP* produced a profit of £2499 16*s*8*d* and Volume II of £2662 *s*7*d*, considerable sums at that date. The copyrights belonged to the Society and in later years *ex gratia* payments were made to Reed's widow. In 1906 the Committee decided that 'in consideration of the continued satisfactory sales of the books a gift be made to Mrs Reed of £100' and in 1914 'a final grant of £100 be made'. The Contract Book of the Society shows that in 1907 permission was given to a French writer to use about three pages of *The Fifth Form* in his Elementary English Reader. In 1909 a Copenhagen publisher was allowed 'to issue a shortened form in English, as a school edition in Denmark, and also for a translation into Danish'. In 1907 the *Review of Reviews* was allowed to publish 750,000 of a 1*d* edition – some years previously they had published a 1*d* edition of 100,000. In 1913 all Reed's books were republished by the Society at 1*s* net each. In 1917 *The Cock House at Fellsgarth* was put into Braille by the National Lending Library for the Blind. Finally, in 1920 the film rights for *The Fifth Form* were sold to a Wardour Street company for £200; during 1921 the scenario was passed by the Society and the film approved for its first showing in December.

Conclusion

In the fourteen years during which Talbot Baines Reed, an active businessman with many other interests, wrote for the new *BOP*, amongst much else he produced six boys' school stories. These were initially serials, but soon published as books which were quickly successful. In the first, *The Fifth Form at St Dominic's*, Reed took elements from Hughes's and Farrar's stories written twenty years before and developed the framework within which he wrote his five other boys' school stories. These became what was expected of Reed, of writers in the *BOP* and, hence, very quickly of what was seen to be a 'proper' boys' school story. This minor genre was marked by four main characteristics: the stories were told – and read – from the viewpoint of boys; they were about hierarchically organised public schools; the character of the hero or heroes developed for good in the way that Tom Brown's, or for ill as Eric's had done previously; and, finally, a well-articulated set of values was explicitly and implicitly involved, which in

Reed's case was still strongly Christian, albeit less obviously so than in *Tom Brown* or *Eric*. The Christianity, too, was less tied to any one theological position. The 'good' heroes, however, were less like Eric than like Tom Brown since there were no 'excess demands for perfection'; boys were now being prepared 'to live an active Christian life in the world as it is' (Rosenthal, 1974: 250).

6

Social structural supports

What has eventually to be explained is what it was that at the time allowed a slow increase in the number of school stories, largely about private schools and mainly in the vein of *Eric*, to occur during the 1860s and 1870s and what then allowed a sharp increase of similar stories, but mainly about public schools which were in the vein of *Tom Brown* to take place from around 1880. Furthermore, some search must be made for reasons why the minor genre became established with the four characteristics that were isolated in the last chapter. In addition, we have noted that literature for young persons and children was starting to show a critical element; attention must also be given to the reasons for that development. In this chapter the state at the time of five social institutions will be considered: first, the economic and the political frameworks; next, the religious and moral structure; fourth, the family; and finally, the contemporary educational structure.

The economic and the political frameworks

Statistics of any nature that can be used for comparing specific categories within the population during the whole Victorian era are hard to find. From 1871 onwards statistical runs built on the same and adequate bases are more common. The total population of England and Wales rose greatly during this period. In 1801 at the first Census the population was 10.5 millions, but between 1871 and 1931 the total population and the population of children and young persons moved as is shown in Table 6.1. Clearly whatever happened to the proportion of children and young

147

Table 6.1 The population (total and the young) 1871-1931 (millions)

Age		1871	1901	1931
0-14	Male	4.102	5.265	4.808
	Female	4.094	5.210	4.712
		8.196 (36.1%)	10.475 (32.2%)	8.620 (21.8%)
15-19	Male	1.085	1.608	1.710
	Female	1.096	1.639	1.725
		2.181 (9.6%)	3.247 (10.0%)	3.435 (7.8%)
Total male and female		22.712	32.528	43.758

Source: D.C. Marsh, 1965: 24.

persons during these years, there was an absolute rise in their numbers during the last three decades of the century and even though numbers fell during the next three decades the absolute numbers of the market for literature for children and young persons in 1931 was still bigger than it had been in 1871. Though there is considerable discussion about how the standard of life changed during these years the consensus seems to favour a pronounced rise up to the onset of the Great Depression around 1876 and a much slower rise thereafter. This larger market had, therefore, an increasing capacity to buy the specialised books and papers produced for them.

Another tendency was at work to increase the size of this potential market. The proportion of the population seen as middle-class was also rising during this same period as Table 6.2 shows. In the first line the growth of the civil service and the development of local government is indexed. The professional occupations here include the Church, the law, medicine, teaching, literature, the arts, engineering and surveying. In the commercial

Table 6.2 Some occupational categories, 1881 and 1901 ('000s)

| | Males | | Females | |
	1881	1901	1881	1901
General and local government	97	171	7	26
Defense	107	168	—	—
Professional	231	312	188	295
Commercial	308	531	8	60

Source: D.C. Marsh, 1965: 118.

category are merchants, bankers and shopkeepers. In all these cases the growth of opportunities for women in clerical work is also seen. The second line covers the army and the navy, only the officers of which would be seen as middle-class, though most of the non-commissioned officers (NCOs) would be able to read, and, indeed, as we know, some did read the *BOP*. This mention of NCOs is not accidental. In the *Edinburgh Review* in 1858 Fitzjames Stephen had written of the increasing numbers of those then starting to follow the pathway from Rugby through Trinity into their working life:

> They are the leaders of everyday English life – what we may well call the non-commissioned officers of English society . . . the clergy, the lawyers, the doctors, the county squires, the junior partners in banks and merchants' offices, men who are in every sense of the word gentlemen though no one would class them with the aristocracy. (1858: 37)

This group of the middle class, the potential market for a public school education and for the genre with which we are here concerned, was clearly rising in numbers and in importance in the later part of the Victorian era.

As will be seen in the fourth section of this chapter the numbers of schools serving every level of society was rising and after 1876 education became compulsory from the age of five until twelve. There was, therefore, an obvious case for an increase in the numbers of literate persons in the working class. In the late 1860s probably 'about 30 per cent of the male working population could not write and about 25 per cent could not read' (Musgrave, 1967: 40). This basis of a wealthier and more literate population provided the market within which entrepreneurs, like E.J. Brett, the pioneer of 'Penny Dreadfuls' were able to make a profit. In 1864 the total circulation of non-daily, London-published periodicals has been reckoned to be of the following order: 2,203,000 weekly newspapers of which more than half were accounted for by such Sunday papers as *Reynolds Weekly*; 2,404,000 other weeklies, of which one third were religious or broadly educational in content; and 2,490,000 monthlies, 'nearly 2 million of which were religious' (Best, 1971: 226). The publishers were keen, as their catalogues showed, to tap this potential market to the full. Novels that were a success with higher-status purchasers were often brought out later in cheap editions and this was as true for children's, as for adult's books. As Salmon wrote:

> Boys books are sold first at four or five shillings – The well-to-do buy them, but if they are ever so good, the poorer lads have no chance of sharing in the benefits to be derived from their perusal.

He congratulated one publisher for bringing out in a sixpenny edition 'some of W.H.G. Kingston's best books' (Salmon, 18866: 340). However, Sutherland in a 'conservative estimate' has calculated that 'for every producer above the literacy threshold there were two beneath it'. Literary novelists were conscious of a huge 'unknown public' of three million readers, yet Wilkie Collins regretted that it was 'impenetrable' (Sutherland, 1976: 5-6).

The constant attempts to tap this new market became more difficult with the onset of the depression both in industry and in agriculture that occurred in the last quarter of the century. A conscious drive to offset these difficulties was made by concentrating on developing new markets in the Empire. Though this may not have led to a much larger sale of books overseas there was a new Imperial spirit abroad in the political air that affected the contents of much that was written. One Act of Parliament and two national, even Imperial, events symbolise this. In 1876 the Royal Titles Act was passed by which Queen Victoria became Empress of India; in 1887 and 1897 there took place the Golden and the Diamond Jubilees, occasions for massive displays of patriotic fervour.

There were other international political events that affected patriotic feeling a little earlier. In 1859/60 there was a scare that Napoleon III would lead a French invasion of Britain. As a result the Volunteer Movement was revived. An associated outcome was the beginning of Cadet Corps in public schools. In 1860 at Rugby a Corps was established in co-operation with local Volunteer Regiments. In 1863 the Volunteers Act authorised the War Office to found such Cadet Units, which grew in number in the 1870s. There was even a corps founded in the East End of London for working-class boys. These units became recruiting grounds for officers for the Volunteers, and for the army itself, especially in the Boer and Great Wars. The post-war economic problems brought about a lowering of their grants in 1923/5 and even led to their discontinuance from 1930 to 1937 (Springhall, 1976: 71 and 87).

There are a number of other indices of the rise of this Imperial spirit. One is a book, *The Expansion of England*, by J.R. Seeley, the Professor of Modern History at Cambridge, published in 1883. This book was based on two series of lectures given at Cambridge in 1881/2, one on the old colonial system and the other on the Indian Empire. The ideas contained in this book were not new and had been around for some fifteen years. They can be summed up very briefly in Seeley's own words, when he referred to 'the simple obvious fact of the extension of the English name into other countries of the globe, the foundations of the Greater Britain' (Seeley, 1971: 12). Seeley has been described recently as 'an imperialist . . . but . . . neither a jingo nor a hack' (Goss, 1971: xiii). His book sold 20,000 copies in two years. The ideas may not have been new, but Seeley's able exposition of them met the new feelings of the time.

If this upsurge of patriotism, often jingoistic in expression, was not to be found in Reed's schoolboy stories, there were other books that did support it. Rider Haggard's *King Solomon's Mines*, published in 1885, sold 5,000 copies in its first two months. But in the work of one writer above all others was this imperialistic spirit to be found – G.A. Henty, who wrote a large number of boys' adventure stories from the 1880s till his death in 1902. 'Twenty-five of Henty's books concern themselves with incidents in British Imperial history' (Huttenback, 1970: 47). His books were immensely popular with boys at the turn of the century so that his stirring view of Empire was transmitted to whole generations of secondary, and hence particularly public school boys during at least the next two decades.

The curriculum of the late nineteenth-century public school still heavily emphasised the classics. In a fine phrase A.P. Thornton has said that '*Kennedy's Latin Primer* . . . proved one of the winding-sheets of Empire' (1959: 31-2). This is a little unfair since even Farrar in the 1860s had shown some keenness for science teaching. But certainly the school history texts of the time in Britain 'became more jingoistic', with a stress on 'the ideal of Empire, description of a noble stereotype compared to inferior races, homilies on the need for patriotic duty' (Chancellor, 1970: 137). Indeed, the same tendency could be found in what to Seeley was one of the extensions of England over the seas, namely Australia (A.R. Trethewey, 1974).

This growing belief in a British imperial mission may have been less pronounced in boys' school stories, but another characteristic that has been noted to have become more common in them was supportive of this feeling, namely the xenophobia expressed in such stories as T.S. Millington's *Some of Our Fellows*. The Germans and Jews were particularly the target for snide or silly comments. One type of publication, however, where jingoism was more pronounced was in comics. The 1890s saw several comics founded, particularly by the Harmsworth Amalgamated Press. *Comic Cuts* (1890) and *The Wonder* (1892) are examples. A prime feature of editorial policy was support for the Empire. One student of popular writers of the time has said that not only did the Amalgamated Press congratulate itself on the way in which its comics built pride in Empire, but 'they had in effect served as useful recruiting agencies for the armed forces' (Howarth, 1973: 89).

But all was not well with Britain in the view of many thinking people. In 1867 Matthew Arnold, son of Thomas Arnold, and himself a school inspector, published his famous book, *Culture and Anarchy*. This was a trenchant attack on the directions in which culture in an industrialising Britain was developing and a demand for, amongst other things, a firm secular moral basis for our culture. The depression caused more questioning which both led to and was fuelled by various Royal Commissions, for example, that on Depression of Trade and Industry (1886). There was, too, a series of major strikes and troubles over the place of trade unions in society throughout those difficult years and these tended to make for inter-class bitterness which amongst other things caused members of the middle class to react by assuming a defensive stance. One result of this was their desire to preserve their class position for their children, especially their sons, through the education system. The obverse of this was the working-class demand, increasingly mediated through the unions and eventually after 1906 through the Labour Party, for more open opportunities for their children to gain secondary, or at least more extended, schooling. The political consensus of the late nineteenth century was breaking down with the growing power of labour and the greater criticism of social inequalities.

In brief, the demographic tendencies of the late-Victorian years increased the potential market for books for both children and young persons. This opportunity remained greater than in the 1870s in absolute, if not in relative terms into the 1930s. The greater wealth in Britain allowed entrepreneurs to build on this change. International politics and the onset of the depression encouraged xenophobia and a jingoistic Imperialism which influenced the content of and the values expressed in the literature offered to this market, especially that for boys. Yet there were well-recognised reasons for criticism, particularly concerning the economic and social conditions of the country, and these would become more obvious as a result of Britain's difficulties in winning the Boer War and during the long drawn-out travails of the First World War.

Religion and morality

Religion, and that means Christianity, was still very central in the minds of many Victorians, certainly to those of the higher social classes – to those, in other words, who could enforce their views from positions of some power. Yet, particularly since the publication in 1859 of Darwin's *Origin of the Species*, the truth of Christianity was no longer accepted with such certainty. The attacks on Christianity did nothing to bring its various branches together to defend it. Thus, the apparent gain by the Roman Catholics in the 1860s had as one result the publication by the Religious Tract Society of a journal, the *True Catholic*, which ran from 1870 to 1876, though never with a large circulation. It stood against 'the perils from the renewed and aggressive pretensions of Romanism' and 'for the vindication and enforcement of evangelical belief . . . to correct the popular misapplication of the word "catholic" ' (Green, 1899: 75).

Yet, if no ecumenical defence movement emerged, the influence of the Broad Church did increase. The position, therefore, of Kingsley was important. He had early in the 1850s attacked Tractarianism. *Westward Ho!* is an example of this aggressive spirit. As the Puseyites, the second generation Tractarians, switched their attention to adorning churches, particularly with statues of the Virgin Mary, the 'muscular Christianity' espoused by Kingsley became important to opponents of High Church tendencies. It was the apparent antithesis of what they so disliked. The Christian Socialists, furthermore, were not in the main political radicals. They admitted the social problems of the working class of the 1850/60s, but mainly sought a cure through 'moral and educational reform' rather than overturning the political status quo (Allen, 1969). But from the late 1850s there was no doubt in some commentator's minds that Kingsley's views, especially as filtered through *Tom Brown*, were liable to produce anti-intellectual adults. It is worth noting that Hughes's second book, *Tom Brown at Oxford*, contained a chapter with the title 'Muscular Christianity'. Yet Kingsley's own Amyas Leigh and his disciple and friend Thomas Hughes's Tom Brown seemed fine and appealing heroes to a middle class in 1860 at the very edge of religious doubt and on the apparent verge of war with another Napoleon. Both heroes continued to set an example, since both books went on selling. As doubt and danger increased, and as Empire became the 'obvious' solution, Kingsley's muscular Christianity gained renewed support, being read as appropriate to the somewhat different circumstances.

There had never been much differentiation between religious belief and morality in the Christian faith, particularly since the start of the Puritan tradition. Kingsley's Christianity translated easily into a moral code of duty to the Queen and Britain. Personal morality too was rooted in the concept of duty and also of honour. Duty to God and one's fellow man was the Puritan legacy. In many, especially Nonconformist, families of mid-Victorian times duty was pursued with great conscientiousness. In particular, work was seen as a duty and, hence, could be connected back to religion. The obverse was that idleness was evil. As has been noted, reading some novels was seen as idleness and, therefore, evil. Yet the movement towards a Broader view of Christianity, amongst Anglicans and others, did allow for some greater opportunity for entertainment. T.B. Reed was able to keep his keen Congregationalist connection apart from his reading and the literary part of his life. If he had not, he would soon have put down Oscar Wilde's novel and resigned from the Saville Club.

The second concept governing personal morality that was

mentioned above was honour. In the context of this book any consideration of honour in the Victorian era must lead to an examination of the increasing use of chivalric terms or metaphors that has been noticed in the school stories of the 1860s, 1870s and 1880s. In the early part of the century the novels of Sir Walter Scott had been responsible for an increased interest in chivalry. In 1822 a book was published anonymously, but in fact written by Kenelm Henry Digby with the title *The Broad Stone of Honour*. This account of the code of chivalry was popular enough to go into a second edition in 1823, sub-titled 'Rules for the Gentlemen of England'. The work was expanded to four volumes and published under the author's name in 1828-9 and again in 1848, but now sub-titled 'The True Sense and Practice of Chivalry'. Finally, in 1877 a fourth enlargement, in five volumes, was published, In the 1823 edition the view is expressed,

> The scholar may instruct the world with his learning, the philosopher may astonish it and benefit it by his researches, the man of letters may give a polish and a charm to society, but he who is possessed of simple faith and high honour, is, beyond all comparison, the more proper object of our affection and reverence.

Morality is here linked as was usual to religion and character is once again seen to be more important than intellect.

When the concept of honour was taken over by Kingsley it became linked to purity. Earlier in the century the true knight fought against what had come to be seen as the contemporary scourges of ignorance, disease and the evil forces of nature. He had now also to fight against the mental disorders and evil forces within himself, against his own passions. Another important influence on the mid-nineteenth-century idea of honour was Tennyson. Between 1859 and 1873 he published the ten parts of his popular poem, *Idylls of the King*. His ethic in these poems has recently been described as 'Live pure, speak true, right wrong, follow the King' (Girouard, 1981: 196). This ethic was very appealing to the public schools and was the one supported by what Bratton has called 'the moral fiction of Empire' (1981: 148).

One paradox resulted from this undertone of chivalry. How should physical violence be treated? There had been a move throughout the century away from the cruelty exhibited in the public schools, in games and in many interpersonal actions and against the excess use of alcohol because this was likely to lead to loss of control and violent action. Fighting in *Tom Brown* and in its successors was hard, but officially controlled. When Loman thrashed Stephen Greenfield in *The Fifth Form at St Dominic's* that was wrong since big boys did not behave thus to smaller boys; it was bullying. Yet the expansion of Empire seemed to demand violent actions. 'Penny Dreadfuls' were criticised as violent and cruel. Yet the *BOP*, acceptable to 'good' parents and emanating, albeit anonymously, from the Religious Tract Society, which incidentally had a very large overseas missionary programme, was also on occasions violent and cruel. 'For a brief period of time Tom Brown's heirs reflected the violence and brutality of an expanding empire' (James, 1973: 98-9).

The schools at all levels had a central role here in inculcating a code of morality, though, as noted, some saw this to be more difficult because the new state schools, though Christian, were non-denominational. In 1890 the writer on 'Penny Dreadfuls' in the *Quarterly* said:

> we must begin in the schoolroom – not necessarily by yielding to the popular argument for technical education for boys and cooking classes for girls at the public expense – but by encouraging the growth of something resembling culture.

The Catechism had gone because it was sectarian; the Bible had followed.

> The result is that we are in the position of the man in the Gospels. We have cast out the unclean spirit of ignorance from the working class mind, and have left it empty, swept, and neatly garnished with 'the 3 Rs'. (*Quarterly Review*, 1890: 170)

There was a feeling that true religion was being ignored. In the public schools religion was becoming more often ritualistic and empty or occasionally repressive in the Evangelical tradition of Farrar which took no account of the nature of the human boy. Hughes's set piece on Arnold's sermon had been transformed into Reed's couple of paragraphs, describing an effect on Stephen Greenfield that was soon forgotten – Eric's moral decline was constantly on his own conscience. And to go back beyond Hughes, Thomas Arnold's own definition of manliness was in terms of an active maturity reached through growth and marked by the cultivation of intelligence and energy in the pursuit of morality within the Christian faith. This ideal was changed into that of Kingsley and of Hughes who stressed the 'masculine and muscular connotations of the word and founds its converse in effeminacy' (Newsome, 1961: 197).

In Arnold's day manliness had been connected to good learning; the link was truthfulness which was as vital to godliness as to good learning. By the 1870s truthfulness was still the link but by then because it joined honour or chivalry to religion. Furthermore, honour was easily related to the muscular Christianity that was apparently so appropriate for an Imperial nation and, therefore, so apt to be the guiding moral concept in the public schools where its leaders were educated.

The family

Much has been written about the intensity of the Victorian middle-class family. Two well-known literary works tell of escapes from such families. One, Samuel Butler's *The Way of All Flesh* (1903), a novel, was a mordant examination of the command, 'honour thy father and mother' as it had affected him, but was not published until after his death because he felt its revelations would be hurtful to relatives still living. The other, Edmund's Gosse's *Father and Son* (1907) was an autobiographical account of his own upbringing. The terrible pressures upon a remarkable boy, an only child, in this somewhat extreme example of the mid-Victorian family are shown in one passage near the end, in which Gosse describes himself at about ten years old:

> Through thick and thin I clung to a hard nut of individuality deep down in my childish nature. To the pressure from without, I resigned everything else, my thoughts, my words, my anticipations, my assurances, but there was something which I never resigned, my innate and persistent self. (IX)

By the 1870s and 1880s the family, however, had handed many of its responsibilities for educating children beyond the nursery years to the schools. These early years were still seen as crucial. Samuel Smiles, the great advocate of self-help and of experience in life as the true educator, still saw that the foundations for future success were laid in early upbringing in the family. 'The nation comes from the nursery' (1859: XII), he wrote. By the end of the century the upper middle class were even handing those years to the nanny. But the idea of family education was a strong one, so that the very wealthy still put their faith in a tutor at home, as we have seen was the case in two of Reed's stories. The small family school, of the type Arnold himself had kept at Laleham before going to Rugby and as described by Frank Smedley in *Frank Farleigh* (1851), was the next best thing. Yet, as *Fraser's Magazine* noted in 1861, 'Private tuition at home is a thing beyond the means of men in general' and 'the alternative of a gentleman to take a few pupils' was only for 'those who can afford it'. The writer was well aware of the disadvantages of the public schools: 'vice reaches its maturity far sooner than virtue.' The ideal role for school masters was not to act as 'teacher, but as guardian and friend' (*Fraser's Magazine*, 1861: 436-8). The legal phrase 'in loco parentis' was beginning to exercise influence. But mothers, as Reed noted, were still concerned about the violence of public schools which were still on many counts barbarous places. One writer observed of boys that 'In the holidays, at home, or on a visit the human boy is very like the savage on the missionary station' (*Saturday Review*, 1882: 449). This sentence neatly encapsulates many of the attitudes towards education, the family and Christianity in late-Victorian Imperial Britain.

As manliness had now come to be opposed to effeminacy the place of women in the family was clearly defined as the opposite of any muscular ideal. The women in Rider Haggard's stories and those of the adventure story writers like him 'sit apart and more than a little above the action; they sit in the place allotted to them by Victorian England: beautiful, passionate, passive, the necessary antithesis to the dominant versions of manliness' (Inglis, 1981: 154). But great restraint had to be shown to women. Excess emotion could not be expressed. Men had openly wept in early Victorian days; as Tom Brown sat in Rugby Chapel after Arnold died 'the tears flowed freely down his cheeks' (II. IX) – his weeping was openly admitted without criticism. This was no longer the case and emotional restraint was the approved way of behaving. Thus, it was that boys at school did not talk of mothers or sisters and ceased showing feelings openly towards even their friends. In *Tom Brown* and stories of that era boys walked around arm-in-arm with each other, but this was no longer true by Reed's time.

This discussion is leading inexorably towards Victorian views on sexuality, both homo- and hetero-, now known to be much more complex than the concept of the double standard portrayed (Marcus, 1966). Marriage, and the family formed by it, were seen as sacred institutions. Even Tom Brown married at the end of *Tom Brown at Oxford* (1861). The separate position of women in Victorian middle-class families – and they at least set the standard for the lower classes – had definite implications for the upbringing of the two sexes and, therefore, for what they were given to read as children. Women had to be protected from evil so that they remained pure and womanly. Men, however, had to know, but to withstand evil, if they were to become manly (G. Avery, 1965: 149). Clearly a different literature flowed from these two sets of assumptions. Boys must read adventure stories and tales of evil overcome, whereas purer and calmer material was needed for girls. Looking back from the standpoint of our uni-sex era we should not be at all surprised that the *BOP* and the school and adventure stories in it were so attractive to girls of the late-Victorian time.

One of the abiding impressions of the earlier chapters of *Tom Brown's Schooldays* is the acceptance of their class positions by all the families in Tom's Berkshire village. But Hughes's and Kingsley's (a country parson himself) nostalgia was for a former era, marked by a lack of class consciousness, that was now past. Many of those in the industrial cities that were supplying the new recruits to the middle class not only felt their class strongly, but aspired to move up the social class ladder. Charlotte Yonge, herself from a rural background, wrote the following passage in a school history textbook:

> We have looked through English history and find that there was never a time when ability backed by industry and uprightness could not raise a man to full power, renown and influence. This is more than ever the case now, when the means of learning are within reach of all, for there is no obstruction in the way. (C.M. Yonge, 1883: 254).

Formal schooling, despite Samuel Smiles's views on life as the great schoolmaster, was seen as important for upward social mobility. Statistics to show this are hard to find, but those for the steel industry are pertinent and available. The percentage of steel manufacturers known to have attended public schools for those in high office in 1865 was 10, for those in office between 1875 and 1895 was 16 and for 1905-25 was 31 per cent (Erickson, 1959: 33). These top industrialists would have been at school some twenty or thirty years before their dates in office, and, hence, the proportions relate to the period under discussion here. The public schools provided an increasingly important educational experience at the time. Not surprisingly one of the themes in the stories referred to earlier was their use to make social connections that might help a boy to hold on to a shaky claim to middle-class status or to move up onto a rung higher up on the ladder than that upon which his father stood.

One sign of this is the importance attached to the choice of school. Much attention was given to the reputation of individual schools, particularly of public schools. In the 1880s and 1890s papers like the *Pall Mall Gazette* and the *Daily News* published tables to show annual records of various schools. In this their successes in the Oxford and Cambridge scholarships, in the army entry examinations and in the Oxford and Cambridge school examinations were tabulated for those interested to read them. Honey has concluded that 'there is plenty of evidence that headmasters took these tables seriously, though the impression they made on parents was less marked' (1977: 246). The point of this argument is that the tables were there and made some impression. As we have seen in Reed's *A Dog with a Bad Name* Mr Frampton, head of Bolsover College, refers implicitly to this ranking system. Honey, using such measures and some others available to him, has been able to categorise the so-called public schools on these contemporary standards rather than, as has until recently been done, on today's Head Masters' Conference (HMC) lists. He created four categories covering the period 1880-1902 and including 64 schools: I – 22 schools; II – 8 schools; III – 20 schools; and IV – 14 schools. We may note that for the period 1885-92 he puts Thomas Hughes's old school, Rugby, into his top Category I and both Reed's school, the City of London School, and Farrar's, King William's College, Isle of Man, into Category IV (Honey, 1977: 264).

For the late Victorians, then, the family was a very important educational agent in early childhood, but except for the very wealthy later education had been handed over to the schools. For the middle class this meant that their sons had to go to public schools if possible. Many of the attitudes learnt previously at home were reinforced at these schools. This was especially true of the emotional restraint coming to be seen as an integral part of the British character. These schools were also now seen to have a crucial relationship to success in life, and, hence, to either preservation of the family's social class position or to upward social mobility for boys.

Education

As hinted above there has always been a problem in defining for statistical or other purposes what a public school is. The real issue is how individual schools were seen at a a given date and that this reality changes through time. In 1866 the Public School Calendar listed three categories: the nine so-called Clarendon schools, upon which the Royal Commission of that name had reported in 1864; these were Winchester, Eton, St Paul's, Shrewsbury, Westminster, Merchant Taylor's, Rugby, Harrow and Charterhouse; the 'old endowed schools' including Sherborne, Oundle, Uppingham and Repton; and the 'schools of modern foundation', amongst which were Cheltenham, Marlborough, Clifton, Wellington and the City of London School. As we have noted, Honey (1977) has successfully developed categories based upon the contemporary status of the schools. The most readily available statistics are those compiled by Bamford, using the 1962 HMC list, and provided care is used in interpretation these can give a fair picture. The numbers of these schools increased throughout the second half of the century; in the 1860s 14 of those in the 1962 HMC list were founded, in the 1870s 7, in the 1880s 10 and in the 1890s 6 (Bamford, 1967: 270). The size of schools also grew. The absolute numbers in these public schools rose from 5,927 in 1866 to 8,696 in 1881, 11,480 in 1900 and 21,521 in 1936. What is significant is that if one expresses the numbers aged 13 to 18 who were boarders in these schools as a percentage of the corresponding age group in England and Wales this index also rose steadily throughout these years, especially after the turn of the century; the percentages were 0.5 in 1866, 0.6 in 1881, 0.7 in 1900 and 1.3 in 1936 (Bamford, 1974: 13 and 22).

By the end of the Victorian era the fifty schools in Honey's highest status categories displayed five characteristics. They were, first of all, 'predominantly Anglican'; this meant that, though there was a chapel, they were not on the whole excessively religious in their emphasis. Most of them, but not all, were boarding schools; after all, even some of the Clarendon schools were day schools. Some could be seen as definitely middle, rather than upper middle class; an example was Bedford Modern. The fees at some were

161

not considered high. Last, 44 of the 50 were in England, and the majority were in the South-East. (Honey, 1977: 284).

Another important characteristic was that these schools had a special relationship with the universities, and more particularly with Oxford and Cambridge. Rothblat (1976: 141) has gone as far as saying that the Oxford-Cambridge style was 'very likely imported from' the public schools. The two ancient universities underwent much-needed academic and administrative reform in the middle of the century. Those in the schools aiming to go up to these universities, and the masters preparing them, were conscious of the style needed and the schools made sure that this was acquired. Another backward influence on the schools was the establishment from 1857 of an examination system for schools run by the universities. This was part of the contemporary general trend against nepotism. Its requirements soon had some influence on teaching in the schools, even affecting the textbooks used, as Gosse pointed out. In *Father and Son* he commented on the new school editions, aimed to meet examination requirements, of Shakespeare's plays (XII).

The increasing scale of the public school system and the greater emphasis upon academic and moral attainments in turn had a backward effect on those schools preparing young boys for entry to the public schools. Honey believes that there were 'perhaps only a score . . . existing by 1850, [but] . . . some five hundred by 1900 and seven hundred by 1925' (Honey, 1977: 126). This development enabled the public schools to require their entrants to be older than in Tom Brown's day. Certainly Reed's new boys were generally in their early teens.

Many preparatory schools were difficult to differentiate from the private schools which were so often portrayed in boys' school stories before the days of the *BOP*. Indeed, quite often, private schools were themselves built on the shells of endowments, as seems to have been the case of Abbotscliff, the school in T.S. Millington's *Straight to the Mark*. The Schools Inquiry Commission into Endowed Schools in England and Wales (1868) was christened by *The Economist* 'the middle class schools commission'. It found 791 schools to fall within its scope in 1865, but thought that, if these endowed schools that fell outside its terms of reference were added, the total could reach about 3000. The eventual result of the recommendations of this report was that in 1874 the Charity Commission was established. This body started the immense task of reorganising many of these often old endowments to meet the contemporary needs for middle-class schools. This work went on throughout the rest of the century. Though most of these new secondary schools stuck to the classical curriculum demanded for university entry, a number did accept funding from the Department of Science and Art, the aim of which was to encourage the teaching of science. The result for the curriculum by the time the Bryce Commission reported on Secondary Education in 1895 was summed up in these words: 'broadly speaking literary subjects have been either virtually ignored or studied in far too perfunctory a manner; while in other cases scientific subjects may have been too much subordinated to literacy' (I: 72). The Charity Commission also redirected endowments towards girls' schools. In 1872 the Girls' Public Day School Trust was founded and by 1891 there were 36 schools under its auspices.

At the turn of the century, and in part following the advice of the Bryce Commission, the 1902 Education Act was passed. This enabled an expansion of secondary schooling financed by taxation and local government rates. The state-provided grammar schools now began to supply the middle class with another and in many cases a higher standard of secondary schooling than could be purchased from many of the private proprietary schools.

Matthew Arnold had for many years proclaimed 'Organise your secondary education' and this was now beginning to happen. But Arnold himself, as an Inspector, was more involved in the expansion of the elementary schools that followed upon the passing of the 1870 Education Act. In 1869 there were 1,765,944 places in inspected schools in England and Wales; in 1876 after the major immediate effects of the Act had been worked out, there were 3,426,318 of which 62.5 per cent of the additions had been supplied by religious bodies. Furthermore, the average attendance at grant-aided schools, which in 1875 was 66.95 per cent, rose steadily after compulsion was legalised in 1876 to become 76.31 per cent in 1886 and 88.11 per cent in 1905 (England only) (Birchenough, 1938: 119-23). This was the main force behind the increasing level of working-class literacy in the last decades of the nineteenth century.

Both the elementary schools and the new secondary schools were deeply affected by the public schools. The values of the public schools and the methods that they had established to impart those values were seen by most of those with power in Britain, and especially by those administering the new schools at both levels, as appropriate and acceptable. Therefore, Hughes's well-known misinterpretation of Thomas Arnold's Rugby became important far beyond the public school readership for which it had originally been intended. The ideas associated with the phrase 'muscular Christianity' were passed on, perhaps with some alteration, to a much wider audience. However, physical fitness and a life dedicated to social service at home or in the Empire were ideas that filtered through to the new secondary schools in a strong form and also, perhaps less strongly, to the new elementary schools. What Newsome has called 'the popular rage for manliness, athletics and belligerent imperialism' (Newsome, 1961: 235) helped to frame and in turn was supported by the educational ethos.

This same period, the 1860s to 1890s, also saw the start of the systematic national organisation of games. In 1871 the Rugby Union was founded; in 1873 the Marylebone Cricket Club established rules for qualifications for county players; in 1877 the All-England Croquet Club took tennis under its wing at Wimbledon; in 1886 the Hockey Association was set up (Tennyson, 1959). This bureaucratisation of sport was in marked opposition to the lack of organisation of leisure time and of many of the games then played at public schools. If nothing else this lack was recognised as a threat to these schools' full control over the all-important process of character building. Cotton and his successor, Bradley, had been important pioneers at Marlborough in the 1850s and 1860s in the process of organising games at school in such a way that loyalty to the school community came through playing in or supporting school teams. House teams were also established, though the latent effect of this rise in house spirit was often to direct loyalty away from the school to the house, as is very apparent in a number of Reed's stories.

The new emphasis on the school community was also expanded to cover those who had left school. Reed mentions this development in the way Old Boys visit the school after leaving. The growth of Old Boys' Associations was strengthened by their continuing to play games together in special teams. Oddly at the very time when examinations were supposedly undercutting nepotism games were helping to usher in a new form of patronage, the 'Old Boy network'. Membership of this network guaranteed, except in the case of 'bounders', that a man had a definite sense of values and a known code of behaviour, thereby providing a reference when applying for a job or when deciding whether a man was socially acceptable. The public schools produced an élite that could easily be identified; those who went to other levels of school entered other, but also known, levels in the social hierarchy.

Games were seen as very important for developing character. They were obviously linked to manliness. They, for example, gave the boys courage to and practice in standing up to opposition. Leaders had to be able to stand out against a majority and school stories, we have seen, emphasised this quality. Games, also, were claimed to use up the physical energy, which today we would probably relate to sexuality, that might otherwise be channelled into such unmanly activities as masturbation or homosexuality. In his book *Health at School* Charles Dukes, who was medical offer to Rugby School, claimed of physical training that it 'tends to induce a well balanced mind and character . . . quick response to call of duty . . . endurance . . . desire to excel, which ultimately becomes a noble ambition . . . and check on morbid desires and sensations' (Dukes, 1905: 336). Sexuality – 'morbid desires' – was a problem for boarding schools to which references are veiled in Reed's and earlier school stories, though the 'taking-up' system is mentioned.

The games cult did not capture all schools equally. The battles involved in its coming are well illustrated in the struggle for power as Captain of School between the Captain of Games and the Captain of the Sixth in Reed's *The Willoughby Captains*. Rothblat believes that the higher the status of the public school the more its aristocratic pupils withstood the innovations in organisation in the late nineteenth-century public schools. Eton and Winchester retained their own forms of house and school government; Eton also refused to accept outside standardisation of its own form of football, keeping as its peculiarity the Wall Game. Reed did not write of such schools, though we shall see a number of books about Eton and Harrow were written, starting in the next decade.

The greater surveillance of what boys were doing at public schools, even in their leisure hours, had another effect. School rebellions were far less frequent. The last rebellion at a major school seems to have taken place in 1900 at Monkton Combe School, a school owned by the headmaster and his predecessor who was, in fact, his father. At this school trouble led to the public ducking of the School Secretary and disorder over several days which led to the head resigning on his own initiative, though under pressure from both boys and masters (Lace, 1969). Rebellions occurred in schools up to the 1880s, but they disappear after Reed's time.

The schools had both influenced and been influenced by the social structure. In the early nineteenth century they had developed a set of values and a way of organising themselves to teach the code of behaviour involved. This had been much admired, but Hughes's version of it in *Tom Brown* had misinterpreted Arnold's original vision. His own version in its turn became the much admired model that eventually, though not immediately, influenced school stories, especially in Reed's work and, as will be seen, those writing after him. It also played a major part in determining the direction in which the new elementary and secondary schools developed. This development was underwritten by the school stories of the time, so that the ideal old boy of any school became a new version, varying with the status of the school, of the old ideal of Hughes. By the late nineteenth century this ideal could be reformulated as a gentleman and a Christian, though the Christianity covered only the very visible behaviour implicit in a Christian code of ethics rather than any deep belief in a revealed religion.

Conclusion

In the period between the 1860s and the 1880s a number of economic and political threats to Britain occurred simultaneously with changes in the family system. This conjuncture encouraged and allowed developments in the educational system in which a particular code of morality, rooted in one interpretation of Christianity, could evolve. As a result the public schools developed so that they were the predominant influences over other new schools founded at various status levels during and immediately subsequent to the period. In this process *Tom Brown* and *Eric* played a part in setting up two different, but competing models of the way in which a Christian gentleman should be educated. Ultimately a reconciliation occurred in the more secular model found in Reed's stories. Reed in these social circumstances wrote a series of stories which firmed up the genre, boys' school stories. These books fell within the limits of the contemporary relations of expectations and the Religious Tract Society acted as a capitalist entrepreneur, though itself in pursuit of the morally based policy of providing worthwhile literature for adolescents. Other publishers soon followed this lead, but in search of profits and with very different outcomes. In the next chapter two exemplars of what was to come will be discussed before in the penultimate chapter the ending of this genre is outlined.

7

Exemplars of Change

Two novels are important in the genre during the next period as exemplars of the great changes that occurred. These are Rudyard Kipling's *Stalky and Co.* (1899) and Alec Waugh's *The Loom of Youth* (1917). They will be closely examined here prior to looking at the more detailed developments in the next chapter. *Stalky and Co.* was written by an already established writer, aged forty-four, for boys, but was also much read by men. *The Loom of Youth* was written by an unknown boy of seventeen for men, but was also read and reacted to by boys. Both were critical of public schools and of some school stories – Waugh more so than Kipling. The genre was not only becoming increasingly critical, but it was, in addition, differentiating into school stories for adults and those for boys with a broad ground in the middle where some school stories could be and were read by both men and boys.

Stalky and Co.

Rudyard Kipling (Carrington, 1955; Wilson, 1977)

Rudyard Kipling was born in Bombay in 1865 and was brought to England in 1871 by his parents who then returned to India where his father was employed in an Art School in Bombay until 1875, when he became Principal of the School of Art and Curator of the Central Museum at Lahore. After an unhappy year with foster-parents in Southsea Kipling went to the United Services College at Westward Ho! in Devon, a new public school founded in 1874 (later to move to London), with the aim of providing a cheap education for the sons of army officers. The first headmaster, Cormell Price, whilst at Oxford one of the William Morris set, was a family friend and known to Kipling as 'Uncle Crom'. It was to Cormell Price that Kipling dedicated *Stalky and Co.* Kipling spent a happy four years at Westward Ho! Due to his poor sight he was unable to play team games, but he spent his time out of doors, swimming, walking, and in escapades which formed much of the material upon which *Stalky and Co.* was to be based. Price encouraged him in his literary bent and made him editor of the school magazine.

In 1882 Kipling returned to India where he remained as a journalist. He spent the first five years on the staff of the *Civil and Military Gazette* in Lahore and the final two years on the *Pioneer* at Allahabad. In 1889 he returned to London through the USA, after the immense success of *Departmental Ditties* (1886), *Plain Tales from the Hills* (1888), and various other Indian poems and stories. Though he travelled widely and, after his marriage to an American, Carrie Balestier, in 1892, lived in New England for four years, he only visited India once more, and then briefly, in 1891.

On his return to Britain, Kipling published his first novel, *The Light that Failed* (1890). This novel was succeeded by four others in the next eleven years, all ostensibly for adults, in three of which adolescents played the major part. These novels were *Captains Courageous* (1897), *Stalky and Co.* (1899) and *Kim* (1901). In addition, in 1892 Kipling, together with his brother-in-law Wolcott Balestier (who died in 1891), wrote *The Naulahka*, in which a young Indian prince plays a minor role. Kipling wrote four other books specifically for children: *The Jungle Book* (1895), *Just So Stories* (1902), *Puck of Pook's Hill* (1906) and *Rewards and Fairies* (1910). He also wrote a number of short stories about children, particularly but not entirely in his earlier years, of which *Wee Willie Winkie* (1888) is an example, and in 1910 he wrote the verses for C.R.L. Fletcher's school text, *History of England*. Kipling was awarded the Nobel Prize for Literature in 1907 and by then had become a major, though not by any means an uncriticised, literary figure in Britain and internationally. His reputation declined somewhat in his later years. He died in 1936 within a few days of King George V with whom he was friendly and seemed to hold many views in common.

Kipling mainly wrote about and for middle-class children. At the end of the Victorian era when the idea of Empire was beginning to be criticised and when Britain's imperial dream was challenged almost for the first time in several generations by, of all people, the Boers, Kipling had three central lessons to teach to children, especially those who were destined to be leaders – or their wives. They were to continue to grow, certainly into adulthood and, if possible, through life; they were to be active; and they were to show initiative, at least when appropriate (Musgrave, 1981).

Growth or 'becoming' was a central feature of the educational philosophy that, around the turn of the century, Dewey was beginning to sketch out systematically and to popularise in the USA. Kipling demonstrates it best in *Kim* and in a less complex way in *Captains Courageous*, in both of which the use of episodes to structure the story is very different in character from their use in *Stalky and Co.* or the *Jungle Books*. In the latter, whatever lessons are emphasised, there is not the same sense of growth through time under circumstances that are often unplanned or at least planned so that the learner is unconscious of their constraint.

Not all becoming nor all activity is necessarily good and a moral code is needed to give direction. Kipling's sense of his country's historical heritage, particularly as it had been worked out in responsibility for the Empire, governed his views of morality. In addition to such individual moral qualities of courage, steadfastness, self-control and forethought as are praised in his well known poem 'If' (1910), social morality was, therefore, important. The young who were to be the leaders in the dangerous years ahead in the early twentieth century were to become committed to their country and its Empire in order to rule with responsibility. Moral integrity for Kipling's ideal children was largely determined socially by the contemporary trials and tribulations of the Empire as he perceived them. This dedication to 'the day's work', a title used by Kipling for a relatively early collection of short stories (1898), was in direct opposition to one strong literary current in late nineteenth-century Britain, the Aesthetes led by Wilde and Beardsley. Kipling, though never the centre of a coterie, served as both a leader and a rallying point for the move from passivity to activity in art. Furthermore, art was not to be isolated from life, but had crucial application to the way life was lived.

Activity could be along lines seen to be eternally good or could be constrained by contemporary social forces. It could, however, take new forms in an attempt to change the world. Kipling was willing to encourage initiative, perhaps rather to counter attacks on the heritage of the past that he saw to be threatened than to create a new social framework. Kipling, very early in his life in India, had felt, in a way akin to his French contemporary, Durkheim, the fragility of the social structure. He wanted to preserve order and had a strong sense of hierarchy, as he showed in, for example, *Stalky and Co.*, *Captains Courageous*, the *Jungle Books* and in many of his stories about army life. Yet he knew initiative and resourcefulness were needed in the world at large – 'Stalkiness', as he had termed it. In India he had seen the need for initiative at quite low levels in the hierarchy of government under stress of crisis.

There is an unresolved tension here between order and change. Dobrée believed Kipling's position to be: 'It is hopeless to try to alter the world' (1964: 42). But this is too simple a description of Kipling's view of the principle upon which children should be educated. Children must grow to take their place in the campaign to stop the moral rot that Kipling saw undermining Britain's position in the world after the late Victorian years and to preserve their country's heritage which included the Empire. In this latter respect Kipling saw one of the reasons for 'bearing the white man's burden' to be to enable the ruled themselves to become mature enough, admittedly by white man's criteria, to rule themselves – 'The cry of hosts ye humour (ah, slowly!) toward the light.' Thus Kipling did believe that education, albeit much of it unconscious learning from experience or in well-chosen settings, which were unrecognised as such by the learners, could help to change the direction in which the world was going.

Stalky and Co.[1]

In 1899, Rudyard Kipling's *Stalky and Co.* was published. It was totally different in style, structure, and moral atmosphere from books based on the model of Hughes and Farrar. Using hindsight we may say that, as so often with Kipling, it was a precursor of much to come. By his own admission, Kipling's aim was didactic. In his autobiography, Kipling wrote of his idea for 'some tracts or parables on the education of the young', which became *Stalky and Co.*: he thought this book to be 'a truly valuable collection of

---

[1] All references are to page numbers in Macmillan's Pocket Edition of the Works of Rudyard Kipling.

tracts'. The style of the book, however, is far from overtly moralising. Indeed, more than once, characters in the book comment on the tradition of Frederick Farrar in such words as 'we ain't going to have any beastly Erickin' ' (137). Kipling never explicitly stated what the lessons were that he was aiming to press home in *Stalky and Co.* The intention here is to make clear one view of what those lessons may have been and to show why these lessons were at the time important to Kipling. *Stalky and Co.* contains nine short stories linked by common characters and – except in the case of the last story – a common environment; a number of other similar stories were written but were considered by Kipling as not worthy of inclusion in the book, although they were later published elsewhere. The stories focus upon the activities of a group of three close friends at Westward Ho!. The main explicit aim of the school was, as already stated, to provide an education for those who wanted to enter the services or some arm of the imperial public service. During Kipling's time there (1878-82) 'eighty per cent of the boys had been born abroad . . .; seventy-five per cent were sons of officers in one or other of the services. . . . looking to follow their fathers' profession' (210). The three friends were Corkran, nicknamed 'Stalky' – in later life Major-General L. Dunsterville; M'Turk – in fact G.C. Beresford; and 'Beetle' – Kipling himself. The stories concerning Stalky and Co., who were described to their faces by King, one of the housemasters in the school, as 'allied forces of disorder' (41), are tersely written, largely in dialogue; have great pace; and abound in comic incidents. Hence the book grasps the interest and is easy to read. Each of the stories can be read separately and demonstrates, as will be shown later, why 'Stalky' was given his nickname and much else besides.

A recent reading of *Stalky and Co.* has concentrated on the fact that Westward Ho! was a school 'in which social position is determined by who can gain physical and psychological control over others' (Piehl, 1978). This emphasis on power is one way of reading *Stalky and Co.* but provides a limiting view, since the lessons that Kipling apparently wished to impart in his 'parables' seem to relate to the aims of control and to the nature of the relationships within the school. These lessons will be shown to concern two main foci: first and more traditionally, the relationships within the hierarchy of the school and, second and, although more uniquely, of equal importance, the expression of initiative within such a hierarchical structure. Control had to be exercised

within a school community which, if only because of the wide
bounds permitted to the boys, stretched out to affect local
shopkeepers and landowners. Yet within this ordered series of
relationships, initiative had to be displayed by at least some of the
boys if the full benefits of the communal educational process were
to be gained.

The hierarchy

The boys formed the lowest rung of the school hierarchy. Within
this group, however, there were important degrees of status,
largely determined by the Form in which a boy was. Third
Formers were at the bottom and acted as Fags, although this
system at Westward Ho! was not a severe one. Fifth Formers
might be allowed to share studies of their own – Stalky and Co.
inhabited Number Five study – and, therefore, have some
privacy. Sixth Formers often, but not always, prefects; regular
exceptions were those older boys who had been rejected by army
'crammers', but who were accepted by the school – they came to
Westward Ho! because of its good record of success in
examinations for entry to Sandhurst. Unlike many public school
boys these had to work at their academic studies if they were to
achieve their aim in life.

The masters formed the middle level in the school, but their
authority, and hence, their status – and the same was true of the
prefects – were not assured; they had to be earned. The boys
constantly and ruthlessly tested their masters; as Stalky put it,
'Not the least good having a row with a master unless you make
an ass of him' (50). One passage in particular indicates the results
of this process in terms of what authority was accepted by the
boys:

> Number Five had spent some cautious years in testing the
> Reverend John. He was emphatically a gentleman. He
> knocked at a study door before entering; he comported
> himself as a visitor and not a strayed lictor, he never prosed,
> and he never carried over into official life the confidences of
> idle hours. Prout was ever an unmitigated nuisance; King
> came solely as the avenger of blood; even little Hartopp,
> talking natural history, seldom forgot his office; but the
> Reverend John was a guest desired and beloved by Number
> Five. (130)

Above all others was the headmaster. At Westward Ho! he had

earned immense respect for a number of reasons. He rarely interfered openly in the running of the school, but when he did, he was considered absolutely fair. Furthermore, he was not, as most headmasters of public schools, a cleric. As Beetle put it, 'But he's awfully fair. He doesn't lick a chap in the morning and preach at him in the afternoon.' Stalky called him 'a downy bird' (131); this was high praise and meant that the head could see through Stalky's ploys and was wise enough to deal with them aptly and quickly. More than once he summarily thrashed the three friends, openly admitting it to be 'flagrant injustice' (128); yet they accepted his punishment with no question. The head ultimately won the school's absolute loyalty by putting his own life in danger in order to save one of his pupils from diphtheria; he sucked the infection from the boy's throat through a tube. For this he was cheered by the school at the final assembly before the holidays. Interpreting this as impudence, he decided to punish the whole Lower School with three hundred lines apiece and the Upper School with a beating. When he was told the reason for the cheering, he let the Lower School off their punishment but stuck to that for the Upper School because of their 'insolence' to the master in charge of 'prep.' before his arrival on the scene. He began to cane each senior boy before shaking his hand and saying 'Good-bye'; the cheering continued and even this man ultimately 'gave it up in despair' (186).

Set slightly apart was the nonteaching staff. Symbolically, the main figure with whom Kipling dealt was 'Foxy', the school sergeant. His status was obviously lower than the masters, but, as in the case of the senior NCO in a battalion, he had direct access to the man in command, here the headmaster. This was accepted by the boys, and the relationship between the head and Foxy was such that the head learnt much more of what went on in the school, perhaps because from a different viewpoint, than he did through his housemasters. Other nonteaching staff are mentioned; in the story entitled 'An Unsavoury Interlude' reference is made to a house servant called Richards, a former naval Other Rank. Stalky and Co. managed to put a dead cat between the floor boards in King's house, whose members had accused their house of 'stinking'. As the corpse putrified, the smell spread through the house. Richards ultimately found the source of the trouble and discovered that the cat had not, as was believed, died there chasing a mouse, but had been placed there. However, his own house loyalty stopped him telling the full details of his discovery to the authorities. ' 'Twas on the born tip o' my tongue to tell, tu, but . . . he said us niver washed, he did. Let his dom boys call us "stinkers", he did. Sarved um dom well raight, I say!' (98).

In all complex organisations, informal groupings develop, which act in many ways contrary to the formal norms of the system. One such was Stalky and Co. One of the most remarkable stories in the book, 'The Moral Reformers', tells of how the school padre, Reverend John, called in the aid of Stalky and Co. to improve the moral tone of their house when two 'crammer's rejects' were bullying a Third Former. Ironically, Stalky and Co. achieved their aim by physical brutality that probably exceeded that exhibited by the bullies whom they were reforming. A reader cannot fail to find something comic in the description of this incident, but equally cannot but ask himself whether he ought to be laughing. The padre knew of their methods but approved of the end.

> 'Boys educate each other, they say, more than we can or dare. If I had used one half of the moral suasion you may or may not have employed – '
>
> 'With the best motives in the world. Don't forget our pious motives, Padre,' said M'Turk.
>
> 'I suppose I should be now languishing in Bideford jail, shouldn't I? Well, to quote the Head, in a little business which we have agreed to forget, that strikes me as flagrant injustice . . . . ' (157)

And off they all went, master (padre) and boys, to bathe together in the sea.

Initiative

In his dedicatory poem at the beginning of *Stalky and Co.* Kipling made clear the manifest aim of the school hierarchy:

> This we learnt from famous men
> Teaching in our borders,
> Who declared it was best,
> Safest, easiest and best –
> Expeditious, wise and best –
> To obey your orders.

But absolute obedience and taking one's expected place in the system was only part of the lesson to be taught and learnt. At this point an explanation of Stalky's nickname is relevant. In the story,

'Stalky', not included in *Stalky and Co.*, but published later, Kipling provides the explicit clue, ' "Stalky" in their school vocabulary, meant clever, well-considered and wily, as applied to plans of action; and "stalkiness" was the one virtue Corkran toiled after' (Kipling, 1923: 133). The repeated message of *Stalky and Co.* is that within the hierarchy of the school, initiative of a certain type is permissible, although if actions infringe rules or exceed the conventional bounds, on discovery punishment must be expected and accepted.

Furthermore, the tacitly accepted values of common sense are all-important – what the dedicatory poem calls, 'God's own Common Sense/Which is more than knowledge'. In 'The Flag of their Country', a Member of Parliament visits the school to give an address on patriotism. So shocked are the boys that their most private values should be discussed in public that they refuse to applaud the Union Jack which the speaker displays as his conclusion: 'he profaned the most secret places of their souls with outcries and gesticulations' (212).

This unwritten code of conduct gave much room for manoeuvre to wily boys. In achieving their enterprises, Stalky and Co. were quite ruthless in the way in which they used others, whether boys, staff or members of the local community. When they wished to get their own back on the Lower Third for assaulting Beetle, they wrecked their form room and destroyed many of the personal belongings of the Third Formers: 'It was a great wreckage and the form-room looked as though three conflicting tempests had smitten it' (60). When they wished to score off the housemaster, King, Stalky managed to provoke a local carrier to throw stones through his study window; flying glass both damaged King's leather-bound books and cut a junior boy who was with him at the time. To cover their late return for roll-call, they tampered with the town gas supply so the lights failed. Finally, in 'In Ambush', they were even capable of causing a local landowner to sack his gamekeeper, fundamentally so that they could have an undisturbed place out of bounds in which to smoke during summer afternoons. They then befriended his successor so that they could the more easily obtain specimens of various wild animals to give to Hartopp, the master who ran the Natural History Society, membership in which allowed them legally to go out of bounds to their smoking place.

Stalky and Co. used not only blatant coercion to carry their enterprises to success. Where possible, psychological pressure was also used. In 'The Last Term' they arranged for a local girl to kiss a prefect in front of them and then used their knowledge of this incident against the prefects who attempted to discipline them for being 'too cheeky to the Sixth' (233).

Conclusion

Kipling, then, presented a paradoxical duo of lessons – on the one hand, obedience to the expectations of a hierarchical system whose core values were implicitly rather than explicitly understood and, on the other hand, the permissibility, even the encouragement, of initiative, pursued by morally questionable means, though in large matters for unquestionable ends. Why did Kipling at the end of the nineteenth century want some schools to pass on these particular lessons?

Kipling began *Stalky and Co.* in 1896 on his return to Britain after living for four years in the United States. The following year was the year of Queen Victoria's Golden Jubilee. During this year Kipling published the poem 'Recessional', with its reminder of the possible passing of Empire ('Lo, all our pomp of yesterday/Is one with Nineveh and Tyre'). In 1898 he published another famous poem, 'The White Man's Burden', the first lines of which were

> Take up the White Man's burden –
> Send forth the best ye breed –
> Go bind your sons to exile
> To serve your captives' need; . . .

Kipling knew and, on the whole, admired the way in which the British exercised their imperial responsibilities in India. In 1891 he had briefly visited the Cape, and in 1898 he did so again, making the acquaintance of Alfred Milner, the High Commissioner, and becoming a close friend of Cecil Rhodes. Under Rhodes's sponsorship he spent some time upcountry, gaining some idea of the size and future problems of what came to be called 'Black Africa'.

Kipling believed in a strong Britain, holding responsible power over a great Empire, especially in its paternal form over less fortunate black people. He was a farsighted man and felt the rumblings of national doubt and the early signs of inefficiency – administrative and also, in his view, moral – which would soon be clearly shown by our conduct of the Boer War. In *Stalky and Co.* he indicated what seemed to him to be the lessons of the times for the public schools, the main source of future leaders for Britain and the Empire at that time.

The causes for Kipling's presumed views have been sought outside the text itself, but supporting evidence can also be found within *Stalky and Co*. First, we may appeal again to the dedicatory poem. Though the schools had to produce

> Men of little showing –
> For their work continueth,
> And their work continueth,
> Broad and deep continueth,
> Greater than their knowing!

they also had to take account that

> Some beneath the further stars
> Bear the greater burden.

Second, we may note that the final story, 'Slaves of the Lamp, Part II', tells of how Stalky, now in the Indian Army, against all odds worsted a group of tribesmen on the North West Frontier, breaking every rule in the book and ending up with an hour's 'wiggin' like a bad little boy' (271) from the Commander-in-Chief himself; this he accepted almost as an honour in itself just as if he were accepting a beating from his former headmaster.

Kipling's book is different in one important aspect from the great majority of the other books of the genre which have been examined previously. Development of character is not a prime focus of the plot. Partly as a result of this, but mainly because of Kipling's own beliefs and experiences at school, organised games play a very minor part in *Stalky and Co*. The structure of *Stalky and Co*. is akin to that of A.R. Hope's books to which reference was made in the last chapter and which take the form of a series of interrelated short tales. *Stalky and Co*. is about a boys' public boarding school and this school is seen from the point of view of the boys. It is very much hierarchical in organisation and aims to inculcate a well-articulated set of values. This does imply development, but this process is not the main business of the book. Because Kipling's aim was didactic it is the values that are central to *Stalky and Co*. There is a basic similarity between much of the schoolboys' moral code in Kipling's book and in Reed's stories. But once again the family is given very little part to play, though in such novels as *Captains Courageous* Kipling did put more weight upon the influence of parents. However, patriotism is very much more important than in previous schoolboy stories, but not in the *English* way in which Thomas Hughes wrote of his country, rather in an Imperial manner that fitted well Kipling's purpose and view of his times.

Reception

In 1891 Oscar Wilde commented on Kipling: 'He is our first authority on the second rate.' A writer of a letter to *The Times*, however, took the view that 'there is no reason why Mr Rudyard Kipling should not select vulgarity as his subject matter, or part of it' (Green, 1971: 104). There was a basic disagreement at the time about the place of realism in fiction. The influence from France of writers like Zola was being felt in Britain and they were seen as realistic in method and attitude. Realism is a very difficult concept to define in literature, since every work of fiction is itself a construct, a set of material chosen from all that is available and, hence, in a sense relative to any other version of the events portrayed. Welleck has written that realism can be seen as 'a system of norms dominating a specific time . . . which we can set clearly apart from the norms of the periods that precede and follow it' (Welleck, 1963: 225). Elsewhere he has defined realism

> as a term to describe a method or an attitude in art and literature – at first an exceptional accuracy of representation, later a commitment to describing real events and showing this as they actually exist. (ibid., 217).

Kipling's writing did always use an immense amount of detail about all manner of situations, whether in school or barrack-room, and it was this approach to which Wilde took exception.

But with his readers this detail was part of his attraction and *Stalky and Co.*, a detailed account of schooling, was an immediate success, certainly in financial terms, though some critics were most unapproving of it. Furthermore, despite disapproval, it continued to sell. The pocket edition first published by Macmillan in 1908 was reprinted in 1909, 1911, 1912, 1913, 1914, 1916, 1917 (twice), 1918, 1919, 1920, 1921, 1922, and 1924 (twice) . . . . This was necessary because *Stalky and Co.* came to be seen as a general work of fiction, not merely as a boys' school story with didactic intent. There was an adult readership from the beginning. Thus, at the *BOP* 'Coming of Age Dinner', held in October 1899, the Archdeacon of London in his speech admitted that he had recently read *Stalky and Co.* He felt that the book did not give 'a just and true picture of schoolboy life' either at the present time or

in the recent past. 'There was no school of importance in the land
to-day where masters were all fools, or the boys quite as given
over to wild escapades as *Stalky and Co.*' (Warner, 1976: 138-9). In
a way Kipling was continuing the critical stance towards school
masters that Anstey had started in *Vice Versa* seventeen years
previously. Indeed, in 1914, Ian Hay, a former schoolmaster, who
became a most successful author himself, took the opposite view
of Kipling: 'He hits the sentimentalist hard. . . . He has drawn
masters as they've never been drawn before. . . . He depicts, too,
very faithfully, the curious cameraderie which prevails nowadays
between boys and masters. (Hay, 1914: 158). Ian Hay's last point is
an interesting one in commenting upon a new development in the
schools, very different from Tom Brown's views of masters as
'natural enemies'.

On 14 October 1899 two London periodicals published
substantial anonymous reviews of *Stalky and Co.* The *Athenaeum*
was, on the whole, favourable to the book, whilst the *Academy*
took a more critical view. The review in the *Athenaeum* thought
that despite its episodic structure the book gave 'a tolerably
complete picture of a certain school organisation – a military
preparatory school in North Devon'. The *Academy* went a little
further, saying, 'Stalky and Co. is the book of empire-makers in
the making.' The *Athenaeum* noted the underlying lesson of the
story called 'The Flag of their Country', 'the abhorrence of
English boys – and, for the matter of that, of English men – of
having their most sacred feelings referred to in public.' This
comment reveals the fact that emotional restraint was now seen as
an important lesson to be learnt or reinforced at school. In
addition, its tone is somewhat at odds with the view that Kipling
in *Stalky and Co.* was an out-and-out jingoist.

Despite its generally favourable comments the *Athenaeum* also
noted 'some slight hits not in the very best taste at Dr Farrar's
books' and in one passage summed up much that many saw as
central, by some to be praised and by others to be condemned, to
the character moulded and approved of in these schools:

> *Stalky and Co.* is almost a complete treatise on the strategy
> and tactics of the British schoolboy – or perhaps one should
> say the British public-school boy. Reverence for the head
> authority and contempt for all other authority, respect for
> moral aspects of physical training, and utter indifference
> towards the training of the intellect, underlies the whole

Stimmung of the book. Mr Kipling has taught the public how Matthew Arnold's Barbarians are trained.

The reviewer in the *Academy* found both *Eric* and *Stalky and Co.* to be wrong about boys; he considered that 'you will find more of him in Tom Brown and Tom Sawyer than anywhere else'. Both reviewers were making rather a similar reading, but the *Athenaeum* saw this as true whereas to the *Academy* this was not so.

As already indicated, whatever the critics thought, *Stalky and Co.* sold. By the 1940s the same battle continued: a true picture versus a jingoistic lack of realism. H.G. Wells, for instance, perhaps predictably, thought 'snob cads' could find a congenial ideology in *Stalky and Co.* 'in which the idea of nasty little quasi-upper-class boys taking the law into their own hands was glorified' (Wells, 1944: 33). Yet this same book was seen to have sufficient literary quality and to be far enough beyond moral reproof to be used apparently quite often as a text for thirteen-year-olds in English lessons in boys' senior schools (Jenkinson, 1940: 124-7).

The Loom of Youth

Alec Waugh

In July 1917 the publisher, Grant Richards, brought out *The Loom of Youth*, an autobiographical first novel by Alec Waugh, then aged eighteen, about his four years as a boy at Sherborne, the English public school. This book was an immediate success. Despite wartime paper restrictions, it ran to seven impressions before the year's end amidst a mixture of critical acclaim and public furore.

Alec Waugh, born in 1898, the elder brother of the more famous Evelyn, was the son of Arthur Waugh. Evelyn once described their father as 'a Man of Letters . . . a category, like the maiden aunt, that is now almost extinct' (Waugh, 1964: 73). He had left Oxford in 1890 with a third class degree and gone into publishing and literary journalism. His name was made by the lucky coincidence that his biography of Tennyson was published a few weeks after Tennyson's death in 1892. He contributed an essay to the first *Yellow Book* and later calculated that he had reviewed about 6000 books in his life. From 1904 to 1930 he was managing director of the publishers Chapman & Hall.

In 1907 Alec Waugh went to a preparatory school at Haslemere, Surrey, prior to going in 1911 to Sherborne, his father's old school, where he was by many counts a success. Sherborne itself was a school that under Nowell G. Smith (1903-1927) was, according to Cecil Day Lewis who went there in 1917, 'pulling out of the last of several crises' though there were 'still swampy pockets left'. His own house was the worst and he was soon initiated into 'immorality'. Certainly, in retrospect, Day Lewis felt that Sherborne was 'a games mad school'; 'the felt centre of school life for most of my generation was not the chapel but the playing field' (Day Lewis, 1960: 105-6; 111-2; 125). In a sense Waugh was lucky in that the First World War broke out in the autumn of 1914 and he returned to a school from which most of the senior boys had left to join the armed forces. Thus, he moved into positions of responsibility more quickly than he might have expected. In what was to be his final year he was captain of his house, in the sixth form, the XV and the XI, and won the school prize for English literature. However, in the middle of the last term of his fourth year an old homosexual episode, long closed, became known to the staff. The normal consequence was expulsion, but due to the time that had passed since the 'offence', Waugh's seniority and his subsequent success at school, the headmaster, despite some opposition from the staff who saw Waugh as rebellious, arranged that he leave at the end of the summer term of 1915. But for this affair Waugh might never have written *The Loom of Youth*; he would still have been at the school that, despite his serious criticism of it, he loved. He himself later saw *The Loom of Youth* as 'a love letter to Sherborne' written to a mistress who had recently ended a long affair (Waugh, 1962: 82). Thus, for Waugh the novel was loving, but critical. In a poem, 'Sherborne Abbey', published a year later, he demonstrated this rebellious love by writing 'For half my wayward heart is buried there'.

When Alec Waugh left school in July 1915 he joined the army. In 1916 he passed into Sandhurst, being commissioned as a machine-gunner in 1917. He wrote *The Loom of Youth* in seven and a half weeks early in 1916 largely during evenings after military training had ended for the day. Having no desire to use his father's position he offered his novel to five other London firms without success. As a result of these refusals he decided to put his book away until after the war, but due to the intervention either of S.P.B. Mais, who had taught him at Sherborne, or of Thomas Seccombe, then Professor of History at Sandhurst and an old friend of Arthur Waugh, the manuscript was sent to Grant Richards who accepted it.

The Loom of Youth[2]

The Loom of Youth is a largely autobiographical novel, tracing the development year by year of the hero, Gordon Carruthers. Waugh on purpose says almost nothing of life away from school. 'I wanted to write about school exclusively' (Waugh, 1962: 40). From the loneliness of Gordon's first day at school through the way fear is overcome in his first house match to the resolution of his feelings about Fernhurst during his final days there the novel is full of detail, economically used to purpose. It is that purpose which must now be analysed.

In Part I, 'Warp and Woof', Gordon soon loses the innocence of the preparatory school. The conversation of his peers 'ran entirely on games, scandal and the work they had not done' (42). He quickly saw 'the sure way to popularity lay in success on the field' (31). He aspired to be captain of his house, School House. Not unnaturally he took to 'cribbing'. During his second year, described in Part II, 'The Tangled Skein', Gordon, having a strong personality, began to rebel against the conformity demanded by masters and senior boys. He did not have the success for which he hoped at games and concluded, 'If he were to remain in the public gaze, he would have to attract attention some other way' (136). He then 'earned a reputation for reckless bravado and disregard of all authority that stuck to him throughout his whole career' (136). But his study mate, Tester, the son of a minor poet, at this time introduced him to Swinburne. As a result, Gordon thenceforth always read much, especially poetry but also came to hate 'the system that had kept literature from him as a shut book' (154).

During the summer holidays before his third year, described in Part III, 'Unravelling the Threads', Arnold Lunn's *The Harrovians* (1913) was published. Gordon was much concerned about the way its criticism affected the Fernhurst that he now loved. He was assured of its truth by a Harrovian friend of his father, who also

[2]All page references are to the Pocket Library Edition, Cassell, London, 1929.

told him that 'it was the system that was at fault, not Fernhurst' (156). He soon forgot his introspective thoughts about the effect of school and though now in the sixth form 'rebellion was . . . at the time almost a religion with him' (183). Tester warned him of his foolishness and the likelihood of expulsion as a result, but, though Gordon realised this to be true, he remained rebellious and still wanted to change things for the better. 'A great battle was before him; he would have to go into it strong. . . . There must be no chink in his coat of mail' (205) – again a metaphor from chivalry. After one of his battles with a housemaster, nicknamed 'the Bull', Gordon was sitting in the Abbey courtyard when a girl sat down beside him and 'smiled at him invitingly. He took no notice' (171). Yet he did spend a few passionate hours with a girl in the middle of one night when as a result of a foolish challenge he broke bounds to go to a carnival in the town. By the summer term Gordon had moved from the classical sixth to the supposedly less rigorous history sixth.

In August 1914 war broke out and Gordon returned to Fernhurst for what proved to be his last year, described in Part IV, 'The Weaving', to find most of the senior boys had enlisted. Unexpectedly 'he had achieved his goal at last' (209). He was captain of the house, in the first XV and first XI, a prefect, and a joint editor of the school magazine. Yet he also now

> saw that for years generation after generation of Fern-hurstians had worshipped at the altar of a little tin god. He saw athleticism, as it really was, shorn of its glamour, and he knew its poverty. It led no whither. (290)

At this time of great self-questioning, despite his lack of religious feeling, he came to feel that 'in the Roman Church at any rate there [might be] something permanent' (309). This foreshadowing of his brother Evelyn's course could have owed something to the thoughts of Michael Fane, hero of Compton Mackenzie's *Sinister Street* (1913) a book mentioned in *The Loom of Youth*. In his last term in a battle for power, Gordon becomes *de facto* head of house in place of Rudd, the boy whose challenge had led him to go to the carnival. 'Now his outward triumph was even more pronounced' (326). He then made eighty-five runs in his last house match. Yet still he felt his school career to be a failure. Only on his last day did he 'see it all clearly':

> He had failed because he had set out to gain only the things

that the world valued. . . . In his haste he had said that
Fernhurst had taught him nothing. He had been wrong. . . .
It had taught him to rely upon himself. (346-7)

Though Gordon Carruthers is central to the novel his
development is traced in his relationship with masters and boys.
Gordon had soon 'learnt to loath all masters in the abstract. They
were all right in themselves' (54). At the moment Gordon leaves
the classical sixth Waugh ironically juxtaposes Kipling's 'Let us
now praise famous men' with a description of cribbing. Tester
had told him, 'The really brilliant men don't take up schoolmastering' (161); the masters were 'all in a groove, all worship-
ping the same tin god' (162). Gordon himself sums up his views at
his last prize-giving:

> There they were, the teachers of youth most of whom had
> never at any time penetrated to the heart of anything. They
> were automata, machines for repeating the same old
> platitudes. (347-8)

Four masters are central to the novel. First, there is 'the Chief',
the headmaster and housemaster of School House. One reviewer
asked how a man portrayed so favourably could have chosen so
bad a staff (*Times Literary Supplement*, 26 July 1917). Since Nowell
Smith had only been appointed in 1909, Waugh's portrayal of the
staff is understandable. Certainly in Gordon's eyes 'the Chief'
seemed, as was in real life the case, 'a brilliant scholar' (162), but
'unassuming' and with 'a clearsighted unprejudiced mind', one
who could appreciate a joke (190-1). But Gordon could not
understand how 'the Chief' with all his wisdom could congratulate him on his work as a prefect and fail to see 'how far his
achievements were below his possibilities' (342). Because
Gordon's admiration of 'the Chief' is so explicit the characterisation in the novel seems less detailed than perhaps would be
expected.

The same is true of another master, who was certainly central
to the purpose of the book, namely Rogers, the chaplain and
officer-in-charge of the Officers' Training Corps. He preached
sermons in chapel which in view of what Gordon knew of the
school and its ethos seemed hypocritical in the extreme. As
Waugh himself later pointed out (Waugh, 1962: 52) the assumed
code of public school morals was that portrayed in Kipling's story
'The Brushwood Boy' (Kipling, 1898). Boys, like the men they

were to become, worked hard (honestly) and played hard (within the rules), spoke cleanly and were 'pure', holding no double standard of behaviour for the two sexes. For Gordon this was clearly hypocrisy. He was, therefore, contemptuous of Rogers. Nor was the situation improved when Rogers preached in chapel against *The Harrovians*. When the war began and the Corps was given more importance, Gordon ragged Rogers, but he 'had never been a king, and it was by no means important to bring his work into ridicule' (282-3).

The opposite was true of 'the Bull', an old Fernhurstian and a housemaster, who had played rugby for Oxford and England and was in charge of school football. Even when 'the Bull' was criticising him for his behaviour, Gordon was 'filled with an immense admiration for this man who thought only of Fernhurst. . . . If only his love . . . had not made him so complete an egoist' (170). A series of clashes, all connected with games, occurred between the two. 'The Bull' came to believe that Gordon put house before school. 'We must not have bad feeling between the houses. Honest rivalry is alright, but there seems so much spite about it all nowadays' (231). Gordon thought that although 'the Bull' claimed to think only of Fernhurst, his real love was for his own house. Yet at his last prize-giving, unknown to 'the Bull', Gordon, somewhat inconsistently perhaps because of his own lack of decision about what he really did believe, 'looked at his old foe [as] a second Garibaldi, with a heart of gold, an indomitable energy, a splendid sincerity, the most loyal of Fernhurst's sons . . . so essentially big, so strong, so noble of heart, that it hardly mattered what he worshipped' (348).

Finally, there was 'Ferrers', in life S.P.B. Mais, who came to Fernhurst in 1913 and was one of 'the Chief's' new men. He was 'willing to get to the boys' level' (212) and, therefore, to many, was, as Tester said, 'an unmitigated nuisance. But . . . he [was] the only man who ever thinks for himself' (162). He was 'so absolutely different from anything that a master had appeared from time immemorial' (177). In his first term he spoke critically of the public schools at a debate, quoting *Sinister Street*. He discovered that Gordon was keen on poetry, invited him to tea and allowed him to use his library. Thus, Gordon entered a world of ideas away from normal school life. Ferrers did not have an easy existence as other masters attacked his 'loyalty' and his 'upsetting, irrational nonsensical notions'. However, he then used 'the only weapon left', his pen, writing many articles on reform of the public schools (Mais, 1916: 93). Gordon gained much from him, but he was not an uncritical disciple: 'The pity was that Ferrers was intolerant of the things he hated, while Buller was intolerant of the things he admired. It was very difficult' (259).

Some of the boys who are important characters are not portrayed in a complex way, possibly because Waugh does not want them to be seen as complex persons. This is true of Lovelace and Mansell, two of Gordon's earliest friends, who in his own words were 'honest Philistines' (183). Even they do not, as had been normal when writing of such boys, use talk 'Embellished with the argot of the Upper Fourth Remove' (Kipling, 1909). Two others are given much fuller personalities. Rudd was

a new type to him. It was clear he had some merits, especially pluck; and yet he was no good at games, and what was more extraordinary, did not seem in the least worried about his failures' (210)

Meeting Rudd and his friendship with Tester helped to widen Gordon's horizons.

Friendships of another nature played an important part at Fernhurst. Rendell, then head of Charterhouse, is reported to have said 'My boys are amorous, but seldom erotic' (Graves, 1929: 35). Amorous friendships usually occurred between older and younger boys. During his first term Gordon was invited by a prefect 'to meet him for a walk', but 'told him in polite language to go to the "devil" ' (43). Tester used to ask Gordon to leave the study as a younger boy was 'coming up here for a few minutes' (101). Romantic friendships were between boys of the same age. Gordon had such a friend, Morcambe, in his last year which made him 'indescribably happy' (295), though 'he knew that [this] friendship would lead to nothing' after they left school (320).

In his first year Gordon had struck up an acquaintance with an older boy, Jeffries, who was 'bunked' (expelled) for an erotic affair. Jeffries's comment immediately following this event is worth quoting in full since it sums up much of what *The Loom of Youth* aims to say:

'Unfair? Yes, that's the right word; it is unfair. Who made me what I am but Fernhurst? Two years ago I came here as innocent as Carruthers there; never knew anything. Fernhurst taught me everything; Fernhurst made me worship games, and think that they alone mattered, and everything else could go to the deuce. I heard men say about bloods whose lives were an open scandal, "Oh it's all right, they can play football". I thought it was all right too. Fernhurst made me think it was. And now Fernhurst, that has made me what I am, turns around and says, "You are not fit to be a member of this great school". And I have to go. Oh, it's fair, isn't it?' (57)

The school is seen as a system but it is the boys who suffer. The novel has a tightly argued thesis, focused around the central flaw in school structure namely, athleticism. In *Stalky and Co.* Kipling by his very omission of any account of organised games criticised athleticism by implication; Waugh did so openly. Two consequences stem from this flaw. First, intellectual matters and academic work are devalued. 'The system . . . loves mediocrity' (20); indeed, 'the one object of the Public School is to produce not great men, but a satisfactory type' (143). Second, within the school prestige depends upon success at games so that a group of older, usually anti-intellectual boys are worshipped by the younger ones. In an all-male, adolescent community emotional and sexually-laden problems are almost inevitable.

The interpretation put upon religion in the public schools aggravated the situation since any boy who had a thought in his head could see that the code of 'The Brushwood Boy' did not rule. This hypocritical stance in a dimension of school life claimed by many supporters of the public school to be central was compounded with a conspiracy of silence about any problems whatsoever that related to sex. In 1922 Waugh wrote that erotic friendship might be disgusting but

> The romantic friendship, on the other hand, is the dawn of love; . . . and because [a boy] experiences this emotion for the first time in an unnatural environment, his natural reaction is misdirected and misinformed. (Waugh, 1922: 160)

This was written after the failure of his own first marriage. It is perhaps too much to read this disassociation of love and its sexual experience into *The Loom of Youth*, but the other points of condemnation were there and were seen to be there by many of those who read the novel in the third year of war when some praised schools like Fernhurst for supplying such fine officers and leaders, whilst others criticised them for producing men who were unable 'to take their proper place in the national struggle for a right and far-sighted civilisation' (143).

Reception

The Loom of Youth was first published in late July 1917, was reprinted five times between July and September. It was a major success, received well both by the reading public and, by and large, the critics. The *Times Literary Supplement* (26 July 1917) described it as 'a most promising first book' by an author with 'something to say' and 'ability to say it', though the book was 'destructive rather than constructive'; the characters were not individually 'overdrawn, but collectively they comprised a caricatured staff'. The book received major notice in the *New Statesman* (4 August 1917) – the characters were so interesting that 'it is their minds, not their external activities, that we bother about'; the *Spectator* (4 August 1917) – 'a picture of the twentieth century schoolboy by himself'; the *Nation* (4 August 1917) – 'attacks upon [the conventions of public school life] are so bitterly resented'; *Land and Water* (9 August 1917) – 'a novel at seventeen'; the *Bystander* (21 August 1917) – compared the author to Lunn who 'started the modern idea that the fetish of games and athletics is ruining our public schools' – Kipling's views were either forgotten or unrealised. A month later 'Wayfarer' in the *Nation* (15 September 1917) saw it as

> an almost miraculous production [with] evils and short-comings . . . and yet I thought it sufficiently delicate. . . . [It is] a revolutionary work – if only the parents of England will read it, and having read it act on it.

Discussion was wide and when the schools commenced their new year in September boys discussed *The Loom of Youth* amongst themselves. Sermons were preached against it at Sherborne (Fernhurst), though C. Day Lewis in his first term there claimed that 'those who had read smuggled copies knew it was true; boys did swear and blaspheme and practise immorality' (Day Lewis, 1960: 112-13). Here can be seen the tendency as time passed to put as great an emphasis on the aspects of morality touched upon by Waugh as on athleticism. Waugh himself possibly compounded his sins by an ironical short piece in the *Nation* (6 October 1917) about a pre-battle church parade which stirred up controversy, apparently even involving Horatio Bottomley (*Nation*, 27 October 1917). Not surprisingly Grant Richards advertised that a new edition of 3,000 was 'nearly ready' (*Times Literary Supplement*, 22 November 1917).

Just prior to this in the *Spectator* (10 November 1917) there appeared an article of some 1,700 words entitled 'The Public School in Fiction' by 'Mere Schoolmaster'. The author claimed that 'the school story' was no longer for 'school boys', but was 'the chief weapon in the armoury of those who assail the Public School system'. Lunn was mentioned, but Waugh was the main target. *The Loom of Youth* was ascribed to 'the morbid imagination of a very unusual boy'. The schools did need careful reform, because they were easy to destroy. The task of the schoolmaster was a difficult one, calling for moral more than academic qualifications. 'The average British schoolboy is unintellectual', but that was the fault of his home. 'There is some truth in what is said about athleticism', but the picture is overdrawn. Once again the school reflects the society. The same arguments were given in answer to Waugh's attacks on honesty and morality. Finally, 'criticism is easy, to appreciate requires penetration . . . it is a young man's book.'

A vigorous correspondence followed in November/December. First (17 November 1917) there came two letters from anonymous schoolmasters supporting the article. There followed (24 November 1917) two more such letters, one in support and one defending Waugh. Finally (8 December 1917), were published letters from a named housemaster from Wycliffe College, focusing on Waugh's 'well-founded indictment' of 'immorality', from Lunn concerning his belief in the truth of *The Loom of Youth*, and from 'A mere schoolboy' claiming the book to be true and to be seen so by public school boys. By Christmas Grant Richards's advertisement in the *Times Literary Supplement* (20 December 1917) read, 'Really if paper and print were at its old price I should print an anthology of reviews of *The Loom of Youth*.'

In December the heavy guns began to fire. A paper by Edward Lyttelton appeared in the *Contemporary Review*. Lyttelton (1855-1942), was a master at Eton (1882-90), headmaster of Haileybury (1890-1905) and of Eton (1905-16). The *Dictionary of National Biography* describes him as 'schoolmaster, divine and cricketer'. He started his article by asserting that *The Loom of Youth* was 'uniformly dull, occasionally unpleasant, and in [his] judgement at least, almost wholly untrue' – a view contrary to much contemporary opinion. 'Whatever is wrong with our Public Schools is the outcome of certain defects of the English character.' That is, defects that were outside the control of the schools. Once again the family could be blamed by the schoolmasters for the boy's lack of intellectual interests. The great value of these schools was 'social training' though even this might disappear without support from outside the school. The strange thing about Lyttelton's attack was that whenever he put generalisations aside Waugh would have agreed with the particular points that he made.

Meanwhile, another schoolboy Martin Browne, an Etonian, spent his last half at Eton in 1917 writing a reply to Waugh. This book, *A Dream of Youth*, was published in 1918. Browne approved of Waugh's work if taken in the right spirit, but saw the public school principle as 'fundamentally sound' – 'the best educational principle we have got'. He thought there to be some truth in what he saw as Waugh's main criticism, namely, 'the tyranny of games', but he claimed that 'The moral atmosphere of *The Loom of Youth* is the thing about it that has most shocked its readers among the general public' (59). Waugh's picture was at this point exaggerated. But to Browne it was this discussion which was crucial because he saw religion as 'the key to the life of the Public School' (77). Out of 132 pages, 7 were given to athletics, 16 to morality – largely, but not entirely to 'impurity', 24 to religion and 30 to chapel services. In the matter of 'impurity' Browne's remedies confirmed Waugh's pictures. Masters should trust boys; the silence now ruling concerning the reasons for remaining pure was to be broken; and attempts were to be made to create more of an atmosphere of home at school.

Browne was not the only schoolboy who answered *The Loom of Youth*. In 1919 another, under the pseudonym of 'Jack Hood', published *The Heart of a Schoolboy*. From the Preface to this book we know 'Hood' was seventeen and not an Etonian. This work consisted of ten short chapters and an Epilogue covering most sides of public school life, but again focusing upon religion and morality, since two chapters were allocated to Morals, including one on 'Impurity', and two chapters to Religion. Though inefficiencies in the workings of the schools were admitted, Hood's book was not at all critical in tone of the system as a whole.

When Waugh returned to England from the German prisoner-of-war camp in which he had been since March 1918, he was frequently asked to lecture on the public schools. He was at this time employed by Chapman & Hall, his father's firm. Ultimately, in 1922, Waugh himself, though then primarily writing as a novelist, produced an analytical account of his views on boys' public schools, *Public School Life*. In this book he showed how mildly critical of the system he really was by the minor nature of the reforms that he advocated. The evils of athleticism and boarding could be eliminated 'were boys to leave school at seventeen instead of nineteen' (Waugh, 1962: 247). Many smaller reforms, for instance, an appeal for a more vocational curriculum, were advocated, but earlier leaving was apparently the main change required. Waugh, who loved his school, wrote, 'I was never against Sherborne, but the popular conception of Sherborne' (Waugh, 1962: 52). Sherborne thought otherwise. His name *and* that of his father were removed from the lists of the old boys' society in 1917. Waugh's name was reinstated in 1933, largely by the efforts of C. Day Lewis and V.C. Clinton-Baddeley (Waugh, 1962: 119) and in due course he sent his own sons there (Waugh 1962: 47).

In his autobiography Waugh wrote, 'I know myself to be a very minor writer' (Waugh, 1962: xiii), but in 1917 when reviewing *The Loom of Youth* in the *Bystander* (20 August 1917) Richard Strauss had written that this work 'will take its place among the few first class school stories which have been published this century'. Its place of importance in this work is an index of that view. Waugh's novel was about the influence of hierarchical schools upon developing boys, seen from the boys' point of view. He produced a sustained piece of critical writing, detailed in nature so that the reader's interest is not diverted by the explicit moralising, yet so that the implicit message goes home. Waugh does not wish us only to laugh at his characters; he wishes – and in 1917 he in part succeeded – us to understand that 'a tin god had to be dethroned' (Waugh, 1962: 120).

Yet his love for his own school somewhat mellowed his criticism so that his readers were able more easily to identify with Gordon Carruthers and to appreciate the problems, particularly those of an emotional nature, that he encountered as he moved up the hierarchy of the school through his 'teens. Parents and others, however, were worried because the attack was directed largely at the moral curriculum of the public schools; this dimension, so closely related to the values seen as crucial to character development in a public school, both affects them more and is more easily understood by laymen than any criticism of the academic curriculum. Furthermore, after three years of war there was a market for doubts about the imperial assumptions of the public schools. Lunn's similar, but less powerful book, *The Harrovians*, published in 1913, did not catch this tide. Reform was not so much in the air.

Waugh himself claimed in the author's note which was substituted for Seccombe's introduction in the 1929 edition that *The Loom of Youth* was 'never meant to be an attack upon a system. . . . It was only because the truth had been so little told about the real life of the public school boy that it was regarded as an attack.' Though there may be some truth in the second sentence, his first remark is undoubtedly disingenuous on the evidence of what Waugh had written in 1922. Certainly Seccombe's original (1917) introduction emphasised the critical element of the novel and in the contemporary climate this was the interpretation commonly given to the book.

Conclusion

Both exemplars examined here fall within the genre as Reed had left it, but neither does so with ease. They were both written from the viewpoint of the boys involved in the schools concerned. Both writers saw the schools as hierarchical organisations. In both books the development of boys is presented though this is much more obviously so in *The Loom of Youth*. In both cases a set of values is to be taught, but here is the rub: the contemporary approved code of public school values is criticised in both books, though for different reasons and in differing ways in each book. This criticism was seen as such by Waugh's readers, whereas Kipling's lessons, being implicitly presented, were read by many more as a more extreme version of the present practice of the public schools.

For Kipling, the Empire and Britain were in danger due to the moral inefficiency of leaders, and this included what in the last chapter were called the NCOs. He had seen this, he believed, at close hand in his travels round the world and more especially in his first brief trip to South Africa in 1898. For Waugh, on the other hand, the problem was not to make the system do its work better, but to make certain changes to the way the schools operated. Initially Waugh seemed to be asking for a massive overhaul, but in the end the changes for which he asked were really rather small. His criticism stemmed from the inefficiencies in fighting the First World War. The leaders, the officers in the armed services, were very largely educated in the public schools and though no one could deny their bravery, they were, according to Waugh, ill-educated academically, unquestioning of the world at large and unfeeling morally, having been reared to be mediocrities on a diet of games and unthinking religion. There was a connection between the two writers in that Waugh saw the quintessential public school boy to be 'Georgie' Cotton, the hero of Kipling's 'The Brushwood Boy'. However, Cotton was a little too 'pi' to have been a member of Stalky's company; we do not know Waugh's views on Stalky.

Both books continued the trend begun earlier and seen in Reed's stories of putting less weight on the family and on Christian moral teaching, but both reflected what was possibly happening in the schools in the emphasis that they gave to fuller relationships between masters and boys, especially where the master was seen to be 'good'. The readership aimed at was still, in the main, middle-class though obviously in view of their large sales both books must have been read more widely. Yet under the social circumstances of the times to exercise influence a book had to be read by the upper middle class and by those in the public schools, because certainly in Kipling's, and to a large extent still in Waugh's times, that was where the future leaders were educated. However, and this again was new, Waugh's book was aimed at, and Kipling's came to be read by, adults rather than adolescents. Out of the genre, boys' school stories, that had helped to pass on the approved social and moral code, was being born a new literary form, the critical school novel for adults.

8

Change, 1890-1930

The quantity of material available for analysis during the years to be covered here is great. This raises two difficulties. First, selection is inevitable, but the aim here must be to examine a wide range of material; thus, some books considered at the time to be of both high and low literary quality will be discussed. Second, the method of organising the material to be presented is a problem. Of the two previous systematic accounts, that of Hicks, when analysing the period 1910 to 1930, used a system of categories partly based on the content of the books examined and partly on the attitudes displayed. His categories were: the day school, the common room, the anti-sentimentalists, the enthusiasts, and the social critics (Hicks, 1933: 27-38). Quigley (1982), covering the whole period from 1857 until today, also used categories to order her material that were based upon literary content. Here, we shall examine books for adults or for general readership, then those specifically for adolescents, in each case emphasising the tendency towards writing in a critical spirit and in the second case focusing especially upon the movement towards the standardisation of the boys' school story. Finally, before drawing some conclusions, the changing social structure supporting the tendencies observed will be very briefly described.

Works for adults, or for general readership

Many of the books written during these years, whether for adults or for both adults and for adolescents, were uncritical and supportive of the public schools. A very few such works were also written about the new secondary schools. Uncritical and critical work will be examined in turn.

Uncritical work

There were a number of books written that achieved some fame in which schools were given considerable space although the main weight of the plot was put elsewhere. In the first volume of Compton Mackenzie's *Sinister Street* (1913) which was, as we have seen, mentioned in *The Loom of Youth* about one third of the space gave an account of Michael Fane's time as a day boy at St Paul's School. There was no criticism of the school and Michael was seen as happy there. The book achieved fame at the time because of some passages relating to his extra-curricular sexual adventures. These led several circulating libraries to ban the book.

Somewhat more emphasis was put by Somerset Maugham on the school in his partly autobiographical novel *Of Human Bondage* (1915). Philip Carey, an orphan with a game leg, is not really happy at his school, in reality King's School, Canterbury. Philip could have gone to Oxford to sit for a scholarship which he would probably have won, but he rebelled against school and his guardian, an old clergyman, and left early to go first to Germany to learn the language and then to Paris as he felt he wanted to be an artist, before he ultimately went to medical school. When almost qualified Philip returned to school and saw the headmaster, a man who had done much to reform the school, in the distance, but never spoke to him. Yet, though Philip did not like his school, the novel is not critical of it or of any other school.

McKenna's *Sonia* (1917) includes several chapters about the schooling of its main characters, including a rather mysterious American, who uses his public school to make him into an acceptable Englishman. The tone is basically uncritical as one quotation, which in its context is not ironical, will show:

> It is probably wise to raise up a class of men who shall be educated and not technically instructed: wide horizons and infinite capacity for learning, constitute an aim sufficiently exalted. That was the aim of Melton; and we were well educated within narrow limits that excluded modern history, economics, English Literature, science and modern languages. We never strove to be practical and had a pathetic belief in the validity of pure scholarship as an equipment for

life. . . . Again, I still hold that character moulding in a great public school is adequate; conceivably, however, a fine character might be moulded in other ways (McKenna, 1917: 70)

One well-received novel, still in print, told of a county grammar school. This was Henry Williamson's *Dandelion Days* (1922). Willie Madieson lives on an isolated farm in the West Country and goes to Colham Grammar School. He is an awkward, shy and diffident boy whose relationship with his father is a difficult one. The story focuses on Willie's friendship with Jack Temperley and his calf-love for Elsie. This novel is one of a series of four, all concerning Willie and his life. In it the school is seen in a neutral way as an inevitable part of Willie's growing up.

There were, in addition, many books for adults that were totally or almost entirely about public schools and which were adult versions of the boys' school story. Several were about Eton. In 1891 H.O. Sturgis published one of the earlier of these adult stories with the title of *Tim*. In this the career of Tim Ebbesley is traced through his preparatory school and at Eton. The main theme of *Tim* is the friendship between Tim and a slightly older boy Carol Darley, whom he knows as home as the local squire's son. Both are together at Eton and their friendship undergoes several strains. Initially, Tim's father on return from India mistakes Carol, a strong good-looking boy, for Tim, physically a weaker boy in whom he is soon disappointed. He forbids Tim from meeting Carol. At school Tim has the usual difficulties in keeping up a friendship with an older boy. Ultimately, after leaving Eton Carol falls in love with Violet, who refuses to share him with Tim. So Tim gives Carol up. He then becomes ill from overwork at school and is brought home, seemingly to die. On his deathbed Carol and Tim are reunited and Tim shakes hands with his father. This theme of conflict with a father is found in other school stories of the time.

Another novel about Eton was Parker's *Playing Fields* (1922). Parker himself was at Eton and Oxford and became editor of the *Field* from 1903 to 1937. In this book the hero's career is again traced from his preparatory school through Eton to Oxford. He does very well at Eton, but his individualistic temperament keeps him from doing exceptionally well. He is in the Shooting Eight, but is not elected to 'Pop'. He misses a scholarship to King's

College, Cambridge, but wins one to Oriel College, Oxford. In a period soon after the publication of Waugh's *Loom of Youth* this was an almost totally uncritical account of a famous public school.

The final book about Eton to be mentioned is Shane Leslie's *The Oppidan* (1922). Once more a near-autobiographical account is presented, from entrance examination to last day at Eton, of the career of Peter Darley. For a reader today this book seems approving of the school, but it was critically compared at the time to *The Loom of Youth*, because Leslie was thought to be 'careless of what damage he may do to his old school, of what wounds he may inflict on his victims' (*Quarterly Review*, 1925: 30). In his book Leslie told of a fire that seriously damaged a house and that could have been the result of some carelessness in administration, and he also mentioned an actual boy as a bully who was recognisable to many and was known to have died in the war. It was the way he told his story not the attitude towards his school that was criticised. Furthermore, the book contains much snobbery and snide comments about Jews, Catholics and 'Continentals'.

Perhaps the most famous approving account of a public school written during these years was not about Eton, but about Harrow. This was *The Hill* (1905) by H.A. Vachell, himself a Harrovian, who became a very successful writer and dramatist – he once had three plays running simultaneously in London. *The Hill* is almost a classic example of the genre. It tells of the school career of John Verney, who comes to a house, the Manor, which 'was showing unmistakable signs of decay'. A new head master diagnosed 'dry-rot', but, upon 'realizing the necessity of cutting it out, was confronted with that bristling obstacle – Tradition' (III). John is a thoughtful, but typical schoolboy. In discussion with his housemaster, Mr Rutford, he says, 'All the same. . . I *would* lie, if I though a lie might save a friend's life. . . . Any decent boy or man would' (III). His friend, Egerton, said of another boy, nicknamed 'The Caterpillar', 'Upon any point of schoolboy honour his authority ruled supreme. He told the truth among his peers; he loathed obscenity; he disliked and condemned bad language' (IV). The house is seen as the central link to the school: 'too many beasts wreck a house, as they wreck a regiment or a nation' (VI). Games were important; one boy, Beaumont-Green, son of a wealthy manufacturer, was a 'funk at footer and a prodigious consumer of "food" at the creameries' (VII). The position of the Sixth and their power within a public school were

VIEW FROM THE FOOTBALL FIELDS.

well defined. When asked by a new housemaster at the Manor about certain ills in the house Lovell, himself a Sixth-former, replied, 'I beg your pardon, sir. I have never considered it my duty as a Sixth Form boy to play the usher' (X). John Verney's character develops into one marked by this set of values after undergoing a number of tests including the risk of expulsion by refusing to 'sneak' on behalf of a friend, a moral dilemma not uncommon in the genre, whether in books for adults or adolescents. *The Hill*'s sub-title was *A Romance of Friendship*.

Friendship in its many forms was emerging as one of the major themes in these stories about schools for adults. This theme had since *Tom Brown* and *Eric* always been taken for granted as one of the relationships through which character developed at school. Increasingly, however, attention was given to friendship as the focal point of the plot and to the fact that friendships between adolescents could take several forms. One story, *Gerald Eversley's Friendship. A Study in Real Life* (1895), indicates that this was the case. The writer was J.E.C. Welldon, the headmaster of Harrow, later to become Bishop of Calcutta. In this book, set in the 1860s, two new boys arrive together at St Anselm's and are put together in the same room. Harry Venniker is the son of a Lord; Gerald Eversley is a scholar and son of a poor and rather narrow country clergyman. Harry fits into school well, Gerald with difficulty. Despite differences in their characters and careers at school they become and remain great friends. Gerald, originally a very devout boy, loses his faith and moves away from his father intellectually. He eventually falls in love with Violet, Harry's sister, and with the help and encouragement of Lady Venniker who is fond of Gerald they become unofficially engaged until Gerald has finished his studies at Balliol, Oxford, and established himself in a career. He wins a fellowship and Lord Venniker nominates him to the Treasury. Three weeks before his marriage to Violet is to occur she falls ill and dies of diphtheria. Very soon afterwards Lady Venniker dies. This tale of the development of and strain upon a deepening adolescent friendship of two boys, markedly different in their characters, is told against the background of a typical public school. Harry is an athlete, Gerald a scholar. Religion is important, especially as Gerald initially was so devout a Christian. A set piece tells of Dr Pearson, the head, giving a sermon on the last Sunday of a summer term. Apart from its romantic tone, this description also approves of Gerald's move at the time from an Evangelical to a Broad Church position:

> 'O sacred beloved spot on earth – the chapel of a great public school! It is there, if anywhere in the world, that worship is realized in its purity, far away from the discords of contemporary creeds.' (IX)

Something of a critical tone does, however, enter into a discussion of the way boys' characters can develop so easily at school by adapting

> themselves to local tone, temper and custom. . . . A public school, then, is the home of the commonplace. It is there that mediocrity sits upon her throne. There the spirit which conforms to custom is lauded to the skies. (IV)

E.F. Benson, a well-known novelist, who was himself born in Wellington College, where his father, later to be Archbishop of Canterbury, was the headmaster, published a successful school story, *David Blaize*, in 1915. Benson was at Marlborough as a boy and his book was of the semi-autobiographical type, usually marked by the name of the hero as its title, with which we are now familiar. In it Benson too put considerable weight upon the possibilities of a seamier side to adolescent friendships. In its review the *Times Literary Supplement* wrote of 'school friendships – those splendours of affections than which only the lucky ones in life experience anything finer', but also commented in carefully chosen words that 'Mr Benson tackles subjects for which a disturbing hint is often considered enough' (30 March 1916).

The great success of some of the books for adults about public schools is shown by C. Turley's *Geoffrey Marten Schoolboy*. This book, first published in 1902, was reissued in 1903, 1905, 1907 (twice) and in 1912 in a popular series which included novels by E.F. Benson, Joseph Conrad, John Galsworthy, Jack London, H. de V. Stacpoole, and H.G. Wells. Turley was at Cheltenham and his book is about that school, here named Cliborough College, What is in many ways surprising is that compared with the careful, if florid, style and controversial matter thoughtfully presented that is found in books like *Gerald Eversley's Friendship*, a book so ordinary in its method and material should by now be achieving a success of this order. The career of Geoffrey Marten is traced from his first term with its fights and bullying through escapades leading on one occasion to near expulsion to a final year of success as a prefect and a member of the first fifteen and the eleven. One or two quotations will indicate that it was not only the plot that was becoming standardised, but also the language used. It must be remembered that this is not a book aimed at a readership of boys as Reed's stories for the *BOP* were, but a book for adults and one which had a continuing success with that readership throughout the Edwardian era. Of a poem in the *Cliburnian* by one boy, Chalmers, 'who was supposed to be literary', Geoffrey Marten says,

> without professing to be a judge of poetry, I must say that it was very fair rot. . . . The fact is that Chalmers was not as most other fellows are, and when anyone is odd at school, some time or other he is sure to be rotted. (XIV)

And this is not a criticism; it is accepted as part of the approved way of behaving in such a school. Of the head of the school Geoffrey Marten says,

> But Wilcox was the sort of fellow who was no good at

anything except talking in Greek grammar, and when anyone is made like that it is best not to take much notice of him, because he is probably irresponsible more than half the time. (XVI)

Writing of the years after 1918 Mack said that 'the unending stream of fiction describing, analysing, criticising and defending the public schools . . . has slackened perceptibly only in the thirties' (Mack, 1941: 327). We shall see that this was certainly true of school stories for boys. However, in regard to the early 1920s Christopher Isherwood, formerly at Repton and then an undergraduate at Corpus Christi College, Cambridge, later admitted that he tried to write such a novel, 'a very typical specimen of the "cradle-to-coming-of-age" narrative which young men like myself were producing in thousands of variations, not merely in England, but all over Europe and in the U.S.' In his novel, a Sixth-former was himself 'writing a novel of public school life; . . . undoubtedly . . . influenced by *David Blaize*; his soliloquies were in Mr. E.F. Benson's most luscious manner' (Isherwood, 1947: 74, 17). A list of school stories for adults written in the 1920s could be long and would include L. Portman's *Hugh Rendal* (1922) about Wellington; E. Raymond's successful *Tell England* (1922) – about a public school career, a fatal wounding at Gallipoli and the attractions of the High Church position; Beverley Nicholls's (1920) *Prelude*, whose hero, Paul, sums up his school experience in this way: the able one in two hundred boys 'educate themselves. For the others – we've got a system going that works – so does it matter?' (Nicholls, 1920: 269-70).

One other writer, however, does deserve more than a mention. He is (later Sir) Hugh Walpole who was born in 1884 in New Zealand. His father returned to Britain to become Bishop of Edinburgh. Walpole, like Maugham, went to King's School, Canterbury and then to Cambridge. For one year he was a master at Epsom after which in 1911 he wrote a story about a school, *Mr Perrin and Mr Traill*. This novel is a pre-Kafka description of the claustrophobic effect of closed institutions. It could have been set in a hospital, a prison or a regiment. It was about 'those crowded, stifled souls buried of their own original free will beneath fantastic piles of scribbled paper, cursing their fate, but unable to escape from them' (Walpole, 1911: 110). Between 1919 and 1927 he wrote the semi-autobiographical Jeremy trilogy, one of which,

Jeremy at Crale (1927), was about his hero's schooldays. This work is not at all critical of the schools and at one point Walpole writes approvingly:

> This great merit in our public school system then – it stiffens your back for anything. It is only the too imaginative who are more than temporarily bruised and even they not for ever. (Walpole, 1927: 80).

Two writers, who in both cases wrote about schoolmasters, but for whom the boys were equally important, will be mentioned. James Hilton wrote in 1934 a very successful short novel, *Good Bye, Mr Chips*, which also became a successful film. This is a sentimental account of a schoolmaster, widowed soon after his late-ish marriage, who gave his whole life to one school and its boys. He eventually became its headmaster almost by default after nearly being dismissed. The story was based on an actual master at the Leys School, Cambridge, and the house opposite in Trumpington Road to which he retired. There was no element of criticism of the school or of Mr Chips's rather traditional ways of running the school or with boys.

Finally Ian Hay, himself at Fettes, was a well-known writer of the war years and the interwar period to whom reference was briefly made in the last chapter. He wrote one novel that must be mentioned, *The Housemaster* (1936). The plot centres on Charles Donkin, aged fifty-five, the bachelor housemaster of Red House at Marbledown, and his battles with a young new head master, but boys are also important to the story, which tells of the effect on Red House when a friend of Donkin's with her three adolescent daughters arrives to stay in the house. As a result of their escapades Donkin is driven in the end to resign, but a governor, who knows his real worth, arranges that the head be offered a bishopric and Donkin becomes head. These events are crowded into six weeks of the summer term. Many elements of the genre are present: house, prefects, sports day and a 'nincompoop' master. Also there is the last mention known to me in such a story of a rebellion which had occurred more than fifty years beforehand in Brown House: 'tired of complaining about their food . . . [the boys] barricaded themselves into their own part of the House, and declined to come out until their grievances were redressed' (Hay, 1936: XIV). But no breath of criticism, except of the young head, really enters into Ian Hay's light-hearted novel.

Critical works

Criticism of schools and discussion of the upbringing of children was in the air around the turn of the century. For example, Henry James wrote three books analysing the move from the innocence of childhood through adolescence in which moral standards must be created and on into adult life when they must be applied: *What Maisie Knew* (1897); *The Turn of the Screw* (1898); *The Awkward Age* (1899). In 1903 on his death Butler's *The Way of All Flesh*, written some thirty years beforehand, was first published, though it did not become a best seller for some years, until Bernard Shaw commented favourably on it in his Preface to *Major Barbara* (1907). This novel was a critical account both of Victorian family life and an early Victorian private school in the period about 1835 to 1853.

One book, *The Thing That Hath Been*, published early in the period in 1895, that is, prior to *Stalky and Co.*, was written by A.H. Gilkes, the headmaster of Dulwich School, one of the major London day schools. The writing, tone and structure are in essence traditional, but the plot is implicitly critical of the older order of the schools. Mathematics is in bad shape at Stratton School. Dr Pincher, the head, decides to consult the Archdeacon who recommends the appointment of John Martin, a Board school teacher. He is appointed on trial and has to face the snobbery of the staff and the boys, but overcomes much of the opposition by his excellent teaching and his straightforward nature. But this straightforwardness is seen by some as tactlessness and offends them. Such persons often on further thought come round to Martin's viewpoint. Eventually one master manoeuvres him out of the school by telling the head what is true, that Martin is not a Christian. Dr Pincher feels he must dismiss him at the end of term, but finds him work as a librarian in London. The type of issues that Gilkes raised can be seen in some remarks to Martin by his enemy, Mr Binning, a senior master of some standing at Stratton School:

'A Public school is not only a place where boys say lessons; it is also a place where they associate together, forming a society, and being trained to play the part of gentlemen of good position in the world. They learn, of course, the ordinary virtues of a man, and they learn also the virtues which especially belong to their class and the right bearing towards the lower orders. This they must be taught, speaking generally, by those who belong to the same class as they do. . . . I speak because I have observed some of the boys often with you, and one boy I know has been at a night school you teach, and I fear that we shall have the school more like a Board school than a public school if this goes on. This mixture of ranks is not good for boys, and your companions should not be theirs. (XIX)

Criticisms of faults other than snobbery was also to be found. In 1899 A.W. Clarke wrote *Jasper Tristram*. On first reading this is a typical school career story. Jasper goes to a preparatory school, is bullied by Orr, the school bully, eventually moves up the school and tries to ingratiate himself with Orr's old friend, Els, though with little success. Els goes to the public school to which Jasper also wishes to go, but because of family circumstances can only do so by winning a scholarship. Orr is also there and makes Els his fag. The old rivalry and struggle for friendship starts again without reciprocation from Els. Jasper grows up an introverted boy, doing reasonably well at school, but not as successful as he might have been. This apparently normal plot, however, hides at least two criticisms of the schools. The first relates to the possibility of erotic, rather than merely amorous, friendships. Els on one occasion went to hand in some Latin verses to Mr Clarke and,

> there, as the correcting still went on, Orr began to give little sly pinches behind. Els did what he could to protect himself by putting out his open hand, but without much effect, for then Orr took to making rapid dabs at his palm with one finger which the boy tried vainly to close all his upon. (X)

The second criticism is implicitly raised by the atypical direction of the development of Jasper's character and is eventually explicitly put into words. Jasper spent one summer afternoon walking alone rather than at games and he asked himself the quite fundamental question, 'Why should one wish to be *manly* rather than the reverse' (XV). This was treachery in a public school boy and also a questioning of the whole ethos of the boys' school story.

A different, but equally deep form of questioning followed in 1907 with the publication of E.M. Forster's first novel, *The Longest Journey*, another novel about a master rather than about boys. In this novel, after taking his degree at Cambridge, Rickie

Elliott became a master at Sawston, a public school. Forster is examining the nature of these schools where our leaders, Imperial and others, were trained. He was concerned at the approved character in the typical public school product. The individual human being was submerged in the group; the emotions, particularly any demonstrations of love, were stifled. What mattered was a surface display of socially approved behaviour. For Forster true humanity was lost and what appalled him was that 'it seemed that only a short ladder lay between the preparation room and the Anglo-Saxon hegemony of the globe' (1907: XVII).

A much shallower, but more overtly critical novel was Lunn's *The Harrovians* (1913), mentioned, as we have seen, by Waugh in *The Loom of Youth* and read, we know, by both adults and boys. This was written as a reply to Vachell's uncritical account of Harrow in *The Hill*. It was based on Lunn's own diary whilst a boy at Harrow and was, therefore, a developmental tale. It was the story of Peter O'Neil, an intelligent, unathletic boy, who became head of his house and managed to beat the captain of the house in a battle for power. In addition to the implicit criticism of athleticism, the low standard of work, the cribbing and the pharisaic nature of school religion were emphasised. When Peter O'Neil is about to be confirmed he thinks about school sermons and sums up what he feels about Harrow:

> 'Consider the lilies of the field' – hardly. Rather, 'Blessed are those that work hard and play hard, for Solomon in all his glory was not arrayed like a flannel at Lords, or a monitor on Speech Day.' 'Blessed are the meek.' No, rather, 'Blessed are those who have a decent self-respect and take a proper place among their fellows. Blessed are those who have a proper sense of their importance. Blessed are those who have as marked a resemblance to the Pharisees as possible by discussing the tone of their House on any possible occasion. Blessed are those that learn to kill the young men of other countries with the quickest possible dispatch.' (139)

Both Hughes and Farrar would have hated the satirical reference to Christianity in the passage. Many of these criticisms are, however, those that Waugh made much of four years later. Lunn took Walpole's view of what the public schools did to individuality:

> The eccentric may suffer, but if he has any genuine

originality it will be submerged – perhaps – but not destroyed. The worst that a school can do is to transform an inefficient artist into a humdrum useful member of society. (44-5)

Yet much of this, for the times, fierce criticism was undermined by the 'Epilogue', in which are given the thoughts of Peter O'Neil on his return to a somewhat reformed Harrow as an old boy:

There was something attractive in the indolent resignation to the theory that public schools existed to turn out gentlemen and not scholars. (309)

After the war there were a number of very critical mentions of public schools in novels for adults. Two of the bitterest critics will be mentioned. One only mentioned the schools in passing in a novel about much else besides. In Richard Aldington's *Death of a Hero* (1929) the experiences of George Winterbourne before the war were outlined – at school, training to be an artist and in his love affairs. The war comes and he joins up to die, like so many others, a pointless death. In one passage Aldington satirises the public schools:

'The type of boy we aim at turning out', the Head used to say to impressed parents, 'is a thoroughly manly fellow. We prepare for the Universities, of course, but our pride is in our excellent Sports Record. There is an OTC organised by Sergeant Major Brown (who served throughout the South African War) and officered by the masters who have been trained in the Militia. Every boy must undergo six months training, and is then competent to take up arms for his Country in an emergency.' (82)

Anti-intellectualism, athleticism, amateurism was the gentlemanly way to an English hero's death.

The other post-war critical novel, Evelyn Waugh's *Decline and Fall* (1928), goes to apparently absurd extremes in its description of a bad private school, but Waugh, who was himself at Lancing, is essentially satirising the main faults of the public schools as he saw them. *Decline and Fall* is another novel about masters rather than boys. Peter Pennyfeather, a serious undergraduate, who wants to be a clergyman, is sent down from Oxford under almost accidental circumstances for becoming drunk, a not uncommon condition there at the time, as Waugh later showed in the earlier chapters of *Brideshead Revisited* (1945). He, perforce, becomes a master at a very second-rate fictitious boarding school, Llanabba Castle. But Waugh's targets were clear and were those that others had also satirised; poor teaching, insensitive relationships, athleticism and, in the case of private schools, the mercenary attitudes of the proprietors.

One other critical novel for adults will be discussed here because it parallels several school stories for boys to which reference will later be made, though in this case it is again about the masters rather than boys of the school involved. This is *For Sons of Gentlemen* (1920) by 'Kerr Shaw', the pseudonym of R.A. Gurney, the headmaster of King Edward the Seventh School, Sheffield, and then of Whitgift. Gurney had taught at a public school before moving to headships of large, partly State-supported, urban, day schools (R. Gurner 1937). In 1924 he had written *The Day Boys*, a plea in novel form for considering the benefits of day over boarding schools. In *For Sons of Gentlemen* he traced the decline of Straye College, a private school claiming the status of a public school in a pleasant London suburb. Gradually through the Edwardian era the school is surrounded by urban sprawl; the pupils change in character and fall in numbers. The school is initially saved by a large donation from Mrs Deane, the founder's daughter, who believes, 'It would indeed be deplorable if the spirit of the elementary school should spread to Straye – adequate as such a school may be thought for the class for which it caters' (V). A wealthy parent, Mrs Bobover, is worried about her son's study companion, 'I have seen him and I do not dislike him, but the question is, who is his father – who *is* his father?' (VI). The war makes things even more difficult and the question of taking a grant from the Board of Education now really has to be faced, but opposition on the staff is strong:

> The bogey of control is good enough for the man in the street, but that's not the real point. It's the outlook, the deadening hand, the touch that kills the spirit. I wonder how many regulations we should fulfill today . . . . But there's a soul in Straye, and so long as the soul's alive. . . . (XIV)

In the end the school applies for a grant, but on inspection is not found up to the Board's standard. Ironically the Inspector who makes this recommendation is the son of a charwoman at one of the houses at Straye and owes his position to the new educational opportunities in the form of scholarships to state secondary schools. 'Believe me,' he tells the head, 'It is no easy thing to condemn one's home. But the system and the power which you have opposed have won. The strife, like the victory, is neither yours nor mine' (XXII), not a nineteenth-century sentiment at all.

The flood of school stories for adults began at the end of the nineteenth century and in many cases novels were written that took the form of the genre as established by Reed, but the concerns of the twentieth century quickly affected the adult school novel. Thus, the critical spirit that was, as we have seen, beginning to be found even earlier, grew stronger and not only was the subject matter of these novels affected by the contemporary administrative problems of education, but there were also severe criticisms, especially after the end of the war, of the code of values so dear to the public schools. This was the code around which the genre itself was written. To the criticisms of anti-intellectualism and athleticism made by Alec Waugh in *The Loom of Youth* was added the condemnation of the social class nature of recruitment to the schools. Furthermore, the reason usually advanced to support this, the provision of the nation's leaders, exemplified by Kipling in *Stalky and Co.*, was to many writers no longer sufficient on the grounds both of inequity and of sheer inefficiency.

Reception

In the *Times Literary Supplement* from its earlier years through to 1939 there was every year in November or early December a section on Christmas Books in which special attention, usually in the form of a separate column or two, was given to school stories, a particularly vivid index of the acceptance of this genre. In 1903 Turley's *Geoffrey Marten Schoolboy* was first reviewed with the comment that there was 'nothing nearer to boy nature than this' (20 November 1903). Almost twenty years later the same book was again reviewed with the comment that it was for boys and fathers (7 December 1922). This is a point that must be made about many of these works in the period after about 1900. We have seen in the last chapter that Waugh had, as a boy, read at home *Sinister Street* and *The Harrovians*. The point may be made that he came from a literary family, but we know too that a sermon was preached against *The Harrovians* at Sherborne. Further, Cyril Connelly and George Orwell shared a copy of *Sinister Street* at Eton and Evelyn Waugh read it at Lancing. Boys were now sometimes reading adult stories about schools just as men had always read stories about schools originally written for boys. The readerships were merging.

What is more, there is evidence within the books that there was an assumption that the average reader, seen to be upper middle-class, though many others read these books, had also read earlier works in the genre. The hero of *Playing Fields*, Marten Wardon, compared his preparatory school Compton Mallory, to the schools about which he had read:

> There was much that was not in the books; much that he had not guessed about from Talbot Baines Reed and the *Boys Own Paper*, which had proved so precisely right about the appearance of the Head Master. (III)

Later, when he reached Eton, 'It was all very much like *Tom Brown* and Marten wondered what could be behind the doors, in the rooms belonging to the Sixth Form' (VII). Yet both Eric Parker (XXXI) and an earlier author, Desmond Coke, in *The Bending of a Twig* (1906) also made clear that these earlier books did not portray the present schools. Coke's story is about Shrewsbury and the arrival there of a boy who had been carefully educated in his country home until the age of thirteen. Before going to Shrewsbury his mother seeks to prepare him by giving him a reading course of indiscriminately chosen school stories including *Tom Brown*, *Eric* and *Stalky and Co*. The result is that the boy arrives, seeking the school bully behind every pillar, hence earning the nickname 'Don Quixote'. This story implicitly indicates the critical views coming to be held of the genre itself.

The reality of the picture of the schools given in these stories was still a major issue. A reviewer in the *Times Literary Supplement* in 1905 wrote:

> We believe the conversation in *Tom Brown*, *Stalky and Co*. and *Tim* to be equally true to nature: we have always hesitated to pronounce those in *Eric* untrue. Taking the books as a whole we find *The Hill* the most widely true of all. (28 April 1905)

Yet this reviewer also felt of *The Hill* that 'school-boy friendships are not fair game for the writers of fiction'. Twenty years or so later a reviewer in the *Quarterly*, commenting on *Hugh Rendal*, *The Hill* and *The Bending of a Twig*, pointed out the use in them of a device whereby two boys, one good and the other bad, compete for the friendship of a third boy. Each novel showed 'a self-sacrifice on the part of the good boy of such a quixotic kind, as not only to be improbable, but a distinct overstepping of the modesty of boy nature' (*Quarterly Review*, 1925: 26-7).

The *Harrovians*, Lunn's answer to *The Hill*, caused some critical comment, though this in no way approached that following *The Loom of Youth*. The *Nation* (6 September 1913) saw the book as 'an astonishingly accurate picture', attributing this to the fact that it was based on a diary. Methuen, the publisher, used the accepted reality of the book to advertise it – 'Probably the best sketch of public school life that has ever been written' (*Times Literary Supplement*, 21 August 1913). Yet the reviewer in the *Spectator* thought that, although each page was true, 'the aggregate effect of the book is . . . untrue' (9 August 1913). In particular, this reviewer praised the passage quoted above about the fate of the eccentric at Harrow as 'a just balancing of the uses and abuses of public schools', an indication of the growth of a more general critical stance towards these schools.

More and more there was an acceptance, albeit reluctant, that school stories for adults, whether about boys or masters, could be instruments of criticism. Thus a review of Beverley Nicholls's *Prelude* saw this book as 'by way of being a counterblast to other novels which have described the public school system' (*Times Literary Supplement*, 19 February 1920). Likewise, Parker's *Playing Fields* was a 'Public School Story', but it is 'quite unlike not only the stories that are turned out by the dozens at Christmas, but also the stories of the modern school of authors who gibe at those conventional narrators'. These suffered from 'the heavy-handed analysis of the reformers' (28 September 1922). When Lunn published a second school novel, *Loose Ends* (1919), one reviewer supposed 'it is necessary that this continued hammering at the public mind in the matter of secondary education should continue, but it is a trifle dreary from an artistic point of view' (*Times Literary Supplement*, 24 April 1919).

Some comments on Walpole's *Jeremy at Crale* are of interest because of a major point to be made about boys', as opposed to adults', school stories. In Walpole's book only one crucial term, that between the Lower Sixth and becoming a prefect, is described rather than Jeremy's whole school career. A reviewer commented, 'Mr Walpole shows a very acute understanding of the possibilities and the limits of the public school novel' (*Times Literary Supplement*, 10 November 1927). There was a genre, an extension of the boys' school story, and some exemplars like *The Loom of Youth* had huge sales, but its characteristics did force restraints upon writers; this is a point to which we shall return after examining the development of the genre in its original form, namely in boys', rather than adults', school stories.

Boys' school stories

The change that can be seen in children's books is symbolised in two books by Mrs F.H. Burnett. In 1886 *Little Lord Fauntleroy* appeared, in 1911 *The Secret Garden*. The first was compelling, but even then seen as sentimental; the second was the story of the development into normal children of Mary Lennox, a nasty mean orphan from India, and her cousin, Colin Craven, a semi-hysterical invalid. Mr Craven told his housekeeper how to treat Mary on her arrival: 'Give her simple, healthy food. Let her run wild in the garden. Don't look after her too much. She needs liberty and fresh air and romping about' (12). This recipe for child care reminds us more of Spock than the usual way of bringing up the young in the late nineteenth-century upper middle-class family. There were earlier signs of this move to more freedom for children. In *Bevis* (1877) Richard Jefferies wrote an account of the boy, Bevis, spending summer days roaming free in the open air close to nature. A world created by and peopled by children became acceptable in literature and now more often also in life. This private world, seen in the secret garden of Mary and Colin and in Bevis's countryside, was described well by Kenneth Grahame, another successful writer for children in *The Golden Age* (1895):

> I went downheartedly from the man who understood me, back to the house where I never could do anything right. How was it that everything seemed natural and sensible to him, which these uncles, vicars and other grown-up men took for the merest tomfoolery? (200)

Boys' school stories had developed as a genre just before this new freedom for children to live within a private world was granted. Its coming was one more influence upon the future course of the genre.

School stories

In 1892 Hodder & Stoughton published *Baxter's Second Innings* by Henry Drummond (1851-97), a Scot, who was a lecturer on theology, and had worked as a tropical botanist and as an evangelist with Moody and Sankey (Lennox, 1901). This little book, subtitled 'Specially reported for the School Eleven' was only fifty-five pages in length and was bound in club colours, black and white diagonal stripes, with the title as a badge on the front cover. It originated as a series of articles for a Boys' Brigade magazine. In it Drummond told how Baxter was bowled for a duck in his first innings for a club by a demon fast bowler. Whilst resting afterwards at home he is visited by the captain who tells him that the bowler is 'temptation'. Baxter says,

> 'I thought we were talking about games'. 'So we are', replied the Captain, cheerily, 'We are talking of the game of Life. . . . Life is simply a cricket match – with Temptation a Bowler. He's the fellow who takes nearly every boy's wicket some time or other.'

He bowls Swifts, Slows and Screws. 'It was a swift that bowled out Peter when the girl sprang that question on him the night the cock crowed' (II). Temptation is not, however, sin. Yielding to it is and will show up on 'the scoring sheet of character' (V). Baxter has a second innings and after a bad first over and a few dangerous moments carries his bat.

The 'cricket allegory' (Lennox, 1901), is a clear descendant of the schoolboy story of the 1860s and 1870s and seems very out of place in the 1890s when Kipling was already writing about children. Yet it shows very clearly that the language and the metaphors of sport, and cricket in particular, had come to be part of general discourse to be applied to diverse topics. This was to be shown again to be true a generation later in the First World War when the imagery of poets, the rhetoric of politicians and the speeches of generals were all marked by their own experiences at public schools and by the assumption that this language and these metaphors were commonly understood by all loyal Britishers (Fussell, 1975). This grip on the public mind of a particular set of assumptions was present by 1900 and owed much to the *BOP* and the school stories of the time. It was sustained and strengthened by the continued and increasing flow of these stories in the Edwardian era.

Ten years later P.G. Wodehouse wrote his first boys' school story. Wodehouse was educated at Dulwich under Gilkes and in 1902 *The Pothunter* appeared, first as a serial in the *Public School Magazine*. By 1905 he had published *The Gold Bat*, *A Prefect's Uncle*, *Tales of St Austin's*, *The White Feather* and *The Head of Kay's*. He then wrote the one school story for which he is still remembered, *Mike*, and soon after *Mike and Psmith*, before moving into other fields to write the works for which he is more renowned. These two stories, now issued in one volume, tell of Mike, originally at Wrykyn, and Psmith, originally at Eton, both arriving at Sedleigh as sixteen/seventeen-year-olds. They are both very good cricketers but refuse to play in pique at being moved to this lower-status school. Eventually more out of self-indulgence than loyalty or pride for their new school they agree to play against Wrykyn and naturally help Sedleigh to win. Wodehouse, like Drummond, wrote a cricket story, though it was also a school story. Yet its whole tone was different. As might be expected of the future creator of Jeeves almost no moral lessons are pressed; indeed, on his arrival at Sedleigh Psmith asks Mike, 'Are you the Bully, the Pride of the School, or the Boy who takes to drink and is led astray in Chapter Sixteen?' (XXXII).

This is a tale of japes – there are fights, water is poured over others; boys break bounds at night. Adults play a small part; the headmaster is rarely mentioned and two housemasters alone have any part in the story, and they are on the whole seen as enemies. There are also far fewer boy characters than in previous school stories which were often peopled with boys to the point of near confusion for the reader. Cricket is all-important; classrooms are barely mentioned except as a site for ragging and as a competitor with the games fields. Religion and the chapel no longer play any part in the story. Wodehouse is writing about a boy's world and for boys' entertainment. The private world of childhood is extended up into adolescence.

Wodehouse was a precursor of much to come somewhat later, because, though some of the tendencies exhibited in *Mike* will be found in other contemporary boys' school stories, most remained rather more serious in tone, retaining an air of agnostic moral didacticism rather than of sheer hedonism. Desmond Coke's books are good examples of the Edwardian story. Coke was at Shrewsbury and became School Captain. He went on to Oxford, where in 1903 he wrote a burlesque version of *Sandford and Merton*. He then became a master at Clayesmore School.

Reference has already been made to his *The Bending of a Twig* (1906) which was satirical of boys' school stories, but approving of public schools. He wrote two other stories: *The House Prefect* (1908) and *The School Across the Road* (1910), the last of which he dedicated 'In gratitude to The Head Master of Clayesmore and all others – whether masters or boys, known friends or unknown – who have written kind things to me about my school stories'.

The School Across the Road tells of a feud between Corunna under Dr Anson, a school of one hundred and twenty boys, and Warren's, a private school of sixty boys, owned and operated on rather easy lines by Mr Warren. The two schools co-operate for the first time on joint manoeuvres for their School Corps; these end in a win for Warren's and a real fight between two senior boys. Warren's soon has to close and is amalgamated with Corunna under the ambitious Dr Anson. The new school is named Winton after the local village. The boys are, however, like 'Oil and Water', as Part II is entitled. Dr Anson makes Wren, one of the boys from Warren's a prefect, but he is a non-athlete and unacceptable to all. Jack Henderson, the best games player at Warren's, is very rebellious and leads a group up to the roof in revolt. Grimshaw, the captain of Winton's, a former Corunna boy, goes up and persuades them to come down and then also persuades Dr Anson that the boys themselves should deal with this matter. Henderson is 'licked' by Grimshaw. After several misunderstandings unity is achieved fortuitously by an external threat. Henderson is captured, whilst out on a training run, by the youths at Dr Costa's Agricultural College for the Training of Young Gentlemen. Both factions join together successfully to release Henderson. Wren suggests to Grimshaw that he call for three cheers for Winton. Dr Anson hears them in the distance and knows his great school is truly born.

Though there are a number of new features here, for example, the place given to the Corps and the lack of all mention of Christianity, the basic characteristics of the genre remain: boys are seen to develop within a structured school which has a set of values. The changes noted fit well with the Edwardian era. Even the closing and reorganisation of schools, reminds us of Shaw (Gurney's) *For Sons of Gentlemen* which was published three years after Coke's book. A more famous account of the reorganisation of a public school was G.F. Bradby's *The Lanchester Tradition* (1914). This was really written for adults by an old Rugbeian, who was a housemaster at Rugby from 1888 to 1920. His novel tells of how the masters at Lanchester reacted to the coming of a new headmaster who planned to change the school and in the end succeeded. After the war calls for educational change became stronger and three stories will be discussed, one of which, *Riverton Boys*, is more in the strict tradition of the genre, whilst the other two, *Day Boys* and *The Champion of the School* in some ways parallel these calls.

Riverton Boys. A Story of Two Schools (1920) was written by K.M. and R. Eady. As the sub-title hints, it is a tale of rivalry between Riverton College and Riverton Commercial Academy. Unlike in *The School Across the Road* these schools were seen to be of very unequal status. Jack Dawson is at the College, but his cousin, Jim, is to go to the academy:

> 'I say, Jackdaw', Eversleigh began again suddenly, 'What shall you do about the other chaps here? You won't tell them, I suppose?'
> 'What?' The Jackdaw roused himself and flushed hotly, 'Why, of course I must. A fellow can't cut his own cousin because his people have sent him to a beastly low school.'

Jack runs a school society called 'the Scalpers' who steal caps from Academy boys and this causes much rivalry and conflict between the boys at the schools. The story revolves around some fireworks, to be used for display by the Academy boys, which 'the Scalpers' steal from an old gatehouse in Riverton. This contains the town museum and its custodian's house – his sons, Ralph and Phil Dunston, are both at the Academy. The fireworks are stolen and let off daringly by 'the Scalpers' in the Academy grounds, but Jack is caught by the head. Meanwhile the gatehouse is burnt out. All think that this is due to the explosion of the fireworks, still believed to be in the gatehouse, but in fact a lantern has been left there by a boy called Dicey when stealing them, and this causes the fire. Phil Dunston discovers Jack's knife and a firework outside the gatehouse. He realises that the fireworks let off at the Academy had been stolen by 'the Scalpers', but is in a dilemma about revealing the truth which would clear the Academy boys of their suspected guilt in the fire, because Jack had earlier saved him from drowning in the river:

> 'But why didn't he tell, and get himself out of the row? You weren't in his school', a wondering Scalper suggested. The Jackdaw positively blushed. 'He couldn't tell, because I

pulled him out of the river that day; and really that was
mostly Wiltshire's doing, as I told him. But just because of
that he would have taken a licking, and been sacked, and not
told. . . . And I call that ripping, don't you?' (XIX)

The last two chapters are set ten years on in the Boer War.
Captain Jack Dawson takes over Frobisher's Scouts (Volunteers),
finding Lieutenant Phil Dunston and Sergeant Dicey to be
members of his new command. Phil now saves Jack's life in a raid
and Dicey gains his commission.

In this story patriotism returns as one of the values to be taught
by the tale, though, somewhat after the manner of *Stalky and Co.*,
the war passages are tacked on the end of a more traditional
school story, in which the schoolboy code of honour seems to be
the main moral didactic element. There is little development of
character, however, as the events occur over a comparatively
short period. The language used is also more notably close to the
manner in which boys were believed to talk. The other two
stories now to be discussed are similarly near to, but not
absolutely within, the genre.

Gurney's *For Sons of Gentlemen* (1920), a novel aimed more at
adults and reviewed as such (*Times Literary Supplement*, 21
October 1926) has been examined earlier. His *The Day Boys*
(1924) seems to be aimed more at a dual readership of boys and
adults and can more relevantly be discussed at this point. Jim
Strang, an upper working-class boy, wins a county scholarship
from his local London elementary school to Stockham County
Secondary School for Boys. He and a new master, Robert
Harcourt, formerly a master at a public school, both arrive at the
start of the new academic year. Mr Harcourt decides Jim could do
well academically and persuades his parents of this. Jim passes his
matriculation well before moving into what is for him the very
foreign world of the Sixth form and spends part of the summer in
Jersey on holiday with the Harcourts, realising vaguely some of
the problems implicit in his possible upward social mobility.
When he enters the Sixth, he realises that he is cutting himself off
from much of his former way of life and friends, but

> To him the school is Life itself. It isn't only work, you
> gather, or games alone, or the societies, or the masters, or
> even the other boys. It's more than that, the whole thing
> together – He can't explain and he knows it sounds absurd.
> But they live and work and talk together, you see, and

Stockham chaps are different from other chaps. (VII)

As Mr Harcourt had expected, Jim wins a scholarship to Oxford, but has some difficulties during his second term. Mr Harcourt, now the head of a county secondary school, visits him and tells him to buckle to and show what boys from such schools can really do. For him the crucial principle is

> 'That our secondary day school boys can rise, and go on, and on, and on, carrying with them that one thing – call it freedom from convention, seriousness, initiative, unsophisticated outlook, what you will – that the day school gives and the public school cannot even understand.' (XIII)

Jim gains first class honours in History. He is appointed junior History master at the public school where Harcourt had taught before going to Stockham. After three years he follows Harcourt's example and leaves to take Harcourt's old job at Stockham. Harcourt himself tells Winfield, Jim's great friend in the Sixth form:

> 'through Strang, and all he stands for, salvation will come to England's schools, the rich and the poor, the old and the new – and there shall be the Highway for the People yet.' (XVI)

Gurney saw the future in the state grammar schools. Frank H. Shaw wanted to model the Elementary Schools along the lines of the public schools. He served in the Flying Corps in the first war as a captain and wrote many books for adolescents in the interwar years, mainly about the sea, but before the war he wrote one school story, *The Champion of the School* (1911). In this book the hero Jack Ambrose has to leave his boarding school because of his father's financial problems and go to the local elementary school. He sees this as an absolute disaster and appeals to his father against the decision. However, a new headmaster, Mr Wilson, comes to Spring Green Elementary School, determined to refashion it. He addresses the school in these words:

> 'Because a school is free it doesn't follow that it is a disgrace to belong to it . . . If the school is worth belonging to, of course, and my desire is to make Spring Green well worth belonging to. It is a free school, and I see a fine lot of boys and girls here. Can't we work together a bit? Don't look on me as your natural enemy – I'm not. I'm willing to stand

your friend, if you'll do the same by me; play the game all through, no shirking.' (200)

Mr Wilson and Jack pull the cricket team together so it begins to win. At this point Mr Ambrose's business is successful again and he wants to take Jack away from Spring Green but he will not leave.

In this story the public school code, or at least some part of it, is moved into a new type of school, but the elementary schools had always had a fairly strong legacy from the Arnoldian tradition. A boy develops through the tale and, although girls are admitted to be pupils too, the story is very much told from the boys' point of view. Despite the resemblance to a normal school story, Shaw very clearly reflects the reforming and critical spirit of many of the stories of the time. In addition, although the style of language used and the nature of the plot is definitely of the twentieth century, the book is not marked by the standardisation that was beginning at this time to be a mark of many representatives of the genre.

Standardisation

The view has been expressed – and indeed the myth about boys' school stories is just this – that books about boys' schools written in the 1920s still conformed to the pattern created by Reed in the 1880s (Crouch, 1962). This has already been shown here to be untrue. But what happened was more subtle than so far demonstrated. There were changes within or around the characteristics of the genre, but those works that remained within the genre also tended to become standardised. Canon C.E. Raven, a theologian and Cambridge don, expressed the result of this process well in an autobiographical work written in 1928:

> Take a juvenile athlete as your chief ingredient, add a wit, a bully, a persecuted fag, an awkward scholar, a faithful friend, a dangerous rival, and a batch of distorted pedagogues; mix these up in an atmosphere of genial romanticism; insert a smoking scandal, a fight, a cribbing scene and sundry rags, and a house match or two; bring them all to the boil when the hero scores the winning try or does the hat trick; serve the whole hot, and with a title associating the dish with an establishment which the initiated can identify; and the suburbs will raid the libraries for the result. (Raven, 1928: 13)

Raven believed that there had been attempts 'like those of Dean Farrar or Mr Kipling' to break out of the pattern, but these were vain protests and the recipe continued to be used despite its total lack of reality.

Some of the problems implicit in the genre had been noted by reviewers in the *Times Literary Supplement* as early as 1912. 'The great difficulty which all writers of school stories have to overcome is the uneventful evenness which makes up the actual life of a boy at a public school' (15 February 1912). Again, and more crucially, a writer 'is required to reveal character while he can exhibit it only in certain conventional situations and in persons who – being underdeveloped and under tutelage – are hardly free agents' (9 December 1915); the tendency for writers of school stories for adults to use masters as the main characters must be related to this difficulty. After the war such comments almost assume the status of a dirge in the Christmas book reviews. 'Adherence to convention, indeed, is the fundamental rule of the game' (25 November 1926). 'School stories are so much alike, and the material from which they have to be made so scanty, that we must give a particular welcome to one who does continue to get a little out of the material' (26 November 1931).

How was this seen to be achieved? This last reviewer notes a story rather like Shaw's *The Champion of the School*. The solution here is the one noted above of widening the range of schools about which stories may be told by using other than public schools. The problem about this course was that so often it attracted critical writers who wished to achieve reforms. Another solution was to widen the range of pupils involved in the stories by introducing, for example, an Australian, a 'raw but virile boy brought up under the rough conditions of colonial life, and thrown unprepared into the highly conventionalised existence of the English public school' (2 November 1929). Publishers also brought out books about Australian and American schools, though there were problems of technical terms, particularly in the latter case (7 December 1922). Yet 'The American school story at its best strikes us at first glance as being better than our best, because it is less trivial and childish.' The American boys were seen as 'younger members of the general community and share in its life and interests' (22 November 1928).

The process of standardisation was in great part due to the narrow conventions set by the expectations held for the genre. Its exact nature and the extremes to which it could lead will be demonstrated by examining first, in detail one story and then in a more general way the magazines, such as the *Magnet* and the *Gem*, which became so popular, starting in the Edwardian era.

Andrew Home wrote some thirteen boys' school stories between 1894 and 1909. Their titles hint at what is true, that they are well within the genre – *Through Thick and Thin* (1896), *From Fag to Monitor* (1896), *Out of Bounds* (1901), *The Boys of Badminton* (1905) and *Well Played!* (1907). His most successful story was *The Fellow Who Won,* first published in 1900 and reissued in 1920 and 1922.

The Fellow Who Won tells of two boys – Ned Duncan, adopted by Dr Templeton, head master of Barford School, in the private hope that he would ultimately succeed him as head, and Edwin Field, a ward of Dr Templeton, who is himself ambitious to outdo Ned. In Part One the boys are juniors, receiving detentions, undertaking illegal boating escapades, carrying out rags in class and using catapults. Field breaks a window with his catapult, but fails either to own up or hand it in to the headmaster, whilst the others, including Duncan, do so and are caned. The school bully, Kenyon, finds out about Field, who spies on him, discovering his drinking and betting activities, so forcing him to burn the catapult. Field now tells Duncan that he has heard 'the Doctor' say all their class will pass their 'Locals'. Duncan stops any extra preparation for these examinations as Field had hoped. Duncan fails and Field is first in the 'Locals'. Field even tries to make Ned appear to be cheating during the examination, but Ned shows himself innocent and does so without giving Field's trick away.

Part Two takes up the story two years later by which time Ned is an excellent games player, but poor at work, whilst Edwin Field is poor at games, but very good academically. Field is also a surreptitious bully. Ned catches Edwin caning his fag, Tommy Medlow, who is Ned's protegée. Ned who is only in the Fifth at once canes Edwin, himself in the Sixth, and arranges for his friend, Roger, to take Medlow as his fag. Roger warns him that Edwin will take his revenge. This he does by secretly poisoning Ned's dog, Gyp. Ned openly accuses Field of this act, but he denies it. Meanwhile Field has sent an anonymous letter to Ned, saying that Dr Templeton is disappointed in him. As Ned has no evidence and as Field denies the poisoning, Dr Templeton tells Ned that he is, as the latter said, disappointed in him and that Ned must publicly apologise. This occurs at the very time Ned is to be given an illuminated address to mark his bravery in pulling up some runaway horses. Ned can take no more and runs away from school to Liverpool with the aim of emigrating to Canada. A day with little money and no food cures him and he returns in the midst of a gale. The dormitories have had to be evacuated because of danger from falling chimneys, but Field has refused to leave. Ned rushes inside and saves Edwin, though both are knocked out as a chimney falls on them. Edwin is severely hurt. In hospital, faced with possible paralysis for life, Edwin admits all his deceptions made to try to outdo Ned and says, 'You've won' (XLVIII). A few years later the two meet en route to South Africa, where Ned now works and to which Edwin, having given up schoolmastering, is going for his health. The ship is holed at night and sinks. Edwin forces Ned at pistol point to take his place in the life-boat so that Ned is saved and Edwin drowned.

The Fellow Who Won is marked by short chapters – there are forty-nine in a normal length book. The sentences are brief, the style is conventional and uncomplicated, as are the ideas expressed, and the characters are prone to use slang. These tendencies can be seen in Duncan's remarks to Field, when discussing Kenyon's bullying of Field early in the story:

> '– only Kenyon's a beast, and the less you have to do with
> him the better. He drinks at pubs, and all that sort of thing,
> Some day the doctor'll get to know, and then he'll be
> expelled, and a jolly good thing too –' (IX)

One can imagine what Hughes, Farrar or even Reed would have made of this situation. There is no standing-up to Kenyon; all is expediency. Above all there is no serious explicit moral didacticism. The nearest Home comes is in a very few sentences like the following, which is taken from the last chapter when Ned and Edwin are on board ship: 'Mr Edwin Field's habitual attitude of mind. Life to him meant – himself; he was a failure therefore life was a failure. Q.E.D.' (XLIX). One recalls the final chapters of *Tom Brown* and of *Eric*. Furthermore, the implicit moralising is simple, compared, even, for example, to that of Reed. In an authorial aside at the start of Part Two Home writes: 'I don't know how you find it in your school, but my view is that you can't judge of a boy till you have watched him grow up among the fellows' (XXVII). Or, again, in relation to the schoolboy's code of honour when Ned had been caught ragging in class:

> 'What an idiot Duncan was', Field remarked to Baily

afterwards, 'not to say whose that thing was straight off! He'd have got off that impot.'

'That's just like Duncan – just like old Ned', said Baily with enthusiasm: 'he'll never get a fellow into a row, he's a trump.'

'Him!' sneered Field; 'I think he's an idiot!'

Finally, there are a number of dramatic incidents, most of which have been included in the resume above. In the middle of one, the stopping of the runaway horses, Home manages to insert the ritual reference to *Tom Brown*, as Ned thinks to himself, 'I must remember that a fellow in *Tom Brown* did it' (XXXIII).

The standardisation in Home's story is obvious, though not excessively so in contemporary literary terms. The worst examples of standardisation are provided by the schoolboy stories that were serialised weekly in such magazines as the *Gem* and the *Magnet*. These two magazines were run by the Amalgamated Press. The *Gem* began on 16 March 1907 and the *Magnet* on 15 February 1908. Both were casualties of the Second World War, the *Gem* ending on 30 December 1939 and the *Magnet*, claimed to be a victim of the paper shortage, on 18 May 1940. The competing publishing houses of D.C. Thomson of Dundee also published a number of successful weekly magazines of a somewhat similar nature: the *Adventure* (begun in 1921); the *Rover* (1922); the *Wizard* (1922); the *Skipper* (1923); and the *Hotspur* (1933). The last of these gave more attention to schoolboy stories and, hence is more comparable to the *Gem* and the *Magnet*.

Almost all the stories in these two magazines were written by one man, Charles Hamilton, usually using the pseudonym of Frank Richards, though elsewhere he used other names, for instance, Martin Clifford and Owen Conquest. In the 1920s Frank Richards was 'turning out copy at the rate of a million and a half words a year'. By his death in 1961 at the age of eighty-four he had written over 7,000 stories under twenty-eight pen names. He will always be remembered for his creation of two schools with two sets of boy characters. In the *Magnet* at Greyfriars were the four best known, the members of Mr Quelch's Remove: Harry Wharton, Frank Nugent, Billy Bunter and Hurree Jamset Ram Singh. In the *Gem* at St Jim's was a slightly less well remembered group led by Tom Merry and including Arthur Augustus D'Arcy. The names of the characters hint at the stereotypical nature of the stories, but two examples from the *Magnet* will give an idea of the extremely standardised material and style used by Richards:

> 'Please sir', gasped Bunter, 'it wasn't me who ragged your
> study!' 'What?' snapped the Remove master. 'You should
> say, "It was not I", Bunter.' 'Oh, sir', said the Oaf of the
> Remove, blinking. 'I never thought it was you –!' 'Wh-a-at?'
> 'It stands to reason you wouldn't rag your own study, sir!'
> (26 October 1929)

Again,

> 'the no-fulness', remarked Hurree Jamset Ram Singh, 'is
> terrific! The esteemed company of the absurd Bunter is not a
> boonful blessing' (8 April 1933)

The childishness of the humour is also worth noting, since in
earlier stories any humour came about entirely from the situations
in which characters were involved rather than from what they
said. Situations recur; remarks are repeated – 'I say, you fellows',
'Chuck it, Bunter'; characters are stereotypical and never change
from year to year – certainly they do not develop within any one
story. Finally, there are no explicit moral lessons. As one writer
put it, commenting in the *Times Educational Supplement* on 'The
Passing of *The Magnet*: An Old Friend Disappears':

> Greyfriars was a school where things happened regularly
> once a week – but where no one and nothing did. The
> excitement was in the midst of a dreamlike stillness; only the
> faint echoes from outside bore a hint of mutability. (25 May
> 1940)

Fred Inglis uses an apt phrase of the best writings of Frank
Richards – 'an unimproving eventfulness' (Inglis, 1981: 118).

In a well-known article in *Horizon* on 'Boys' Weeklies', written
in 1940, George Orwell noted that 'the mere survival of such
papers into the nineteen-thirties is rather a startling phenomenon'
(Orwell, 1940: 196-7). What is remarkable is not so much that
Richards wrote so much, but that he sold so many copies for so
long. There was no mention of religion or of sex; no war, no
poverty and no social classes; all foreigners were cardboard
figures. There was nothing violent beyond schoolboy ragging.
Indeed, the implicit moral code was a decent one compared with
some American magazines for adolescents. Orwell had no doubt
about the origins of these magazines. They did not owe so much
to those writing schoolboy stories at the date of their inception,

for example, to Desmond Coke. 'They are much more like Tom Brown's Rugby than a modern public school.' Greyfriars and St Jim's had no Corps; games were not compulsory; nor was there a school uniform. 'But without doubt the main origin of these papers is *Stalky and Co.*' (Orwell, 1940: 181).

Frank Richards answered Orwell in the next-but-one issue of *Horizon*. He was unconcerned about and unconvinced by Orwell's criticisms. A 'writer for young people should still endeavour to give his young readers a sense of stability and solid security, because it is good for them, and makes for their happiness and peace of mind.' As to Orwell's remarks on his presentation of foreigners Richard merely commented bluntly, 'foreigners *are* funny'. Orwell's arguments which accused Richards of practising implicit teaching went straight past Richards:

> To conclude, Mr Orwell hopes that a boy's paper with a Left-Wing bias may not be impossible. I hope that it is, and will remain impossible. Boys' minds ought not to be disturbed and worried by politics.

Richards's extreme conservatism – in the early summer of 1940 too – and anti-intellectualism may be judged by his final sentence:

> If there is a Tchekov among my readers, I fervently hope that the effects of *The Magnet* will be to turn him into a Bob Cherry! (Richards, 1940: 355)

Reception

As the standards achieved in schools surpassed the learning of little more than the 3 Rs the problem of what children should read in class became more obvious. As early as 1886 an angry parent whose daughters were at Pangbourne School had complained to the Education Department about 'a book . . . that is titled *Ivanhoe* . . . I object to her reading it on moral and religious grounds.' Around the same time there were complaints about the poem 'John Gilpin' by supporters of temperance and about 'The Lady of the Lake' as 'having an immodest tendency' (Lowndes, 1969: 10). Under the relatively decentralised British system of educational administration, however, decisions about what books were to be used in class were taken at local levels. Advice did, however, come from the centre and in its Report for 1910/11 the new Board of Education commented on the need 'in any well-equipped school [for] a small library of fiction consisting of historical novels and books of adventure; *Tom Brown's School-days* . . . ' (24). As we have seen *Tom Brown* and *Stalky and Co.* were in fact still read by numbers of schoolboys down to 1940. By this date too 'bloods' like the *Gem* and the *Wizard* were being used in English lessons as teaching material. Jenkinson found in his survey that half of secondary school English teachers used such magazines 'occasionally at any rate' and in senior elementary schools a third used them 'apparently rather more than occasionally' (Jenkinson, 1940: 131).

The mid- and late-Victorian schoolboy classics – 'Victorian Adventures' – had kept their high reputation. Publishers still found them profitable books. Thus, for example, in 1923 Humphrey Milford issued 'a uniform edition of some of the late W.H.G. Kingston's once widely popular books for boys' (*Times Literary Supplement*, 29 November 1923), though his two school stories were not included. Four stories by Henty were companion volumes in this same series. In 1930 works by Ballantyne and Kingston were reprinted and welcomed by reviewers in the *Times Literary Supplement*. The Religious Tract Society reissued two of Reed's books, *The School Ghost* and *Roger Ingleton Minor*, 'wholesome cheery tales, with less moralising than characterised so many school books of their day'. *Tom Brown* was also reissued and it,

> as of old still takes pride of place among the classics of school life. Even Tom Hughes did not quite succeed in painting the normal public school boy to the life, though he came nearer than anyone in a task which remains beyond the reach of art. Talbot Baines Reed nearly succeeded in *Some of Our Fellows* and *St Dominic's*, which is worthy of a place beside *Tom Brown*. (20 November 1930)

Another reviewer, writing in the *Quarterly* about schoolboy stories both for adults and children, was 'prepared to make a first class in which *Playing Fields* would definitely be senior, and *Tom Brown* second' (*Quarterly Review*, 1925: 40).

Critics clearly still gave the major authors here discussed an important place, but what were adolescents reading? Jenkinson's study has already been referred to on several occasions. This covered 1570 boys and 1330 girls, aged twelve to fifteen plus, in 11 secondary and 17 senior schools in urban areas. Secondary schools, at which some fees were paid, were state-provided schools which prepared pupils up to university level and hence tended to recruit mainly from middle-class homes, whilst senior schools were funded according to the lower level provided by the elementary code and were free; they, therefore, consisted largely of working-class pupils. Jenkinson asked not only what books were being used in schools, but what had been read out of school in the last month. Ninety-seven per cent of the boys claimed to read some books. Of the twelve-year-olds in secondary schools 42.8 per cent read adventure and 14.0 per cent school stories; by fifteen the percentages were respectively 36.2 and 5.3. In senior schools a different tendency was found: at twelve 53.3 per cent read adventure and 12.2 per cent school stories and by fourteen there had been little change, as the percentages were respectively 51.6 and 11.5 (Jenkinson, 1940: 15-16). The lower-class adolescents continued to read school stories, certainly up to the minimum legal age for leaving school.

Jenkinson also reported what books these adolescents claimed to have read. *Treasure Island* was the most popular amongst both secondary and senior school boys at twelve and thirteen with about one quarter of respondents claiming to have read this book. *Tom Brown's Schooldays* was named by just over 4 per cent of secondary and just under 5 per cent of senior school boys, the proportion declining with age. *Stalky and Co.* received one mention amongst the fourteen-year-old secondary school boys (Jenkinson, 1940: 36-44).

If the old classics were still holding their own with many readers and most critics, what of the new books? Jenkinson does not mention these, though publishers continued to bring them out, and presumably this was profitable, particularly for the Christmas market. The critics had varying responses. Wodehouse's early school stories were not well received. He was seen as derivative of *Stalky and Co.* (*Times Literary Supplement*, 20 November 1903; 11 November 1904). *Mike* was seen on publication as 'a very fair picture of school life' (*Times Literary Supplement*, 7 December 1909). But once he had succeeded in wider fields, views of Mike and Psmith stories, the only ones to achieve any lasting success, changed a little. When *Enter Psmith* was reissued in 1935 a critic wrote:

> The most obvious difference between this and Mr Wodehouse's later writings is that at moments he takes schools and schoolboys rather more seriously than, in his recent

works, he takes anything in the outside world. (*Times
Literary Supplement,* 7 March 1935)

A case of damning with faint praise if ever there was one!

Throughout the period from 1902 to the 1930s reviewers in the
Times Literary Supplement noted such adult stories as those by
Coke on their publication and in its Christmas number there were
columns on 'School Tales' before the war and on 'Books for Boys'
after the war. Two points emerge. First, school stories for both
adults and boys were now seen to have a possible political function.
The reception of *The Loom of Youth,* described in the last chapter,
makes this very clear. However, reviewers of boys' school stories
also noted this tendency and, furthermore, there was not only the
opportunity to criticise the schools, but to support them as they
were. Thus, in 1934 one reviewer made the general comment about
the 'propaganda' function of boys' school stories; there was 'a
certain flavour of propaganda in favour of the public school system
and its traditions' (*Times Literary Supplement,* 22 November 1934).
It was to this that Orwell had drawn attention in relation to the
Magnet and the *Gem,* though Frank Richards could not or would
not recognise the force of the argument.

In his consideration of Coke's *The Bending of the Twig* the
reviewer asks 'What we would ask *is* the conventional school
story?' He then lists *Tom Brown, Eric, Stalky and Co., The Hill,
Tim, Hugh Rendal* and one other story. He concludes, 'Each of
these books is as different from the rest as the career at school of
one boy is different from that of another' (*Times Literary
Supplement,* 23 February 1906). This is a striking confirmation that
the characteristics of the genre earlier drawn from Reed's
institutionalisation of it were the correct ones and were still
perceived in the Edwardian era as forming the pattern of
expectations implicit in the genre. In the sentence cited above
there is the expected assumption of the development of a boy in a
school under the influence of a set of values.

The second war brought an end to the *Gem* and the *Magnet,* but
a decline in the number of boys' school stories being published
was first noted in the First World War. In 1914 in a Christmas
review of 'School Tales' the reviewer in the *Times Literary
Supplement* commented, 'School tales, probably by accident rather
than design, are appreciably fewer than usual this year –
particularly those for boys' (10 December 1914). The 'accident'
seemed to be a sign of things to come. This review also draws to

attention the growth of school stories for girls, a development to be considered briefly in the next section. 'School stories' ceased to be indexed as a category in the *Times Literary Supplement* in 1916, being given two brief paragraphs in 1917. 'War Stories' were, however, now worthy of a full column. In 1918 'Books for Boys' included works by Edgar Wallace and four war stories by Percy F. Westerman, but only two school stories, one of which was a collection of short stories about the same school. 'For the moment school stories have lost their popularity' (*Times Literary Supplement*, 12 December 1918). This situation continued. In 1920 no school stories were included in the review headed, 'Books for Bys' and if one scans the advertisements in the Christmas number, only two publishers named school stories; Nisbet mentioned 'Some Good School Tales', three in total, two of which were by women, and Blackie advertised two new girls' stories by Angela Brazil.

In 1929 a reviewer commented,

> The once fairly plentiful output of stories of school life has been shrinking in recent years and this year the number is small enough to raise a question whether the shrinkage is a symptom of some real change in the taste of modern boy readers. (*Times Literary Supplement*, 21 November 1929)

The stories were thought to be fundamentally unchanged, though details had been altered to try to bring them up to date. Modern slang was used; motor bikes and lawn tennis now took their place. In the stories, tips from rich uncles had risen with inflation and were paid in paper money, not gold. In 1930 a slight improvement in numbers but not quality was noted (*Times Literary Supplement*, 20 November 1930). In 1932 there was 'a heavy drop to not more than a third of the number produced a few years back' (*Times Literary Supplement*, 24 November 1932). The obvious explanations were advanced. The slump was seen as not entirely to blame. There was also a 'want of freshness' and a lack of reference to the changed circumstances in life outside the schools. Finally, in 1939 a reviewer of 'Boys' School Stories' developed more fully the argument earlier advanced about a change of taste and had some views on the age of readership:

> The modern boy's interest in practical books on flying, high-speed locomotives and any kind of engineering enterprise or scientific achievement tends to make the story of

school life less popular than it was, and nowadays boys undoubtedly outgrow this class of book earlier than they did formerly. . . . It is probable that the present readers of the school story are mainly those between ten and thirteen, so that books dealing with life at a preparatory school make a particular appeal. (*Times Literary Supplement*, 5 November 1938)

From the evidence of the books cited here there does seem to have been some tendency to include a section about the hero's career at his preparatory school in twentieth-century school stories, both for adults and boys, but those entirely about preparatory schools seem rare.

Who, then, bought and read the magazines often known as 'bloods'? Orwell more or less agreed with a reviewer in the *Times Literary Supplement* of 1938 when he wrote that public school boys read them till the age of about twelve; boys at 'cheap private schools' for 'several years longer', but that they were 'certainly read by working-class boys as well' (Orwell, 1940: 82-3). Evidence was published within the year that would support Orwell's views. Table 8.1 summarises the situation as found by Jenkinson in his survey. The pupils in the secondary schools, largely middle class, read 'bloods' less as they grew older; the pupils in the senior schools, mainly working-class, continued to read much the same number of 'bloods' until the compulsory school-leaving age. The most popular of the magazines, and the order of popularity were much the same at all three ages and in both types of schools – they were: the *Wizard* as the most popular, followed by the *Hotspur*, the *Rover* and the *Skipper*. In the secondary schools *Modern Boy*, a magazine in which science fiction and adventure stories were more frequent than school stories, was more popular with younger boys than the *Magnet* or the *Gem*, though the *Magnet* overtook *Modern Boy* at fourteen and fifteen. The *BOP*, now a pale reflection of its former glory, had about the same level of popularity as the *Gem*. In the senior schools the *Magnet* was more popular at all ages than the *Modern Boy* and the *BOP* was not mentioned at all (Jenkinson, 1940: 68-70).

The serial stories in these magazines were both very different from and very much the same as those written by Reed in the *BOP* which had set the pattern for the genre; they were different in that so many of them were extremely standardised. The accusation levelled against *Tom Brown* and *Eric* that they lacked

Table 8.1 Number of schoolboy magazines read in a month
by age and type of school

Age	Secondary schools		Senior schools	
12+	(11.8)	3.7 per boy	(5.7)	4.2 per boy
13+	(17.5)	3.0	(7.3)	4.0
14+	(34.4)	2.0	(10.3)	4.0
15+	(49.1)	0.8		—

( ) show %s who made no answer
Source: Jenkinson, 1940: 64-5.

reality is much truer of these successors of those books. In
addition, all mention of religion had gone. Moral dilemma, and
hence the opportunity for, even implicit, didacticism, had either
disappeared from the plots or such material had become
simplified. The language and general literary style too was simpler,
marked by much slang and by repetitions. It was, of course, in
large part this simplicity and the stereotypical nature of the stories
that made them so attractive to many young and many older, but
less educated readers. Frank Richards would have had some
difficulty in writing the thousands of stories he did if he had
written like Hughes or Farrar or, for that matter, like Reed.

Girls' school stories

Nineteenth-century books for girls centered on family and home.
Towards the end of the century some school stories were written
and published, but the modern girls' school story owes much of
its development and character to Angela Brazil (1868-1947) whose
first story, *The Adventures of Philippa*, was published in 1906
(Cadogan and Craig, 1976). Prior to this we have seen that girls
were reading boys' school stories and the *BOP*. This tendency
continued so that in 1917 a reviewer in the *Times Literary
Supplement* went so far as describing 'the modern girl [as] the chief
reader of books for boys' (13 December 1917).

Many girls' school stories were written during the interwar
years as can be seen from the references made by the reviewers

quoted in the last section. Their nature, and probably their readership, is well described in a quotation from a review, entitled 'Girls at School', in the *Times Literary Supplement* during 1938:

> The bulk of the vast public who devour this form of reading matter is made up of girls who cannot hope to attain the giddy heights of boarding school. For them these blazer-bedecked heroines fill the places that the film stars occupy in the thoughts of their older sisters: like the romantic film the school story is an escape from reality. (15 November 1938)

Jenkinson's survey supports this interpretation. He found that less than 1 per cent of girls did not 'claim to read some book in the last month'. Table 8.2 presents relevant data.

Table 8.2 Girls claiming to read a book in the last month by age, type of book and type of school (%s)

School type	Age	School story	Home life	Adventure
Secondary pupils	12+	22.3	33.5	17.6
	13+	16.6	23.0	22.3
	14+	12.4	18.0	24.7
	15+	—	15.5	22.5
Senior pupils	12+	24.9	30.0	21.8
	13+	26.3	20.2	20.2
	14+	23.2	16.2	16.2

Source: Jenkinson, 1940: 173-4.

The pupils at the senior schools, recruiting mainly from the lower social classes, continued to read school stories in all the age ranges, whilst the percentages of those who were largely middle-class in the secondary schools fell away dramatically. Jenkinson's evidence shows that the school stories read were in the main not boys' school stories. He did, however, find that amongst fourteen- and fifteen-year-old girls at secondary schools *Stalky and Co.* was the most popular of Kipling's books, though it was not a widely made choice. There were also weekly magazines for girls. The

Amalgamated Press ran two: *School Friend* (1919-29) and *School Girls Own* (1921-36). Northcliffe himself imposed a strict code upon the writers: the word 'rotten' was banned for a time. The editor, in his turn, made a set of rules for the stories: cheats, liars and spiteful girls were not to prosper; smoking, drinking and swearing were forbidden; sex was out of the question (Cadogan and Craig, 1976: 231). Girls did read these magazines, as Table 8.3 shows.

Table 8.3 Number of school girl magazines read in a month by age and type of school

Age	Secondary		Senior	
12+	(14.0)	2.0 per girl	(16.5)	2.7 per girl
13+	(14.8)	2.0	(6.4)	3.3
14+	(34.0)	1.3	(7.5)	4.2
15+	(66.0)	0.6		—

( ) show %s who made no answer
Source: Jenkinson, 1940: 211-2.

Some girls did read boys' magazines and the percentages of these readers rose with age. They were 31.5 at fifteen for secondary schools and 26.6 at fourteen for senior school girls (Jenkinson, 1940: 217). The magazines read most of all were the *Wizard* and the *Hotspur* with the *Magnet* in the secondary schools, but with the *Gem* in senior schools. Neither *Modern Boy* nor the *BOP* were mentioned by girls. The teachers in girls' school used these 'bloods' as teaching material considerably less than their male counterparts, but, as was also true for the male teachers, they rarely tried to repress them.

Girls were still reading boys' books, but very much less than formerly, because they now had a literature of their own, though it bore the marks of its origins in boys' stories and of the origin of girls' schools which in so many respects were trying to do what boys' school did, but better. There was, however, a tendency for girls to read boys' magazines and this included those like the *Wizard*, the *Magnet* and the *Gem* which concentrated upon boys' school stories.

Changes in the social structure

The social, political and economic conditions in Britain were vastly different after the First World War from those around the turn of the century, but, particularly in the field of education, the crucial point to be remembered is that many values, attitudes and structures embodying these values were handed on from one period to the next and often with much support. The apparent calm and so-called progress of the late-Victorian years might be seen to have ended and a critical spirit to be at work in an endeavour to repair the damage done by the war and the depressed economic conditions, but it worked very largely from a set of assumptions constructed in the last century. Above all it relied on leaders trained to be what Howarth has christened 'Homo newboltiensis' or 'Newbolt man' (Howarth, 1973: 4-10).

Patriotism was important. Indeed, the demands for service for and duty to the nation were paramount as was graphically shown in the trenches from 1914 to 1918. A character marked by admiration for athleticism, a faint philistinism, emotional restraint and deference to authority, all of which were obviously related to what had been learnt in the public schools, was expected in national leaders. Because this was so, the leaders of the country and of its armed forces were followed into the war without question and this loyalty withstood the immense carnage that followed. For some years now colonial and trade rivalry, particularly with Germany, had led many to think that preparations for war were essential. Nationalism had been encouraged throughout the Edwardian era by the building up of the Volunteers/Territorial Army and the official encouragement of the celebration of 24 May as Empire day. The rapid acceptance of Baden-Powell's suggestion, made in the early 1900s, of the founding of the Boy Scouts built on and in turn supported this patriotic spirit.

But there was ground prepared for this militaristic and patriotic fervour. In December 1899 a simple questionnaire was given to some 600 English boys (N = 302) and girls (N = 289), aged eleven to thirteen. One question asked, 'What man or women of whom you have ever heard or read would you most wish to be and why?' Six of the first eight choices by boys were military heroes and included Kitchener, Nelson, Wellington and Baden-Powell. Shakespeare came fifth and Gladstone eighth. Interestingly, Kipling was thirteenth. For the girls Florence Nightingale was first choice and Gladstone second, both receiving about 15 per cent of the choices, but amongst the girls military heroes including Wellington, Nelson, Napoleon and the boy's equal first choice – with Kitchener – Sir Redvers Buller, were also popular (Dodd, 1900).

History textbooks at this time continued to support the view that 'the soldier was the hero rather than the villain of society'. In the Revised Code for Elementary Schools of 1899 twelve of the thirty stories dealing with the period from 1688 to modern times that were recommended reading for eleven-year-olds were 'wholly devoted to wars or war heroes' and these included Gordon and Baden-Powell. In the Edwardian era history textbooks appear to have become more supportive of war and its heroes. There was some tendency to justify violence and cruelty in terms of expedience, though there was also a growing concern about poverty. The texts for schools catering for both the middle and working classes all exhibited those tendencies (Chancellor, 1970: 70 and 89).

Nowhere is this almost dogmatic certainty in actions on behalf of Britain, provided they were entered into after earnest thought and could be supported from a Christian position, more apparent than in the heroes in John Buchan's adventure stories, mainly written, and so popular, in the interwar years. Many of these were intended for and achieved the dual readership of adolescents and adults. Buchan, a son of the Manse, was a Presbyterian, a conservative and a romantic, a not uncommon Scottish type, who went through his education, including Oxford University, on scholarships, filled many important posts, and ended his career as Lord Tweedsmuir, Governor-General of Canada (Himmelfarb, 1960). He was almost a living example of one of his own fictitious heroes.

There was much talk at the end of the war in 1918 of starting anew. Government and political parties announced many plans and aspirations, particularly in the field of social policy. In 1918, for example, before the end of the war, a new Education Act was passed. One of its main enactments was to extend part-time continuation education to all who left school at the minimum school-leaving age. In the light of the existing knowledge of economic theory in the days before Keynes's *General Theory* was published in 1936 the economic circumstances, first in the early 1920s, and then after 1929, made the fulfilment of such policies seem impossible. Furthermore, many of the taken-for-granted assumptions of pre-war politics had come to be questioned. This can be attributed both to the growth of the Labour Party since the 1906 election, a party beginning to question much of the existing social structure, and to the criticism that arose during the travails of a war that was almost lost. Patriotism was no longer necessarily always to be unquestioned. Even the upper middle class was open to this apparent disloyalty. There was, for example, the widely reported motion that 'this House will in no circumstances fight for its King and Country' passed by 275 votes to 153 by the members of the Oxford University Union in February 1933.

The generation responsible for this motion and moved by the feelings behind it had not fought in the war. Nor had many of the older generation. And the numbers of those between twenty and forty who had were severely depleted by the casualties suffered during the war. There was, therefore, a great opportunity for what Martin Green has called 'the undermining of the fathers'. A young, inexperienced and idealistic generation could shoot over the heads of the experienced and often cynical few at the discredited older leaders to whom previously deference had been accorded of right. The authors of the fathers were Kipling, H.G. Wells, Arnold Bennett and John Buchan. The young, some of whose critical attacks we have already noted, included Richard Aldington, Evelyn Waugh and George Orwell (Green, 1977: 86-95).

There was change too in the structure of the family. Views of children had altered. The beginnings of these new views have been noted in some children's literature in the late nineteenth century. The nice naughty child had begun to replace the earnest good child as an ideal. Freud's *Three Essays on Psychoanalysis*, one of which was on infantile sexuality, was published in 1905 and his ideas began to be influential even before the war, though not without opposition. As his biographer Ernest Jones noted, 'This assault on the pristine innocence of childhood was unforgivable' (Jones, 1955: 13-4). But one source of support for psychoanalytical views of the child was the growth in importance of the helping professions. Social workers and to some extent teachers were trained to hold a psychological view of the child that owed much to psychoanalytic theory. Freud too gave support to the growing doubt in revealed religion. This questioning of religion had other sources, particularly the general move away from deference to any traditional agent of respectability. The young now tended to question not only their fathers, but all in authority and this included those in the Church, the law and the schools.

Certainly the sanctions against disobedience of all types grew less stern. In part this was due to a lower tolerance of physical violence so that the floggings and canings reported so often in public schools now grew less common. Indeed, the incidence and severity of corporal punishment seems to have fallen throughout the period from 1900 to 1939 in elementary schools, both those run by the state and by the churches (Musgrave, 1977). Both in families, particularly in the middle class, and in schools, especially when progressive in their ideology, more subtle forms of individual and social persuasion tended to replace the physical techniques used in the nineteenth century. Rewards came to be given more emphasis than punishments. Children at home were not thrashed or at school beaten; they were ignored. For some such techniques were more traumatic in their use than the straightforward old types of punishment. For others they were seen to be lax and to cause the ill-discipline often complained of in young people. Evelyn Waugh, writing in the *Spectator* in 1929, and in an early example of his intransigent conservatism, said

> the only thing that could have saved the younger generation from anarchy (since they had no fathers) would have been a rigid school discipline. But unfortunately the schoolmasters came back from the war with a jolly tolerance of everything modern. Children who should have been whipped for disobedience were encouraged to think for themselves. (13 September 1929)

Pressures within families were greater because families were now on average smaller at every social class level. They were smallest in the interwar years amongst clerical workers in particular and in the middle class in general. This restriction on family size appears to have been a conscious reaction to bad economic conditions and was apparently an attempt by the lower middle class to ensure that their offspring at least enjoyed the benefits of a secondary education at a time when those with education suffered less unemployment and had more chance of either holding their social class position or achieving upward social mobility (Floud, 1954). In such tendencies are to be found the social roots of the continuing demands for an education in the public schools, particularly in those of lesser status which had lower fees, and for places in the new state-provided secondary schools.

The statistics showing the continuing increase in the proportion of the age group in public schools were quoted earlier. There was a parallel rise in the number of pupils in the new secondary schools about which Gurner wrote in such glowing terms. These schools had come into existence quite recently as a result of the 1902 Education Act and were supplied by the local authorities, though about half of the funding came from the central Treasury. Their growth may be judged from the following figures. In 1904/5 94,698 pupils attended grant-aided secondary schools; in 1937/8 the number was 484,076, of whom 8.3 per cent were in the sixth form (1911/12, 5.7 per cent) (Osborne, 1965: 136).

In many respects these schools grew in the image of the Arnoldian public school. Indeed, it was to something of the status of those older schools to which many first-generation grammar school parents aspired. However, some parents from the upper middle class, and particularly from the professional groups, recognised the truth of many of the current criticisms of these public schools and their traditional form of education. In this view the schools were criticised not as Kipling had done because they were not producing the men who would maintain the British Empire, but just because this was what they were attempting to do. In trying to achieve their aims they gave no chance for individuality to develop; they stressed the body at the expense of the soul; they emphasised intellect at the cost of the emotions; and, finally, they were single-sex schools, thereby not only discriminating against women, but preventing the normal sexual development of both sexes. As a result there was a growing support for the new 'progressive' schools, though it was not until 1938 that anyone wrote a school story at least in part about such a school. Then Reginald Turner's *Bring Them Up Alone*, a novel for adults, told of the moving of a boy from a public school to a coeducational progressive school. Progressive ideas were also strong in the teachers' training colleges and by 1939 had begun to have an influence in some elementary schools (Selleck, 1972). We can find the beginnings of this influence in Mr Wilson's handling of the Spring Green Elementary School – in his methods of proceeding rather than his aims, which were in tune with many found in traditional public schools.

Conclusions

The life of the genre petered out in the interwar years. Two tendencies were at work. One was a movement towards diversification; the other was that towards standardisation. Diversification meant that books about schools were written for adults as well as for boys, or sometimes for both readerships. In addition, whereas in the classical exemplars of the genre the stories were supportive of the schools and the social structure within which they were set, now the genre was being used both to criticise the schools, their educational beliefs and their exclusiveness and to suggest or support alternative forms of educational organisation. Rebellions in the schools were now nearly unknown, but 'dry rot' was admitted by some who recommended reform. Others, like Lunn and Alec Waugh, initially seemed to want radical change, but their love of their old school held them back in the end and they joined the reformers. Others yet again wrote in support of a grafting of the best of the old onto the newly developing state system. The second tendency, that towards standardisation, was marked by a stereotyping of the plots, the characters, the style and the material offered, seen in its most extreme form in the stories in such weekly magazines as the *Gem* and the *Magnet*. Furthermore, the morally didactic element so important early on disappeared entirely in these stories. Billy Bunter would be the symbol of this second tendency and Gordon Carruthers of the first.

One point must be clarified. In their original form the stories were fulfilling a propaganda function too, but of a very different order. They were supporting a set of values held by those in power and largely admitted by the ruled. This was no longer the case. The stories, both for adults and for children, were now part of the fray. When the stories were not written with some political aim they often fell victim to the tendency of standardisation. Compare *Tom Brown* or *Eric* with the *Gem* or the *Magnet* or even, and this is a fairer comparison, with Home's *The Fellow Who Won*; there is no mention of Christianity, seen as the basis of the moral code to be learnt; there is no explicit, and not much implicit, moral teaching of more than the traditional schoolboy's code of honour; academic work was important for some in the 1860s, in 1900 it was, except for the Army class at Westward Ho!, a source of japes and jokes – and usually childish ones too; a healthy attitude towards games had been replaced by a hearty fanaticism.

These changes were too great for the genre to remain viable. Writers reacted to changes in the social structure – to the new views of education, to the critical attitudes of schooling and the family, and to new views of religion and morality. Their publishers knew that books by the average writer, men like Coke or Home, would sell. The link between the existing expectations of readers and writers in a capitalist economy must be the publisher. When new authors came to them with new ideas that did not fit current expectations, either their own perceptions or their view of those of the potential readers, they were wary. This was true, as we have seen, of Anstey's *Vice Versa*. It was true, too, of Alec Waugh's *The Loom of Youth*, which was refused by several publishers. Kipling was an established author when he wrote *Stalky and Co.* That book was, too, more subtly subversive and only within the existing school and social system.

Any genre is marked by a set of expectations. To use 'genre' as an analytical tool is in a way to bow to a form of essentialism however much one may in the end deny this concept in its absolute sense. The pattern of expectations, the characteristics that mark the genre, and the relation between those who held these expectations, are all seen, at least temporarily, as relatively fixed, albeit by social construction, not by any appeal to philosophically derived essences. Genre is, therefore, to be seen as a temporary relatively unchanging pattern in people's minds. When that pattern no longer meets the problems that it was evolved to cope with, then the genre must itself change, decline, or disappear.

Evelyn Waugh was an outstanding and innovatory writer, even though he was of a conservative temperament. In September 1945, as the Second World War ended, he started a 'novel of school life', having re-read the diaries he wrote as a boy at Lancing. The title was to be *Charles Ryder's Schooldays*; Charles Ryder was a character in his earlier novel, *Brideshead Revisited*. Chapter I, 'Ryder by Gaslight', was published in the *Times Literary Supplement* in 1982 (5 March 1982). He never wrote more than this first chapter, because the book seemed to him to be about 'as untopical a theme as could be found'. Despite the renewed interest in education because of the 1944 Education Act and in the light of the recent election of a Labour government this was probably a reasonable judgment at that time. But though on the evidence of Chapter I Waugh's book would not have been an outstanding work, even of the quality of his brother's novel in 1917, yet whatever the social conditions some writer of genius

could have taken the genre and remade it as men like Hughe
Reed and Kipling had done. That writer has not yet emerged so
that the genre now consists of a residue from the past to which
few new additions are now made.

9

Conclusions

At the beginning of this study the point was made that this is a case study. It has traced the development and decay of one minor literary genre, the boys' school story. The conclusions, therefore, inevitably are of two kinds. Some definite findings can be reported that are of a social historical nature, that relate in the main either to the literary or educational history of the period 1860 to 1940. These concern the actual historical development of boys' school stories that has been set out here. Second, however, there are a number of points of a theoretical nature that can be made. These relate to the sociologies of literature and of culture, although, since the material here presented relates to children and schools there are some implications also for the sociology of education. Yet, because this is a case study, no sociological conclusions of general validity are possible. Only speculative points can be made which must ultimately be tested in other case studies, some suggestions for which are made, or by research especially designed to examine one or more of these specific points alone. The social historical conclusions will be presented first prior to examining matters of sociological concern.

Social historical conclusions

One finding that is patently obvious concerns the so-called 'flood hypothesis', that *Tom Brown* gave birth to a flood of similar stories for boys. This is just not true. There were a few school stories for boys before Hughes wrote his tale. There were a very few such stories for adults. After the publication of *Tom Brown* came *Eric*, and the school stories of the 1860s and 1870s were in many respects far more like Farrar's than Hughes's book. They were about private schools, usually small; their Christianity was more overt and less Broad Church; their plots lacked much emphasis on team games; and, finally, patriotism played a very minor role. When Talbot Baines Reed began his comparatively short, but intensive period of writing for the *BOP* – he wrote all his stories in a little over ten years – he inherited a tradition of boys' school stories that, even in the 'penny dreadfuls', was not the commonest type of boys' literature. The adventure stories of writers like Kingston or later Ballantyne and Stevenson, were more common and, probably, more influential. Reed, however, amalgamated the slightly different patterns provided by Hughes and Farrar and wrote morally didactic boys' school stories that for another thirty years provided the expectations to future writers, readers and publishers of such stories. These expectations were also accepted by literary critics and new works were measured against the pattern given to these books by Reed. A minor genre had been born, or, perhaps, it would more represent what had happened to say that it had been mutually constructed.

Nor was there a flood of adult literature following on the publication and widely acclaimed success of *Tom Brown*, be it noted, as a book for both boys and adults. One or two recognised authors tried to write adult school novels, as did Mrs Wood. The only author who wrote such a book that succeeded did so against his own expectations. Anstey believed *Vice Versa* to be a book that adults could read, but it was a success largely with adolescent boys. The flood of books for adults about schools appears to have begun in the 1890s. The generation brought up on *Tom Brown*, *Eric*, and their successors together with the younger men who had been the earliest readers of Reed's works formed the readership for these novels – for books like *Gerald Eversley's Friendship* or *Jasper Tristram*. But what has straightway to be noted is that almost at once some of these adult books became critical. For example, *The Thing That Hath Been* was first published in 1894, but the great era of the critical school novel was really ushered in by Lunn's *The Harrovians* in 1913, though the social and historical circumstances surrounding the publication of *The Loom of Youth* made this latter book more of a *cause célèbre*. The tradition had become diversified. The real flood might be seen to have been the massive output of standardised boys' school stories, and those for girls too, of the 1910s and 1920s, more especially for the

Christmas present trade and the stories in such 'bloods' as the *Magnet* and the *Gem* of which Frank Richards was the progenitor.

Throughout this rather complicated history of the genre a number of elements recurred in the plots. From early in the nineteenth century through to 1936 we find mention of school rebellions. The establishing and defence of legitimate authority, both at home and in the Empire, meant much to those in power during these years. Rivalries between boys, not only between athletes, but also between an athlete and an academic boy, were common. False accusations were also frequent. Masters are rarely central to the plot, but are seen as enemies by the boys involved. An explanation of all such elements can rightly, but too obviously, be sought in the social and historical circumstances of the time. The crucial point to note about all these common elements is that they provide opportunities for boys to stand against others or against the majority or even against adults. This was a key quality in the version of manliness that the schools were dedicated to teach. The recurrence of such elements in the plots was implicit in the genre because a well-understood moral didacticism was central to the genre and the courage to stand up for oneself, especially against the majority, was a vital part of it. Indeed, the one element present in nearly every boys' school story, even those written prior to *Tom Brown*, is representative of this quality. This is the outright condemnation of any boy who 'sneaked'. Such a boy would be outlawed by his peers and seen to be developing a doubtful character by the masters.

Yet, though, except perhaps in the standardised stories of the twentieth century, there was always some moral code that was presented overtly as worthy of learning, some elements in that code changed through time; an example was the growing restraint to be shown in openly displaying emotion. The code was fundamentally that of the upper middle class and was marked by two qualities above all else, deference to authority within a hierarchy and an abhorrence of lying. In addition, a sense of duty towards one's family, one's group, one's friends and the school was encouraged. But the mode of expression or tone of the code changed. Patriotism for Hughes was expressed through a deep attachment to rural England; for Kipling it meant service to maintain the Empire. Perhaps oddly the patriotic element tended with time to be given less emphasis in these stories. What has to be remembered is that there was a whole series of alternative sources for the creation and support of patriotic feelings. The adventure stories of Haggard, Henty, Westerman and Buchan all continued to show such feelings strongly, even if the critical adult school novels of the 1910s and 1920s did rather the opposite and even if the patriotic element is totally absent from standardised boys' stories like *The Fellow Who Won.*

This issue is of some importance, because since the 1930s one relatively influential view in the field of children's literature, apparently first stated by Helen Martin (1936), has been that 'there is a possible relation between periods of intense nationalism and the children's literature at the time'. She based her hypothesis upon a content analysis of a number of well known books for children from several nations, written over the last few decades, correlating her findings with the history of the nation concerned. From the evidence available in this present study of boys' school stories the process is obviously more complex than Martin originally believed. She may be right, but only if one grants that not all forms of children's literature need exhibit patriotic fervour, as it is exhibited more intensely in some forms rather than in others. Different types of children's literature must be balanced against one another.

Since the moral code that is to be learnt from reading boys' school stories changed through time the character of the heroes in the stories also changed through time. The qualities present in what Howarth (1973) has called 'Newbolt man' were only approved for a short period around the turn of the century. The muscular Christianity of Hughes differed greatly from its successor and 'Newbolt man' was in turn very different from 'scholarship man' of *The Day Boy* and even more different from his successor today, found in such novels as Bradbury's *The History Man* (1975). Yet in all its varieties it is the code of those who are being educated in all probability to hold greater or lesser power. In the nineteenth-century version the code was for the upper middle class, sponsored, as they were, for power. In the interwar years that code was still to be found in a somewhat attenuated form in books like Hay's *The Housemaster*, but there was too a meritocratic version to suit the advent of the scholarship holder. Neither was now overtly Christian or patriotic. One must view the didactic function of this genre in a comparative setting to realise that it is not at all unique. In her study of the socialising effect of children's literature in the Soviet Union O'Dell has shown how 'The moral Code of the Builders of Communism' is marked by six main virtues: 'collectivism, discipline, love of work, patriotism, proletarianism, internationalism and atheism' (O'Dell, 1978: 32). There was a firm code, parts of which paralleled that taught by the British genre. Thus, team spirit in Britain matched collectivism in the USSR, discipline was common to both, a sense of duty paralleled the love of work, patriotism was found in both and lastly Christianity was taught rather than atheism or, indeed, a belief in Communism.

Children's literature in Britain was rooted in didacticism so that from its earliest beginnings this genre was read as didactic, as strong approval for a definite cast of character. This is important in itself, because the type of character emphasised changed through time. Prior to the publication of *Tom Brown* and *Eric* the few school stories written presented a view of the moral qualities to be taught in schools that, though to some extent prefiguring later developments, was much influenced by Evangelical ideals, but after Hughes and Farrar wrote there was a gradual movement towards a Broader Church and more 'muscular' view, which put less stress on overt signs of Christianity and supported the form of personality that was found in what came to be called 'the public school type'. The literary flowering of this process is to be found in the works of Talbot Baines Reed. By the end of the century boys' school stories indicated quite clearly that the inculcation of certain moral, rather than intellectual, qualities was seen as the main aim of elite secondary schooling. This had immense implications for the new state secondary schools and also for secondary schooling throughout the British Empire. The important part played by the first generation of boys' school stories in this connection is clearly shown by the direction of the attack mounted by the writers of the critical stories after about 1900. Their main target, as *Stalky and Co.* and *The Loom of Youth* demonstrate, was the nature of the personality developed in the public schools and celebrated in these stories for boys and novels for adults.

Effects of the genre are very hard to measure. It is rare to find such definite effects of literature on society as O'Dell reported when the publication of one book led to the formation of the Timurite groups of adolescents to help in the war effort. The claim has been made that *Nicholas Nickleby* had such an effect. There were many schools like Dotheboys Hall 'in 1838 doing a roaring trade round about Bowes and Barnard Castle . . . *Nicholas Nickleby* very nearly put the whole lot out of business' (Clinton-Baddeley, 1957/8: 381). We have seen that the publication of *Tom*

Brown and *The Loom of Youth* made many people think about the aims and methods of the public schools. What is of more interest and more difficult to tease out is the long-term result of the presence of the genre over several decades so that generations of boys grew up reading its greater or lesser books or the yearly additions to their number.

Clearly throughout the whole period members of all social classes have read representatives of the genre, either in its high-quality or in its standardised form. We know *Eric* was read by working-class boys. The *BOP* had a readership through all social classes as did the 'bloods' of the twentieth century. But members of each social grouping, male and female, men and adolescents, middle- and working-class, will construct very different texts from the same book. Some boys in the upper middle class read the genre to prepare themselves to go to a public school. If this had not been the case Coke would not, indeed could not, have satirised the stories as he did in *The Bending of a Twig*. Others must have found support for their values in the books or Kipling could not have been so rude about *Eric* as he was in *Stalky and Co*. Others, again, must have read the 'penny dreadfuls' for entertainment, but this was at least to Kipling demeaning, as his friend 'M'Turk' pointed out in his autobiography, and this implies some effect. Working-class boys read the stories at home and at school. *Tom Brown* was recommended for inclusion in the library of state elementary schools. Many of Reed's books and others like his were given as Sunday School prizes. In the interwar years 'bloods' were used by teachers as teaching material in senior schools. They were also read massively outside school.

From around the turn of the century children were given much more freedom to create their own private worlds and their literature supported this position. *Bevis* and *The Secret Garden* are examples of this tendency. The literature that children read helps them to people their private play world, as all parents know. Books for adolescents will have a parallel effect in supporting this older age group in their private world. So upper middle-class boys reading boys' school stories are supported in their view of the social structure. These schools about which they read are the schools to which they will go or are at and the code described is the right one for them. They, as Kipling knew, are to be rulers, so they must read books fitting them to be rulers. They will learn the code of behaviour for those who assume that they will themselves be superior. Those in the lower levels of the middle class can see clearly in such literature where their aspirations must lie. The place of the mid-Victorian 'success' story was filled first by reference to upward mobility in school stories and then as the secondary school system was expanded by the modern merito-cratic boys' school story. For the working class the position was very different. They could learn that they were in the main excluded from such opportunities and could begin to adjust to their future adult position of relative political powerlessness. They early read of the qualities of superiority of those who were to be their leaders in war and peace, and could learn to make heroes of these men. The amateur players in county cricket and even as late as the 1930s in the football league are symbols of and reinforced this process.

Ogilvie wrote that

> No other kind of school has ever had the benefit of such propaganda and thousands of boys who were being educated at public expense or at piffling private schools dreamed wistfully of the glorious life they could only read about. (1957: 183)

In sociological terms what we are discussing here is the way in which the genre helped the successful operation of the hegemonic process in Britain during these years. This interpretation may be seen as speculative, but it is supported throughout by appeal to evidence internal to the books themselves. Furthermore, it is reinforced by a consideration of the adult books published as we have seen, from the 1890s on.

The uncritical novel for adults about schools had to be well constructed and well written to attract a readership. Raven's quoted recipe hints at one of their main markets, those who knew the particular school concerned. Such books would also be readable by many who knew the type of school concerned. They were read in a spirit of nostalgia and gave support to the *status quo*, both social and educational. It was only because this was the case that Longmans would or could publish both Martin Browne's and Jack Hood's answer to Alec Waugh's *The Loom of Youth*. The critical novels are a crucial test of the whole hypothesis. They caused many hard words. Figures from the ruling class, like Lyttelton, former Headmaster of Eton, were stirred to defend the schools with vigour and literary critics in journals supportive of the *status quo* wrote stinging remarks about propaganda novels. Criticism by these novelists of the hegemonic process at work drove those with an interest in keeping its operation unchanged into defensive measures.

Sociological conclusions

In the past, considerations of boys' school stories have been either literary, psychological or historical. Hicks's pioneering study in 1933 was comparative, dealing with Britain and Germany, but his method and conclusion were literary in essence. For example, Hicks wrote, 'The English novelist, ignoring on the whole the day school, has gone to the source of the best narrative, that is, the public school' (1933: 118). The reason for writing about public schools was entirely literary in nature. No real possibility of sociological explanation was entertained. More recently, Quigley's (1982) approach was literary and historical in that she traced the development of boys' school stories, without really differentiating them from school stories for adults, through time using criteria of literary excellence. Her conclusions were somewhat different from those reached here, particularly in two respects: since she gave no attention to the precursors of *Tom Brown's Schooldays* or to the period between Hughes and Farrar and Reed, her interpretation tends to be a version of the flood hypothesis in which Hughes's roots in the past are ignored and Farrar's influence on the future is overlooked. One major historical study, that by Mack (1941), used school stories as one of its major primary sources, though more weight was put upon those written for adults than for boys. Mack traced changes in social attitudes towards the public schools by examining books written throughout the period since *Tom Brown*. More recently, Mangan (1981) has to a minor extent used examples from this genre to illustrate the emergence and consolidation of athleticism as an educational ideology in the public schools. The reasons for writers choosing to write boys' school stories have been attributed to various psychological mechanisms by a number of different writers. C.A. Alington in 1936 felt that 'a public school novelist *in posse* existed when 'a cleverish boy' felt his merit to be 'insufficiently appreciated' (1936: 228-9). A more recent writer, Gathorne-Hardy, who has some expertise in the educational field, advanced an explanation for writing school stories based on the working-out of unconsummated homosexual love (1977: 180).

To some extent the research questions asked by literary critics, historians and psychologists differ from those asked by sociologists. There is no monopoly of discipline over any area of primary source material. Sociological approaches to the analysis of the career of a genre can be variously based. A homological account would put the development of the genre side by side with the apparently relevant historical events. This is not so useless a procedure as some attacks on it would make it seem. Clearly the content of boys' and adult school stories changed through time and no very subtle analysis is needed to explain this. Day schools and lawn tennis were introduced because they were now part of the educational and social scene at large. But although this type of analysis may point to a source of change it does not clarify the mechanism. Lodge points us in the right direction when he describes 'literature as a system of possibilities, of which the corpus of literary works is a partial realisation' (1981: 4). Yet even these words, after their use of the concept of potentiality in the world 'possibilities', slip in the direction of fixity or ultimate stability by speaking of 'partial realisation'. Because of problems of this nature the analysis here has been in terms of writers, readers and middlemen. Those who fill these social positions create the texts about which we speak, but the texts of any author are reconstructed variously by readers of different natures or at different times. Comments will be made about each of these three social positions prior to some final remarks concerning the concept of genre.

Writers

In an essay, entitled 'What is an Author?' Foucault has written of the very few authors who 'occupy a transdiscursive position'. As examples he names Homer, Aristotle and the Church Fathers. Such writers produced theories, traditions, or disciplines 'within which new books and authors can proliferate'. Foucault also speaks of a second category, 'initiators of discursive practices', and sees the writers of nineteenth-century Europe as included here. The distinctive contribution of such writers is that they not only produced their own books, but the possibility of and the conventions governing other works. Foucault is somewhat doubtful about applying this concept to novelists, since he sees those who follow after the initiators as no more than 'imitators' (Foucault, 1977: 130-2). Yet this seems an unduly limiting view, because it totally ignores the way in which their imitations are reconstructed by succeeding generations of readers. It also does not make enough of the fact that at some point an individual with the help of his publisher and readers does bow to a new pattern of expectations and initiatives. No sociological analysis, however much weight it puts upon social structural considerations, can ignore the part individuals play in negotiating their place in that structure or in achieving the creation of innovation within that structure as a result of carrying off successfully an act initially defined as deviant or, more likely in the literary field, writing in a way not seen before, that is, creating their own new niche in the literary sector of the social structure.

Hughes and Farrar in the late 1850s wrote books that built in a prefigurative way upon various emergent elements in the literary world of their times. They inserted themselves successfully into a niche in the social structure, which was at a time of rapid industrialisation, particularly for the middle class, characterised by a growing concern with education outside the family. These two writers, and indeed their publishers, had no idea that their books would be best sellers and would lead to a profitable trade in writing imitations of them. Talbot Baines Reed, then a comparatively unknown writer, at the request of the editor of the new *BOP*, likewise gradually, and again in a prefigurative manner, over a very few years institutionalised a pattern of expectations that built on the works of Hughes and Farrar and their imitators who had largely tended to follow Farrar's example. A genre was now born; Reed's pattern was dominant. At the turn of the century, Kipling, an established author, seen by his readers in a certain light, found space in the historical moment of the Boer War to renew the patriotic element in the genre. But he was critical of the genre itself and some of the values expressed in it, and in the succeeding period of social change, both before and after the First World War, writers for boys and adults were able to find space to write critically of the schools and of the genre.

Althusser sees literature as being uniquely capable of revealing and even rupturing dominant contemporary ideologies. This is true, but sounds merely radical, whereas books can rupture an old ideology and create in its place a conservative or a more conservative one. This was the tendency of school stories. Even the critical ones did no more than suggest that the mechanism of the schools should be revamped in order to make them more efficient. Furthermore, the Althusserian position makes the suggested process sound automatic, whereas it depends upon readers reconstructing a text in a given way. In 1913 Lunn's *The Harrovians* was not constructed by readers in the same critical way in which was Waugh's *The Loom of Youth* in 1917. Both made the same attempt and had the same intent to rupture, in a minor way, the ideology governing the schools. Furthermore, writers can be mistaken about the effect that their books may have, as was Anstey, when he thought that he had written a book for adults rather than one mainly for boys. The author constructed by readers may not be the one expected by the writer. Finally, in a capitalist society the whole process depends upon the writer finding a means of publishing his work. Similar middlemen exist in non-capitalist societies, although possibly with greater, certainly with different, powers of censorship.

Middlemen

Those publishing novels for adults operate within a pattern of related expectations. This is partly determined by residual literary tradition, partly by contemporary historical circumstances and partly by publishers' views of likely choices made by potential readers. Chaney has rightly pointed out that 'popular art is produced *for* an audience' (Chaney, 1979: 9). Macmillan did not publish *Tom Brown* as a work of popular art. Nor, certainly initially, did Hutchison, the editor of the *BOP*, publish Reed's stories as popular works, though that is what they became, contributing to the growth of a popular market in boys' school stories, of which the yearly crop of school stories at Christmas up to the 1920s was the index. Writers were meeting the publishers' needs to make a profit by themselves making a living out of becoming a known type of author. Frank Richards was the example *par excellence* of this.

Sociologists of literature are familiar with this process, but have always written of it in relation to books for adults. It becomes more complex when books for children or for adolescents are considered. The middlemen who may have some influence on the process of publication and of construction of a text are more extensive. Thackeray had written of 'the young girl standard' but not of how this developed or who was responsible for ensuring it was followed. From the evidence of this case study some of the stuctures within which expectations about children's literature are generated can be seen.

Even if there is no consensual force at work such as public

opinion about what children should read there is a belief, perhaps open to manipulation by the Mary Whitehouses of this world, that there is. Indeed, one of the aims of writing in the weeklies or the monthlies about this subject clearly is to create the impression of a public opinion existing, that is, to work on the relations of expectations. Publishers like the Religious Tract Society were, however, very conscious of what they thought ought to be published in the *BOP* or their other publications and also of what they thought Christian parents would allow their children to read. Where an opinion did not exist such a publisher saw himself as an agent of respectability making sure that the innocent young were not defiled, that is, ensuring that the young grew in the version of respectability approved of by that agent. In the nineteenth and early twentieth century circulating libraries also sanctioned what should be published and public libraries, or their committees, may today fulfil a similar role.

Soon 'experts' in children's literature evolved. Charlotte Yonge, herself a writer for girls, was one of the earliest. Nor must it be forgotten that one of the groups that she was aiming to influence was Sunday School teachers, themselves responsible for choosing prizes, usually books, for their pupils. A little later Edward Salmon was another such expert. He was an innovator in that he cited data gathered by questionnaire upon which to base his views, though the data was not so complex as that gathered in the 1930s by Jenkinson, himself a university lecturer on Education, and more particularly on the teaching of English. These experts tried to influence both parents and those *in loco parentis*. Children were not seen as necessarily capable of making wise choices on their own, so that they must be helped and experts set out to influence the children at second hand through those who could help them.

Teachers are the most obvious group who stand *in loco parentis* to children and where literature is concerned the teachers who will have a possible influence on choices of what will be read are primary teachers who are responsible for the early stage of English teaching and at the secondary level the specialist teachers of English, though teachers of foreign languages will have a comparable position in regard to older pupils' choices of books written in languages other than English. Teachers are much influenced by what material is available to them. Thus, we saw English teachers in the interwar years using both examples of the genre and 'bloods' like the *Magnet* and the *Gem* in their English lessons. In addition, they are dependent upon the resources of their school, including its library, which, as we have noted, can be influenced by the Inspectorate through advice, reflected in annual reports to the Minister.

But the power of middlemen does not end in the classroon or the school. As has been shown elsewhere (Musgrave, 1982a), those who train teachers influence how they perceive what should be read by their pupils. Furthermore, school libraries have now become larger and more specialised, so that school librarians are specially trained for their task. These librarians influence what is available in school libraries and advise children and teachers how to use their book stock. Finally, the availability of libraries varies very greatly between countries. Thus, in 1965 Americans bought 14 books per household and borrowed 13; comparable figures for the British and French were 4 and 38, and 10 and 1 (Kermode, 1975: 23). Clearly, the opportunities for different groups of middlemen, acting largely as agents of respectability, to influence children's choices of reading matter varies culturally.

A useful study could be made to investigate the language and values of the books that evolve from this process of 'censorship' as approved for use in schools at different levels of society. We know that works like *Tom Brown* and *Eric* were read in schools up to and around 1900 and we know, setting aside the values, explicit and implicit, in these books, that the language used in them was very different from that used in the daily speech of many of the pupils concerned. *Stalky and Co.*, in which the speech was less literary and more realistic, was used in the 1920s/1930s, but so too was the *Gem*, whose speech was more akin to a perhaps unrealistic version of the slang of a certain type of public school boy. Today everyday speech forms are common in the literature studied in schools. Whereas a case can be made that down to the 1930s the language forms read were supportive of hegemony, is this still the case when the language of the dominated class is so readily studied in schools?

Readers

Though the genre continued through the period after its institutionalisation by Reed until its decay in the interwar years books within it were constructed differently by readers through-out the period. This obvious point can be seen in the way *Tom Brown* passed from a best seller to a classic to be read in school almost within twenty-five years. *Eric* was always criticised, but in its earlier years in a very respectful way. By 1899 Kipling's heroes in *Stalky and Co.* thought nothing of its overt moralism. The 'penny dreadfuls' were effectively replaced in the 1880s for many readers by the *BOP* and then by its standardised imitators, the 'bloods' of Frank Richards and his imitators. They too in their turn became material that could be used in schools for teaching purposes, presumably both to teach reading and to form a critical basis upon which to build the more approved literary expectations known as good taste.

But a more subtle process was also at work, relating to the growth of an adult readership for school stories. Some adults read boys' school stories. Yet other writers were able to find a space in the literary output of the times to insert in much greater quantity than ever before adult school stories. Many of these fell absolutely within the genre. They were uncritical tales of the development of a boy, told from his point of view, at a boarding school, learning the approved moral code. Others, however, to meet the more complex characterisation expected in novels for adults found the need to make masters rather than boys their heroes. Others, again, used this new development to criticise both the schools and the moral code celebrated in boys' school stories, and sometimes even the genre itself. Alec Waugh criticised both Kipling's values and boys' school stories in *The Loom of Youth*.

There had been critical boys' stories in the 1880s, but the real stream of adult school stories, some of them critical, started to flow in the 1890s and was in full flood after the end of the war. What seems to have happened is that the generation brought up on *Tom Brown* and his successors in the 1860s/1870s had become adult readers in the 1880s/1890s and could form a readership for an adult version of what they had been, and had, themselves, expected to read as boys. This intergenerational cultural process allowed the emergence of an adult version of the school story which in the social and historical circumstances of the time could easily become critical. To use a concept found in analysis of the mass media a 'sleeper' effect was at work. But, if this was how this development occurred, a theoretical point of some importance can be made, which once again demonstrates the benefits of using children's books as a basis for analysis in the sociology of literature.

The Russian writer Shklovsky enunciated a 'law of the canonization of the junior branch'. According to this the materials and methods of such 'sub-literary' genres as thrillers or romances come to provide devices through which literature renews itself (Bennett, 1970: 58). In the case of school stories those for boys a generation later provided exemplars for a new adult fictional form, which in some cases became so critical in tone that the world of adult fiction was made more lively. Two points emerge. First, there could be a case for searching for other examples of non-adult literature being canonised in this way. Second, there could also be some advantage in bearing in mind that changes in adult literary taste, that is, in the expectation of adult readers, may be born in some way in what they read when young a generation or so earlier.

Genre

The concept of genre has here proved to be a profitable and worthwhile analytical tool. Without doubt in the case of boys' school stories for a period from the 1880s to at least the 1930s this genre was a phenomenological reality in the literary world of Britain. Yet, it was a changing reality and the view of genre stated at the end of the last chapter is the one that is to be pressed here. Genre is not an essentialist concept, but any genre does have a temporary and a socially negotiated reality, which forms a social factor that influences and is influenced by the behaviour of writers, middlemen, and readers.

The interesting quality of this particular minor genre is that its characteristics, the pattern which formed the genre, was a very narrow one. It was so limiting, for example, that it could not easily accommodate its usage for adults – boys were replaced by adults as central figures. A genre is a solution to a perceived literary problem. Hughes and Farrar wanted to teach a particular set of values for boys, largely of the upper middle class. They evolved a way of doing this. Some fifty or sixty years later the problem perceived by writers had changed. Kipling saw it differently for boys and Alec Waugh for men. A little later still Alec's brother Evelyn moved from criticism to satire, a totally new solution, rarely adopted by others since. But due to its limitations, upon which the critics in the *Times Literary Supplement* regularly commented, certainly during the interwar years, the genre could not cope with the demands put upon it. No doubt the genre could have survived if there had continued to be a strong demand for works of moral didacticism of the old type, but due to structural change there was not. The genre, therefore, began to decay, so that examples of it today remain only as residues from a past era, a source for us today to learn of the problems and solutions of times now past.

So far the points made about the genre have been general. There is one specific point about school stories and those for boys in particular, that must be explored. Many writers have said that the genre was a particularly English creation. Perhaps, in passing, this Englishness should be stressed. Only two stories, both for adults and both about one of the few Scottish public schools, namely Loretto, are known to me (Freeman, 1891: Connell, 1930). So far only one comparative study, that of Hicks (1933), has been written. Hicks compared British and German school stories. The genre to which the school story may most readily be compared is the German *Bildungsroman* of which the school is never the main focus, since the emphasis of these stories is always upon an individual's development, not upon his growth into a social being within a well defined group, as was the case in the English school story, whether written for adults or for boys alone. Furthermore, the German secondary schools were almost entirely day, not boarding, schools, and seen as agents of academic, not of moral, education. Therefore, the conditions for the growth of the genre in Germany at least were unpropitious. Comparative work on the place of English school stories in such English-speaking countries with boarding schools as Australia or New Zealand would, however, add a further perspective to this case study.

Finally, what is happening to the genre today? Several of the books that have played an important part in the development of the genre have recently been given new exposure by their presentation as television serials. This is the case for *Tom Brown*, *Vice Versa* and *Stalky and Co*. From the comments of reviewers and personal observation of these serials they are not seen today as school stories, but as historical costume dramas. Their didacticism and the code to be learnt according to the expectations of the nineteenth-century and early twentieth century are no longer perceived as crucial elements. These books are not, therefore, constructed on television as members of the genre.

Stories about schools are, however, sometimes still published. Two may be briefly mentioned, one American and the other English. Cormier's *The Chocolate War* (1975) a book popular with secondary-school English teachers throughout the English-speaking world, tells about the way funds were raised by the boys selling boxes of chocolates in an American Catholic school. Those administering the school used the informal social structure of the school to pressure boys to sell quotas. One boy stood out against this and was cruelly bullied. There are elements here that are comparable with parts of *Stalky and Co.*, since, as we saw, in one story the Padre used the trio of Stalky and Co. to stop bullying in the school and did not ask about the rather violent means that were used to that end. However, Kipling's book was didactic, unlike *The Chocolate War*, and was not permeated with a tone of physical violence, whereas Cormier's is. Cormier's book can more easily be termed, and this is a phenomenologically recognised contemporary minor genre, 'an adolescent problem story' set in a school.

Much the same can be said of Wood's *A Period of Violence* (1977). In this work the ageing head of Seacliffe Comprehensive School dies of a coronary and his deputy, Mr Dickens, aged forty-eight, takes over, determined to tighten up discipline, which he believes has become lax under Mr Fairborn. The result is not so much a planned rebellion as that large numbers of the school run amok, doing much damage to property and indirectly causing one girl to be seriously hurt when she is run over by a car. During the story the hero and his girl friend are described having sexual intercourse on two occasions. Once again we have a story about the problems of adolescence set in a school.

These two contemporary school stories, one a so-called American adolescent problem novel, pose again an issue raised in the first chapter. This concerns what happens if the parent genre, the novel, develops fundamental expectations greatly at odds from those ruling for the sub-genre, here the boys' school story. Clearly the tone of these last two stories has something in common with the pessimistic nature of many contemporary adult novels. Yet, though a critical spirit may have invaded the genre soon after it was institutionalised at the time of Reed, pessimism is really only found in such bitter inter-war books as Aldington's *Death of a Hero*. Only in very recent years can this same spirit be found in stories for adolescents. Therefore any effects of the contemporary changes in the novel in assisting the near-death of the minor genre must be indirect. The exact mechanism would seem to be that the values expected in these stories were optimistic and pessimism in adult stories was one more strain on the narrow limits of the diversified genre. The coffin of this minor genre was nailed with nails of diverse nature, but this was not one of them.

Conclusion

Clearly the last book quoted, *A Period of Violence*, was set in a comprehensive school to match the contemporary historical circumstances. The content of novels or changes in them can be analysed in this homological way, though this method of analysis does not provide for a mechanism of causation. Any full explanation for the existence of adolescent problem stories must be made, as was done for boys' school stories, by examining the relations of expectations of writers, middlemen and readers and by noting how these are mediated by the operation of publishers or their equivalents in non-capitalist countries. Such an analysis, focusing upon relations, can lay bare the structure implicit in the genre itself and thereby force attention, as has been the case in this study, upon the social supports for and the contradictions to that structure. These supports and contradictions, as worked on in history by individual writers and middlemen, and by readers in various social positions, provide the incidents that comprise the biography of any literary genre.

Bibliography

Primary sources

Books

Adams, H.C. (1861)
Schoolboy Honour.
Adams, H.C. (1872)
The Doctor's Birthday.
Aldington, R. (1929)
Death of a Hero.
Anstey, F. (1882)
Vice Versa.
Ballantyne, R.M. (1857)
Coral Island.
Banks, G.L. (1872)
The Manchester Man.
Barbauld, A.L. (1792-6)
Evenings at Home.
Benson, E.F. (1915)
David Blaize.
Bradby, G.F. (1914)
The Lanchester Tradition.
Brontë, C. (1847)
Jane Eyre.
Brontë, C. (1853)
Villette.
Browne, M. (1918)
A Dream of Youth.
Butler, S. (1903)
The Way of All Flesh.
Clarke, A.W. (1899)
Jasper Tristram.

Coke, D. (1906)
The Bending of a Twig.
Coke, D. (1910)
The School Across the Road.
Connell, J. (1930)
Lyndsesay. The Story of a Boy.
Cormier, R. (1975)
The Chocolate War.
Day, T. (1783-8)
Sandford and Merton.
Dickens, C. (1839)
Nicholas Nickleby.
Dickens, C. (1854)
Hard Times.
Disraeli, B. (1844)
Coningsby.
Drummond, H. (1892)
Baxter's Second Innings.
Eady, K.M. and R. (1920)
Riverton Boys. A Story of Two Schools.
Edgeworth, M. (1796)
The Parents' Assistant.
Ewing, J.H. (1878)
We and the World. A Book for Boys.
Farrar, F.W. (1858)
Eric or Little by Little.

Forster, E.M. (1907)
The Longest Journey.
Freeman, R.M. (1891)
Steady and Strong.
Gilkes, A.H. (1895)
*The Thing That Hath Been or a
Young Man's Mistakes.*
Gosse, E. (1907)
Father and Son.
Hay, I. (1936)
The Housemaster.
Hilton, J. (1934)
Goodbye Mr Chips.
Home, A. (1900)
The Fellow Who Won
Hood, J. (1919)
The Heart of a Schoolboy.
Hope, A.R. (1870)
My Schoolfellows.
Hope, A.R. (1873)
Stories of Whitminister.
Hughes, T. (1857)
Tom Brown's Schooldays.
Hughes, T. (1861)
Tom Brown at Oxford.
Kenyon, E.C. (1883)
*Jack's Heroism. A Story of Schoolboy
Life.*
Kingsley, C. (1855)
Westward Ho!
Kingston, W.H.G. (1851)
Peter the Whaler.
Kingston, W.H.G. (1860)
Ernest Bracebridge or Schoolboy Days.
Kingston, W.H.G. (1860)
*Digby Heathcote or The Early Days
of a Country Gentleman's Son and
Heir.*
Kipling, R. (1898)
'The Brushwood Boy' in *The
Day's Work.*
Kipling, R. (1899)
Stalky and Co.
Kipling, R. (1909)
'The Puzzle' in *Actions
and Reactions.*
Kipling, R. (1923)
'Stalky' in *Land and Sea Tales.*

Kipling, R. (1937)
Something of Myself.
Lawrence, G.A. (1857)
Guy Livingstone.
Leslie, S. (1922)
The Oppidan.
Lunn,A. (1913)
The Harrovians.
Mackenzie, C. (1913)
Sinister Street.
McKenna, S. (1917)
Sonia.
Mansfield, R.B. (1860)
*School Life at Winchester College or
The Reminiscences of a Winchester
Junior.*
Marryat, F. (1838)
Mr Midshipman Easy.
Martineau, H. (1841)
The Crofton Boys.
Maugham, W.S. (1915)
Of Human Bondage.
Millington, T.S. (1883?)
Straight to the Mark.
Millington, T.S. (1886?)
Some of Our Fellows.
Nicholls, B. (1920)
Prelude.
Reed, T.B. (1880)
*The Adventures of a Three Guinea
Watch.*
Reed, T.B. (1881)
The Fifth Form at St Dominic's
Reed, T.B. (1882)
My Friend Smith.
Reed, T.B. (1883)
The Willoughby Captain.
Reed, T.B. (1885)
*Reginald Cruden. A Tale of City
Life.*
Reed, T.B. (1886)
Roger Ingleton Minor.
Reed, T.B. (1886)
A Dog with a Bad Name.
Reed, T.B. (1887)
*Follow My Leader or The Boys of
Templeton.*

Reed, T.B. (1887)
The Master of the Shell. A School Story.
Reed, T.B. (1891)
The Cock House at Fellsgarth.
Reed, T.B. (1892)
Tom, Dick and Harry.
Reed, T.B. (1897)
A Book of Short Stories.
Reed, T.B. (1905)
Parkhurst Boys.
Reed, T.B. (1930)
The School Ghost and Boycotted.
Shaw, F.H. (1911)
The Champion of the School.
Shaw, F.L. (1878)
Castle Blair. A Story of Youthful Days.
'Shaw, K.' (1920)
For Sons of Gentlemen.
Sherwood, M.M.B. (1818)
The History of the Fairchild Family.
Sinclair, C. (1839)
Holiday House: A Book for the Young.
Smedley, F. (1851)
Frank Fairleigh or Scenes from the Life of a Private Pupil.
Smiles, S. (1859)
Self Help.
Smith, A. (1831)
The Fortunes of the Scattergood Family.

Sturgis, H.O. (1891)
Tim.
Thackeray, W.M. (1850)
Pendennis.
Trimmer, M.M. (1788)
Fabulous Histories.
Trollope, A. (1881)
Dr Wortle's School.
Turley, C. (1902)
Geoffrey Marten Schoolboy.
Vachell, H.A. (1905)
The Hill.
Walpole, H. (1911)
Mr Perrin and Mr Traill.
Walpole, H. (1927)
Jeremy at Crale.
Waugh, A. (1917)
The Loom of Youth.
Waugh, E. (1928)
Decline and Fall.
Welldon, J.E.C. (1895)
Gerald Eversley's Friendship. A Study in Real Life.
Williamson, H. (1922)
Dandelion Days.
Wodehouse, P.G. (1909)
Mike and Psmith.
Wood, H. (1867)
Orville College.
Wood, K (1977)
A Period of Violence.
Yonge, C.M. (1853)
The Heir of Redclyffe.

Journals

The Boys' Own Paper
The Times Educational Supplement
The Times Literary Supplement

Secondary sources

Books

Alington, C. (1936)
Things Ancient and Modern
Longmans, London.

Anstey, F. (1936)
A Long Retrospect
Oxford University Press, London.

Avery, G. (1965)
Nineteenth Century Children
Hodder & Stoughton, London.
Bamford, T.W. (1967)
The Rise of the Public Schools
Nelson, London.
Bamford, T.W. (1974)
Public School Data
Institute of Education, Hull.
Banks, J.A. (1954)
Parenthood and Prosperity
Routledge & Kegan Paul, London.
Bennett, T. (1979)
Formalism and Marxism
Methuens, London.
Beresford, G.C. (1936)
School days with Kipling
Gollancz, London.
Best, G.F.A. (1971)
Mid-Victorian Britain, 1851-1875
Weidenfeld & Nicolson, London.
Bratton, J.S. (1981)
*The Impact of Victorian Children's
Fiction*
Croom Helm, London.
Birchenough, C.E. (1938)
History of Elementary Education (3rd
edition)
University Tutorial Press, London.
Cadogan, M. and Craig, P.
(1976)
You're a Brick, Angela!
Gollancz, London.
Carrington, C. (1955)
Rudyard Kipling. His Life and Work
Macmillan, London.
Cawelti, J.G. (1976)
Adventure, Mystery and Romance
University of Chicago Press,
Chicago.
Chancellor, V.E. (1970)
History for their Masters
Kelly, New York.
Chaney, D. (1979)
Fictions and Ceremonies
Arnold, London.

Cook, E. (1969)
The Ordinary and the Fabulous
Cambridge University Press,
Cambridge.
Coveney, P. (1967)
The Image of Childhood
Penguin, Harmondsworth.
Crouch, M. (1962)
*Treasure Seekers and Borrowers.
Children's Books in Britain 1900-
1960*
The Library Association, London.
Dainton, F.J.H. (1958)
*Children's Books in England, Five
Centuries of Social Life*
Cambridge University Press,
Cambridge.
Dalziel, M. (1957)
Popular Fiction 100 Years Ago
Cohen & West, London.
Dixon, B. (1977)
*Catching Them Young 2: Political
Ideas in Children's Fiction*
Pluto Press, London.
Day Lewis, C. (1960)
The Buried Day
Chatto and Windus, London.
Dobrée, B. (1964)
The Lamp and the Lute (2nd edition)
Cass, London.
Dukes, C. (1905)
Health at School (4th edition)
Rivingstons, London.
Dunning, E. and Sheard, K.
(1979)
Barbarians, Gentlemen and Players
Australian National University
Press, Canberra.
Ellis, S.M. (1931)
Wilkie Collins, Le Fanu and Others
Constable, London.
Erickson, C. (1959)
*British Industrialists: Steel and
Hosiery*
Cambridge University Press,
Cambridge.

Eyre, F. (1971)
British Children's Books in the Twentieth Century
Longmans, London.

Farrar, R. (1904)
The Life of Frederick William Farrar
Nisbet, London.

Fussell, P. (1975)
The Great War and Modern Memory
Oxford University Press, New York.

Gathorne-Hardy, J.A. (1977)
The Public School Phenomenon, 1597-1977
Hodder & Stoughton, London.

Girouard, M. (1981)
The Return to Camelot
Yale University Press, New Haven.

Graves, R. (1929)
Goodbye to All That
Cassell, London.

Green, M. (1977)
Children of the Sun
Constable, London.

Green, R.C. (ed.) (1971)
Kipling: The Critical Heritage
Routledge & Kegan Paul, London.

Green, S.G. (1899)
The Story of the Religious Tract Society
Religious Tract Society, London.

Griest, G.L. (1970)
Mudie's Circulating Library and the Victorian Novel
David & Charles, Newton Abbot.

Gurner, R. (1937)
I Chose to Teach
Dent, London.

Hay, I. (1914)
The Lighter Side of School Life
Foulis, London.

Hicks, W.R. (1933)
The School in English and German Fiction
Soncino Press, London.

Honey, J.R. de S. (1977)
Tom Brown's Universe
Millington, London.

House, H. (1942)
The Dickens World
Oxford University Press, London.

Howarth, P. (1973)
Play Up and Play the game. The Heroes of Popular Fiction
Methuen, London.

Inglis, F. (1981)
The Promise of Happiness
Cambridge University Press, Cambridge.

Isherwood, C. (1947)
Lions and Shadows
New Directions, Norfolk (Conn.).

Jenkinson, A.J. (1940)
What Boys and Girls Read?
Methuen, London.

Jones, E. (1955)
Life and Work of Sigmund Freud (Vol II)
Hogarth, London.

Kingsford, M.G. (1947)
The Life, Work and Influence of William Henry Giles Kingston
Ryerson Press, Toronto.

Lace, A.F. (1969)
A Goodly Heritage
Monkton Combe School, Monkton Combe.

Lennox, C. (1901)
Henry Drummond. A biographical sketch
Melrose, London.

Lodge, D. (1981)
Working with Structuralism
Routledge & Kegan Paul, London.

Lofts, W.O.G. and Adley, D.J. (1970)
The Men Behind Boys' Fiction
Baker, London.

Lowndes, G.A.N. (1969)
The Silent Social Revolution (2nd edition)
Oxford University Press, London.

Macherey, P. (1978)
A Theory of Literary Production
Routledge & Kegan Paul, London.
Mack, E.C. (1941)
*Public Schools and British Opinion
since 1860*
Columbia University Press, New
York.
**Mack, E.C. and Armytage,
W.H.L.** (1952)
Tom Hughes
Benn, London.
Mais, S.P.B. (1916)
A Public School in Wartime
Murray, London.
Mangan, J.A. (1981)
*Athleticism in the Victorian and
Edwardian Public School*
Cambridge University Press,
Cambridge.
Marcus, S. (1966)
The Other Victorians
Weidenfeld & Nicolson, London.
Marsh, D.C. (1965)
*The Changing Social Structure of
England and Wales: 1871-1961*
Routledge & Kegan Paul, London.
Martin, R.B. (1959)
*The Dust of Combat. A Life of
Charles Kingsley*
Faber & Faber, London.
Morrison, S. (1960)
*Talbot Baines Reed. Author,
Bibliographer, Typefounder*
Cambridge University Press,
Cambridge.
Musgrave, P.W. (1967)
*Technical Change, the Labour Force
and Education*
Pergamon, Oxford.
Musgrave, P.W. (1968)
*Society and Education in England
Since 1800*
Methuen, London.
Newsome, D. (1961)
Godliness and Good Learning
Murray, London.

O'Dell, F. (1978)
*Socialisation through Children's
Literature: The Soviet Example*
Cambridge University Press,
Cambridge.
Ogilvie, V. (1957)
The English Public School
Batsford, London.
Osborne, G.S. (1965)
Scottish and English Schools
Longmans, London.
Palmer, J. (1978)
The Thriller
Arnold, London.
Quigley, I. (1982)
The Heirs of Tom Brown
Chatto & Windus, London.
Raven, C.E. (1928)
A Wanderer's Way
Hopkinson, London.
Ray, G.N. (1945)
*The Letters and Private Papers of
William Makepeace Thackeray* (Vol.
IV)
Oxford University Press, London.
Richards, F. (1952)
The Autobiography of Frank Richards
Skilton, London.
Riesman, D. (1956)
*Constraint and Variety in American
Education*
University of Nebraska Press,
Omaha.
Rockwell, J. (1974)
Fact in Fiction
Routledge & Kegan Paul, London.
Rosenthal, L.M. (1974)
'The child informed: attitudes
towards the socialization of the
child in nineteenth century English
children's literature', unpublished
Ph.D. thesis, Columbia University.
Rothblatt,S. (1976)
*Tradition and Change in English
Liberal Education*
Faber & Faber, London.

Salmon, E. (1888a)
Juvenile Literature as it is
Drane, London.
Seeley, J.R. (1971)
The Expansion of England
University of Chicago Press,
Chicago.
Selleck, R.J.W. (1972)
*English Primary Education and the
Progressives, 1914-1939*
Routledge & Kegan Paul, London.
Sharrett, B. (1982)
Reading Relations
Harvester Press, Brighton.
Springhall, J. (1976)
Youth, Empire and Society
Croom Helm, London.
Stanley, A.P. (1844)
*Life and Correspondence of Thomas
Arnold D.D.*
Fellowes, London.
Sutherland, J.A. (1976)
Victorian Novelists and Publishers
Athlone Press, London.
Thornton, A.P. (1959)
The Imperial Idea and its Enemies
Macmillan, London.
Warner, P. (1976)
The Best of British Pluck
Macdonald & Jones, London.
Watt, I.F. (1957)
The Rise of the Novel
Chatto & Windus, London.

Waugh, A. (1922)
*Public School Life: Boys, Parents,
Masters*
Cassell, London.
Waugh, A. (1962)
The Early Years of Alec Waugh
Cassell, London.
Waugh, E. (1964)
A Little Learning
Chapman & Hall, London.
Welleck, R. (1963)
Concepts of Criticism
Yale University Press, New York.
Wells, H.G. (1944)
'42 to '44
Secker & Warburg, London.
Wertham, F. (1954)
Seduction of the Innocent
Rineholt, New York.
Williams, R. (1976)
Keywords
Fontana, London.
Williams, R. (1977)
Marxism and Literature
Oxford University Press, Oxford.
Wilson, A. (1977)
The Strange Ride of Rudyard Kipling
Secker & Warburg, London.
Yonge, C.M. (1883)
English History Reading Books,
vol. 5
National Society's Depository,
London.

Journal articles, etc.

Alderson, B. (1971)
'Introduction' and 'Postscript' in
T.B. Reed, *The Fifth Form at St
Dominic's*
Hamish Hamilton, London
Allen, P. (1969)
'Christian Socialism and the Broad
Church Circle', *Dalhousie Review*,
49(1),58-68.

Bamford, T.W. (1975)
'Discipline at Rugby under Arnold',
Educational Review, 10(1),
November, 18-28.
Clinton-Baddeley, V.C. (1957/8)
'Benevolent Teachers of Youth',
Cornhill, 169(2), 360-82.

Dodd, C.I. (1900)
'School Children's Ideals', *National View*, XXXIV, 875-89.
Empson, W. (1935)
'Alice in Wonderland', in *Some Versions of Pastoral*.
Escarpit, R. (1970)
'The Act of Publication: Publication and Creation', in M.C. Albrecht, J.H. Burnett, M. Griff (eds), *The Sociology of Art and Literature*
Praeger, New York, 396-406.
Floud, J.E. (1954)
'The Education Experience of the Adult Population of England and Wales as at July, 1949', in D.V. Glass, *Social Mobility in Britain*
Routledge & Kegan Paul, London.
Foucault, M. (1977)
'What is an Author', in M. Foucault (ed.), *Language, Counter-Memory, Practice*
Cornell University Press, Ithaca (N.Y.).
Fraser's Magazine (1861)
'Public Schools', LXIII, 434-40.
Goldmann, L. (1973)
'Genetic Structuralism in the Sociology of Literature', in E. and T. Burns (eds), *Sociology of Literature and Drama*
Penguin, Harmondsworth, 109-23.
Gordon, W.J. (1913)
'The Boys' Own Paper. The Hutchison Memorial' (mss)
Religious Tract Society, London.
Gross, J. (1971)
'Introduction to J.R. Seeley: *The Expansion of England*'
University of Chicago Press, Chicago.
Harrison, J.F.C. (1957)
'The Victorian Gospel of Success', *Victorian Studies*, I(2), 155-64.

Himmelfarb, G. (1960)
'John Buchan: An Untimely Appreciation', *Encounter*, September, 46-53.
Hutchison, G.A., (1897)
'Introductory Sketch. The late Talbot Baines Reed, as Boy and Man', in *T.B. Reed: A Book of Short Stories*
Religious Tract Society, London.
Huttenback, R. (1970)
'G.A. Henty and the Vision of Empire', *Encounter*, XXXV, 46-63.
James, L. (1973)
'Tom Brown's Imperialist Sons', *Victorian Studies*, XVIII (1), 89-99.
Johns, B.G. (1867)
'The Books of Fiction for Children', *Quarterly Review*, 122, 57-62.
Kermode, F. (1975)
'London Letter', *New Republic*, 173(5&6), 23.
Lang, K. (1958)
'Mass, Class and the Reviewer', *Social Problems*, VI(1), 11-21.
Laurenson, D. (1969)
'A Sociological Study of Authorship', *British Journal of Sociology*, XX(2), 311-25.
Lewis, C.S. (1969)
'On Three Ways of Writing for Children', in S. Eggoff (ed.), *Only Connect*
Oxford University Press, Toronto.
Lewis, N. (1971)
'Preface to *Tom Brown's Schooldays*', in Thomas Hughes, *Tom Brown's Schooldays*
Penguin, Harmondsworth.
McDowell, M. (1973)
'Fiction for Children and Adults: Some Essential Differences', *Children's Literature in Education*, no. 10, 50-63.

Martin, H. (1936)
'Nationalism in Children's
Literature', *Library Quarterly*,
VI(4), 403-18.

Musgrave, P.W. (1977)
'Corporal Punishment in Some
English Elementary Schools, 1900-
1939', *Research in Education*, No.
17.

Musgrave, P.W. (1978)
'*Stalky and Co*. re-read: a Taste of
Things to Come?', *Children's
Literature in Education*, 10(4), 186-
93.

Musgrave, P.W. (1979)
'The Publication of "The Loom of
Youth": an Incident in Public
School History', *Australian and
New Zealand History of Education
Society Journal*, 7(2), 43-54.

Musgrave, P.W. (1981)
'Kipling's View of Educating
Children', *Australian Journal of
Education*, 25(3), 211-23.

Musgrave, P.W. (1982a)
'From Chummy Innocence to
Concerned Individualism: A Case
Study in the Sociology of
Literature', *Australian and New
Zealand Journal of Sociology*, 18(2),
162-71.

Musgrave, P.W. (1982b)
'From Brown to Bunter: the Birth
of a Minor Literary Genre', in S.
Murray Smith (ed.), *Melbourne
Studies in Education, 1982*
Melbourne University Press,
Melbourne.

Orwell, G. (1940)
'Boys' Weeklies',*Horizon*, 1(3),
174-200.

Piehl, K. (1978)
Letter to Editor, *Children's
Literature in Education*, 9(4), 198-
201.

Quarterly Review (1860)
'Public School Education',
CVIII(1), July, 387-424.

Quarterly Review (1890)
'Penny Fiction', 171, 150-71.

Quarterly Review (1925)
'Public School Stories', CCLV, 19-
29.

Richards, F. (1940)
'Frank Richards replies to George
Orwell', *Horizon*, 1(5), 346-55.

Salmon, E. (1888b)
'Should Children Have a Special
Literature?', *Parents' Review*, 337-
44.

Saturday Review (1882), 'Boys',
22
April, 449.

Scott, P. (1975)
'The School and the Novel: "Tom
Brown's Schooldays" ', in
B. Simon and I. Bradley (eds), *The
Victorian Public School*
Gill & Macmillan, Dublin.

Sime, J. (1895)
'In Memoriam. Talbot Baines
Reed', in T.B. Reed, *Kilgorman. A
Story of Ireland in 1798*
Nelson, London

Spectator (1861)
'Tom Brown at Oxford',
2 November, 1288-90.

Stephen, J.E. (1858)
'Tom Brown's Schooldays',
Edinburgh Review, CVII, 217, 172-
93.

Tennyson, C. (1959)
'They Taught the World to Play',
Victorian Studies, II(3), 211-22.

Times (1857)
'Tom Brown's Schooldays',
9 October.

Townsend, J.R. (1971)
'Introduction' to F.W. Farrar, *Eric
or Little by Little*
Hamish Hamilton, London, 9-14.

Trethewey, A.R. (1974)
'Social and Educational Influences
on the Definition of a Subject:
History in Victoria, 1850-1954', in
P.W. Musgrave (ed.) *Contemporary*

Studies in the Curriculum
Angus & Robertson, Sydney.
Webb, R.K. (1958)
'The Victorian Reading Public', in
B. Ford (ed.), *From Dickens to Hardy*
Penguin, Harmondsworth.
Yonge, C.M. (1867)
'Children's Literature of the Last Century', I, II and III, *Macmillans Magazine*, XX(2, 3 and 4), 229-37, 302-10 and 448-56.
Yonge, C.M. (1887)
What Books to Lend and What to Give
National Society Depository, London.

Index

271

Index